W9-AFK-520

STUDIES IN HISTORY, ECONOMICS AND PUBLIC LAW

Edited by the
FACULTY OF POLITICAL SCIENCE
OF COLUMBIA UNIVERSITY

Number 572

THE OLD DOMINION AND NAPOLEON BONAPARTE

A STUDY IN AMERICAN OPINION

BY

JOSEPH I. SHULIM

THE OLD DOMINION AND NAPOLEON BONAPARTE

A STUDY IN AMERICAN OPINION

BY

JOSEPH I. SHULIM

AMS PRESS
NEW YORK

COLUMBIA UNIVERSITY
STUDIES IN THE
SOCIAL SCIENCES

572

The Series was formerly known as
Studies in History, Economics and Public Law.

Reprinted with the permission of Columbia University Press
From the edition of 1952, New York
First AMS EDITION published 1968
Manufactured in the United States of America

Library of Congress Catalogue Card Number: 68-59263

AMS PRESS, INC.
NEW YORK, N. Y. 10003

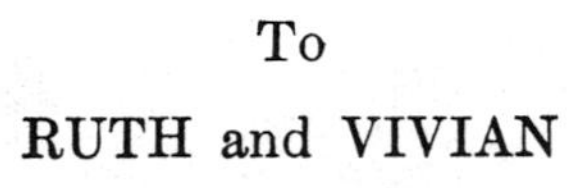

To

RUTH and VIVIAN

PREFACE

ATTEMPTS have been made to arrive at conclusions concerning the attitudes of a society by a selection of expressions of opinion for the entire country. I have employed another method: an exhaustive study of an especially prominent region within the particular nation. I have endeavored to analyze thoroughly the opinions held by contemporary Virginians concerning the "Little Corsican."

Although Virginian opinion had its local peculiarities, it was not, on the whole, divorced from that of the rest of the nation. Virginian editors frequently reprinted editorials from non-Virginia journals as a means of expressing their own opinions, thereby demonstrating the existence of a basic core of American opinion. The political leadership provided by Virginians to the federal government necessarily gave their opinions added national significance.

Though Virginia was not unique, it was especially rich in Republican opinion, in the opinion of nationally distinguished individuals, and in that of the predominantly local sect, the Quids. The minority Federalists were also to be found in the state.

The organization as well as content of this study has been determined by the character of the material. Purposes of clarity necessitated, for the most part, an analytical division of the attitudes into three natural segments: opinion of French domestic developments, and of Franco-European and Franco-American relations. Since Napoleon Bonaparte was a product of the French Revolution, I have included an analysis of the attitudes toward the revolution, with emphasis on the later phase. Moreover, the obverse of certain aspects of Virginian opinion of France was the attitude toward other European countries, especially toward its inveterate foe, Great Britain. Such attitudes have been analyzed when pertinent. Since, furthermore, opinion at times resulted in acts, the latter have also been examined.

As important as the opinion itself is its origin. I have, consequently, attempted, wherever possible, to ascertain the factors in the creation of the attitudes of Virginians toward Napoleon.

In general, the pattern of Virginian opinion of Bonaparte had become fixed by the end of Jefferson's presidency. The developments from March, 1809, through 1815, therefore, have merely been outlined.

I wish to express my gratitude to Professor Carlton J. H. Hayes of Columbia University for his tolerance, sympathetic encouragement, and assistance, and to Dean John A. Krout, also of Columbia University, for his consideration, advice, and critical appraisals; and to my colleagues, Professor Arthur C. Cole for his editorial criticism and many other helpful suggestions, and Professor Bernard H. Stern for his unstinted and valuable advice on various problems. Many librarians have been of help, particularly Dr. Thomas P. Martin, formerly with the Division of Manuscripts in the Library of Congress. I owe a debt of gratitude to my friends, Mrs. Anne Gainen, who prepared most of the typescript of the several drafts regardless of the time and energy involved, and to Mrs. Natalie Matenko, who helped assiduously with the proof. Last, but not least, I thank my wife, who, by her assistance in manifold ways in the preparation of this volume and by her steadfast encouragement, made its realization possible. None of the above, however, should be charged with any of the failings this work may have.

J. I. S.

TABLE OF CONTENTS

CHAPTER I

THE OLD DOMINION IN TRANSITION

WESTERN civilization in the late eighteenth and early nineteenth centuries witnessed a newly-born American republic buffeted by European revolution and war. Those were the stormy years when France, in its attempt to reorganize and modernize its own institutions, aroused a Europe still largely content with its traditional organization. The issues of the French Revolutionary and Napoleonic eras were almost as crucial for Americans as for Europeans. The young republic was still an economic and cultural appendage of Western Europe.

One of the original United States, Virginia, was particularly aware of the problems created by old Europe. "It was the leading State of the Union during all the Time of my Residence in America," wrote Augustus J. Foster, one of the British ministers at Washington during the period.[1] It was the most populous of all the states.[2] Virginians were in control of the new federal administration from 1789 to 1815, with the sole exception of the presidency of John Adams. It was the Old Dominion that produced such diverse personalities for the national scene as Thomas Jefferson, the inspired spiritual founder of American liberalism, and practical politician and creator of the Republican party; James Madison, constitutional philosopher and lieutenant of Jefferson; James Monroe, persevering aspirant to the presidential succession; George

1 Sir Augustus John Foster, *Notes on the United States of America Collected in the Years 1804-5-6-7 and 11-12* (MSS., Library of Congress: hereafter, LC), II, 126. Virginia's leadership remained largely unchallenged until the eve of the War of 1812.

2 See *Second Census Of The United States; Return Of The Whole Number Of Persons Within The Several Districts Of The United States...* (Washington, 1801) and *Third Census Of The United States; Aggregate Amount Of Each Description Of Persons Within The United States Of America... In The Year 1810* (Washington, 1811).

Washington, one of the chief architects of the new federal régime, a stanch Federalist in his later days; John Marshall, biographer of the first President, who, by his pronouncements from the highest tribunal in the land, buttressed the new political structure and gave moral encouragement to the declining Federalist party; and the eccentric young John Randolph of Roanoke, stormy petrel of the Republican administrations and heart and soul of the Republican malcontents, the Tertium Quids. These were some of the Virginians who lived and acted during the years of the rise and fall of the "Little Corsican."

The opinions of Virginians concerning the French Revolution and Napoleon Bonaparte were determined by a complex of forces, either continuing or transitory. Some were present in the economic and social history of the state.

Whether France or its enemy Great Britain was the market for Virginia tobacco [3] was of great significance, especially to economically-minded tobacco growers.

During the colonial period, Great Britain had imported all of the American tobacco in accordance with its mercantilist regulations, but had reëxported most of it to the European continent. Approximately ninety per cent of the imports of the island kingdom from 1770 to 1774 were thus reshipped, with France taking nearly one-third of the total reëxports.[4] After the revolution, Great Britain reëstablished, to an important degree, its position as entrepôt for the American tobacco trade,

3 Virginia was still the state exporting the most raw tobacco for the year ending September 30, 1792, with 61,203 hogsheads as against Maryland, which was second, with 28,992. [*American State Papers...*, Class 4, *Commerce And Navigation,* vol. I (Washington, 1832), p. 161. The hogshead varied in weight. For example, Jefferson indicated that his hhd. of tobacco made in 1800 varied from 1342 lbs. to 1719 lbs. *Expense Accounts of Thomas Jefferson, 1791-1803* (MSS., New York Public Library: hereafter, NYPL), entry for February 13, 1801, p. 130.] Virginia's primacy undoubtedly continued throughout the period 1789-1815.

4 The extensive smuggling, of course, is not taken into account. Lewis C. Gray, assisted by Esther K. Thompson, *History of Agriculture in the Southern United States to 1860* (New York, 1941), I, 255.

though direct trade between the United States and other markets naturally developed.[5]

No statistics seem available as to the exact proportions of Virginia tobacco that were consumed in Great Britain and France respectively in the Napoleonic era. Much of the tobacco was still imported by the former.[6] Great Britain retained for its own consumption the prime quality tobacco, the "sweet scented," and then resold the second-grade to the continent.[7] Whether France obtained its second-grade tobacco directly or indirectly from the United States, the French market was an important one for Virginia tobacco during much of the period.[8]

5 According to Joseph C. Robert, *The Tobacco Kingdom. Plantation, Market, and Factory in Virginia and North Carolina, 1800-1860* (Durham, No. Car., 1938), p. 10, the British dominated the export trade in the 1780's almost as completely as they had in colonial times.

6 *V.* Timothy Pitkin, *A Statistical View of the Commerce of the United States of America...*, 2nd ed., with additions and corrections (New York, 1817), pp. 157-8, Table No. VI.

7 *Vide* various speeches in Congress, in particular, those of Senator William B. Giles, January 23, 1810, in *Annals Of The Congress Of The United States,* 11th Congress, 2nd Session, vol. I, col. 538, and of Representative John W. Eppes, February 26, 1810, *ibid.,* 11th Cong., 2nd Sess., vol. II, col. 1452.

8 See Giles' speech in the Virginia House of Delegates on January 8, 1800; reported in the Richmond *Examiner* of January 10, 1800. Also *cf.* Timothy Pitkin, *op. cit.*, pp. 157-8, Table No. VI. Contemporaneous official French statistics show much larger imports of American tobacco than do the American. See E. Buron, "Notes and Documents. Statistics on Franco-American Trade, 1778-1806," *Journal of Economic and Business History,* vol. IV (November, 1931-August, 1932), pp. 571-580; *Affaires Étrangères, Correspondance Politique, États-Unis* (Photostats, LC), vol. LIV, pt. 7, fol. 481, and vol. LXIV, pt. 5, fol. 400ᵛ.

Restrictive acts by the American and foreign governments hindered the tobacco export trade, especially in the latter half of the Napoleonic period. The British duty on tobacco imports, heavy enough in colonial times, was gradually increased until it reached 3s. 2d. by February, 1815. France abolished the fiscal monopoly in 1791, replaced it by increasingly high duties on leaf tobacco, particularly for that imported in non-French vessels, and then reëstablished the tobacco monopoly in 1810. French commercial policy—among other factors—thus helped reduce American tobacco imports after 1810 to minor proportions. The remaining nations of Europe, by and large, imitated the British or French policy.

Certain good tobacco lands in Virginia, not subject to the usually rapid rate of soil exhaustion, continued to yield prime quality crops throughout the late eighteenth and early nineteenth centuries. Especially noted for its fine quality was the tobacco raised on the banks of the James River and to the south of it.[9] Coarser types generally prevailed elsewhere.

When the market for prime or second-grade tobacco was endangered by restrictive acts in the United States or abroad, especially after 1805, tobacco growers in Virginia became concerned. Under the circumstances, an agriculturist producing exclusively or mainly secondary types of tobacco might, if he thought in terms of economic returns, interpret the acts of the Napoleonic government more favorably than one who cultivated prime quality tobacco.

The supremacy of tobacco as the market crop in Virginia had been challenged by wheat or other grains since the latter part of the colonial period. Land exhausted by tobacco was turned over to grain. Periods of low tobacco prices led to temporary diversification of crops. Most important of all in creating a more permanent shift during the years of the French Revolution and Napoleon was the increasing dependence of warring European powers upon foreign grain. But the uncertainty of the grain market or occasional high prices for the Indian plant brought a return to the old crop. Many planters combined the cultivation of wheat and tobacco, stressing one or the other on the basis of their interpretation of market conditions. Nevertheless, the tendency away from tobacco as the staple in the late eighteenth and early nineteenth centuries was clearly evident.[10]

The shift was more pronounced in certain areas than in others. By the Napoleonic era, tobacco had been abandoned

9 Duke De La Rochefoucault [*sic*] Liancourt, *Travels Through The United States of North America... In The Years 1795, 1796, And 1797...*, trans. by H. Neuman (London, 1799), II, 55. According to the author, this tobacco was almost exclusively sent to Richmond.

10 Avery O. Craven, *Soil Exhaustion as a factor in the agricultural history of Virginia and Maryland, 1606-1860* (Urbana, Ill., 1926), 72 ff.

mostly in the oldest settled part of the state, the Tidewater.[11] In this region wheat was grown especially in the rich alluvial lands of the river valleys. In the remainder of the Tidewater it seems that corn was becoming the principal market crop.[12] The northern counties of the Piedmont were leading producers of wheat in the period of the Napoleonic régime. Wheat was the chief market crop in many parts of the Valley of Virginia, especially the northern counties. In the Trans-Alleghany region, its production was also rising rapidly.

The Old Dominion was, therefore, a great wheat and flour exporter in the period. The wheat and flour of the northern counties of the Piedmont and Valley left the United States through Alexandria, Baltimore, or Philadelphia; that of the Trans-Alleghany went down the Mississippi to New Orleans for export. That which was produced in other sections was channeled through the eastern towns of the state.

The chief foreign consumers of American wheat and flour in the Napoleonic era were Great Britain, the Iberian peninsula, the West Indies, and Canada. The Anglo-French war, by hindering the purchase of grain on the continent, compelled the British to seek it in the United States. Between 1800 and 1812, the United States ranked second in the exports of wheat to Great Britain with 1,169,572 quarters; while Prussia was first with 3,017,471 quarters.[13] The needs of the British armies in the Peninsular War caused unprecedented shipments of wheat and flour from the United States to Spain and Portugal, especially from 1811 through 1813.[14] The British West Indies

11 Virginia may be divided into four regions on the basis of its geography. The Tidewater is the coastal area, bounded on the west by the "fall line." The Piedmont extends from the "fall line" to the Blue Ridge mountain range. Between the Blue Ridge and Alleghany mountains lies the beautiful Valley of Virginia. The Trans-Alleghany section was later to become the major portion of West Virginia.

12 Barley was another important grain in many parts of the Tidewater.

13 W. Freeman Galpin, *The Grain Supply of England During the Napoleonic Period* (New York, 1925), p. 194.

14 *Vid.* W. Freeman Galpin, "The American Grain Trade to the Spanish Peninsula, 1810-1814," *American Historical Review*, vol. XXVIII (October, 1922-July, 1923), p. 24, n. 5.

were likewise provisioned from the same source, the exports coming usually from Norfolk, Alexandria, Philadelphia, Baltimore, and New York.[15] Unlike certain years in the preceding decade or so, metropolitan France imported very little wheat or flour from the United States during the Napoleonic era. It even exported grain to its enemy, England, on several occasions. The French West Indies, however, were provided with flour and grain by the American Republic. New Orleans grain, which included the grain of the Trans-Alleghany region of Virginia, was probably the chief source of supply for the French and Spanish West Indies.[16] After the renewal of war with France in 1803, Great Britain had easily seized Tobago and Santa Lucia in the French West Indies. Martinique was conquered in 1809 and Guadeloupe in 1810. British areas thus became the prime consumers of American wheat and flour during the Napoleonic era.

A tendency toward a more sympathetic appraisal of British actions could be expected on the part of those planters or farmers who, cultivating wheat exclusively or mainly at a particular period and concerned about their economic interests, found that their market was a British region. With the British buying the bulk of American wheat and flour after 1808, this pro-British proclivity spread among economically-minded wheat growers in Virginia.[17]

Besides tobacco and grain, the Virginia countryside marketed many other commodities in the period of Napoleon. The livestock trade long flourished in the Valley and Trans-Alleghany. Cattle, sheep, and pigs were driven to market in Baltimore or Philadelphia. The Trans-Alleghany also sent animal products

15 W. F. Galpin, "Grain Trade of New Orleans, 1804-1814," *Mississippi Valley Historical Review*, vol. XIV (March, 1928), pp. 501-2.

16 *Ibid.*, p. 501.

17 For confirmation of this interpretation of the opinions of wheat growers see, for example, Jefferson to Madison, April 27, 1809; *The Papers of Thomas Jefferson* (MSS., LC), vol. CLXXXVII, p. 33276. Also, Sérurier, the French minister at Washington, to the Duc de Bassano, July 12, 1812; *Affaires Étrangères, Corr. Pol., États-Unis*, LC, vol. LXVII, pt. 4, fol. 260v.

down to New Orleans. The cotton plant was cultivated in many parts of the Old Dominion, primarily for use on the plantation, the region of commercial cotton production being limited mainly to the southeastern part of the state.[18] In 1800, three-fourths of the cotton of the United States was produced in Virginia and the Carolinas.[19] The chief consumer of American cotton was Great Britain. Could this partly account for the southeastern congressional district of Sussex, Southampton, Surry, and Isle of Wight counties reëlecting Edwin Gray so long as he desired it? This representative opposed the anti-British tendencies of the national administration from December, 1807.[20]

The real income of the agriculturist as well as the ultimate destination of his produce had some influence upon his attitudes. The size of the harvest was one of the factors determining his income. John Randolph of Roanoke, for example, complained continuously of poor crops from 1810 through 1814. To aggravate matters, markets were frequently curtailed by restrictive measures placed upon commerce by the American and foreign governments and, ultimately, by the war with Great Britain. The price the agriculturist received for his produce fluctuated. While tobacco prices for most of the Napoleonic period were indifferent, when not low, wheat prices were occasionally good.[21] The index of the wholesale prices of agricul-

18 Gray, *History of Agriculture*, II, 687.

19 James C. Ballagh, ed., *The South in the Building of the Nation*, vol. V, *Economic History, 1607-1865* (Richmond, 1909), p. 113.

20 Minor commercial products of eastern Virginia included clapboards, shingles, barrel staves, and other forest products. The western sections of the state also produced hemp and flax for sale.

21 For tobacco prices see, *e. g.*, Arthur H. Cole, *Wholesale Commodity Prices In The United States, 1700-1861; Statistical Supplement. Actual Wholesale Prices Of Various Commodities* (Cambridge, 1938). For wheat prices see Arthur G. Peterson, *Historical Study of Prices Received by Producers of Farm Products in Virginia, 1801-1927* (Virginia Polytechnic Institute, Virginia Agricultural Experiment Station, Technical Bulletin 37, March, 1929; Blacksburg, Va.), p. 72, Table 1; p. 175, Table 85a; and pp. 23 ff.

tural commodities was lower than the industrial index in 1799, but the agricultural led from the second half of 1800 through 1801, and again from December, 1804, through July, 1805. In the periods 1802-November, 1804, August, 1805-1806, and in 1807, the two indexes fluctuated closely around the same level. From 1808 till late in 1815 the divergence between the two became greater and greater, with industrial commodities much higher than agricultural, especially during the War of 1812.[22] The real income of the Virginia planter or farmer—except for those who raised grains exclusively—was thus much lower in the second half of the Napoleonic era than in the first half. Here was part of the economic background for the War of 1812.[23]

Hostility to Britain was fostered also by the character of the plantation system. Though there were many farmers,[24] the planter, especially the large planter, was more important in the life of the state and in its opinion. Yet the plantation system of capitalistic agriculture based upon slave labor had been increasingly in decay since the middle of the eighteenth century.[25] Even the greatest planters during the period of the French

22 The description of price developments is based on the information on Philadelphia prices to be found in Anne Bezanson, R. D. Gray, and M. Hussey, *Wholesale Prices in Philadelphia,* 1784-1861 (Pennsylvania University. Wharton School of Finance and Commerce, Industrial Research Department. Research Studies, XXIX, 1936), Chart II facing p. 4, pp. 21 f., 354-5, 356, 365. *Cf.* George R. Taylor's description of the economic condition of the western farmer in his "Prices in the Mississippi Valley Preceding the War of 1812," *Journal of Economic and Business History,* vol. III (1930-1931), pp. 148-163.

23 *V. infra,* p. 270.

24 *Vid.* Ulrich B. Phillips' distinction between a plantation and a farm; *Plantation and Frontier,* I, 72-3, of *A Documentary History Of American Industrial Society,* ed. by John R. Commons, Ulrich B. Phillips, *et al.* (Cleveland, 1910). For the degree of slaveholding in Virginia see Gray, *op. cit.,* I, 482, 531.

25 Edward Channing, *A History Of The United States*; vol. IV, *Federalists and Republicans* (New York, 1938), pp. 390-1. Ulrich B. Phillips, *American Negro Slavery...* (New York, 1929), p. 366.

Revolution and Napoleon were constantly complaining of their straitened circumstances.[26]

The plantation system, originally "a phase of the colonial expansion of capitalism," [27] had remained inextricably intertwined with the British economy throughout the colonial period. Through the system of factorage the Virginia planters had become by the American Revolution, as Jefferson expressed it, "a species of property annexed to certain mercantile houses in London." [28] Friction between Virginia planter and British merchant inevitably became a prominent feature of the relations between the colony and the mother country. The hostility which many a planter felt toward Great Britain during the American Revolution is thus quite comprehensible.

The problem of the pre-revolutionary debts continued to plague Anglo-Virginian relations for many years afterwards and intensified anti-English feeling among the Virginian aristocracy. Finally, by the Convention of 1802 the national government agreed to pay £600,000 sterling to the British government as a settlement for all outstanding claims against Americans.[29]

The planters of Virginia, meanwhile, accumulated new debts. After the American Revolution, they had established economic

26 Jefferson, with about 10,000 acres and 200 slaves in 1796, was requesting a loan from a Dutch banking firm. [Jefferson to N. & J. Van Staphorst & Hubbard, February 28, 1796. *Jefferson Papers*, LC, vol. XCIX, p. 17038. This letter is incorrectly dated 1790 in Paul L. Ford's edition of *The Writings of Thomas Jefferson* (New York, 1892 ff.), vol. V, p. 144.] In fact, he was beholden continuously throughout his maturity to British, Dutch, and American creditors. His situation was so difficult by 1815 that he had to sell his cherished library of about ten thousand volumes to the government for the Library of Congress.

27 Gray, *op. cit.*, I, 303. *V.* Gray's brilliant analysis of the plantation system as a phase in economic evolution, pp. 302 ff.

28 *The Writings of Thomas Jefferson*, H. A. Washington, ed. (New York, 1857), IX, 251. Answer to questions by M. de Meusnier, *c.* 1785.

29 For the history of the debts see Isaac S. Harrell, *Loyalism In Virginia, Chapters in the Economic History of the Revolution* (Durham, 1926), pp. 127-78.

relations, similar to those of colonial days, with merchants or factors in Virginia. The old story repeated itself. The Richmond *Virginia Gazette and General Advertiser* wrote on July 18, 1807, that most of the planters were then in debt to the merchants.

Though some planters maintained cordial relations with their resident factors,[30] others developed the natural antipathy of debtor toward creditor.[31] A large proportion of the merchants in the late eighteenth and early nineteenth centuries were still agents or partners of British houses, although increasing numbers were American. Even the latter, however, were largely dependent on British capital.[32] Therefore, the hatred of planter for merchant capitalist retained in Virginia, to an important degree, the form of hatred for the merchants of a foreign country, the old enemy, England.

The planter of Virginia was the owner of a complex institution. The plantation was largely self-sufficient in its agricultural life, raising a variety of products for home consumption, besides a market crop or crops. It also satisfied its needs for manufactured commodities in varying degrees at different times and places. The period between 1775 and 1815 was the heyday of domestic manufactures in the state.[33] The commercial restrictions following 1807 and the war with Great Britain greatly stimulated household industry.

Sometimes planters produced manufactured wares for sale. Jefferson is an example. At first acting as his own overseer, he began about 1794 to use twelve young slaves between the ages of ten and sixteen for the production of nails. The mer-

30 *E. g.*, Jefferson.

31 Planters sought all kinds of protection from the state government, in times of depression particularly, against the recovery of debts. In general, many were dilatory in repayment. This lack of punctuality was commented upon by foreign and native observers alike. *V.* La Rochefoucault Liancourt, *Travels*, II, 93, 114, and other passages; and Jefferson to William Short, April 15, 1803, *William Short Papers* (MSS., LC), vol. XXXII, p. 5714.

32 *Vid. infra*, p. 25.

33 Gray, I, 455.

chants of the neighborhood, however, fearing the wrath of the importing houses, refused to take his nails. Jefferson thereupon decided to retail at wholesale prices, plus five per cent commission to the retailer, through small shopkeepers at Milton, Charlottesville, and Staunton. As importers could not compete with a manufacturer who retailed at wholesale prices, Jefferson defeated the "effort of the general system of Scotch policy to suppress every attempt at domestic manufacture." So he wrote in 1796.[34] In addition to his nail "manufacture," Jefferson had a grist mill and a "merchant mill" valued in 1809 at $900 and $10,000, respectively.[35]

Since the plantation was now again self-sufficient to an important degree, its trade was mainly limited to the sale of its commercial crop and the purchase of luxuries. The little that the planters did buy was their undoing, because the net return from their annual crop was frequently less than the interest on debts and the cost of the few things purchased.

Impoverished as they might become, the planters of the Old Dominion, nevertheless, continued to live their lives of luxury. Perhaps not as given to unrestrained pleasure as their colonial ancestors, the planters still retained many of the divertissements of their forbears. Though he might be called "Mister," the large planter was truly an aristocrat, as much so, if not more than any titled individual on the other side of the Atlantic.[36] Did he not own human beings as chattel property? Where in Western Europe could an aristocrat claim such a privilege?

34 Jefferson to Thomas Mann Randolph, January 11, 1796. *Jefferson Papers*, LC, vol. XCIX, p. 17006.

35 Samuel Greenhow to Jefferson, October 25, 1809; *ibid.*, CLXXXVIII, 33538. For the manufacturing and commercial interests of an eighteenth century large planter see Louis Morton, *Robert Carter of Nomini Hall, A Virginia Tobacco Planter of the Eighteenth Century* (Williamsburg, Va., 1941).

36 The Virginia planters had become so aristocratic by the late eighteenth and early nineteenth centuries that duelling became a popular means of settling personal disputes. See Thomas J. Wertenbaker, *Patrician and Plebeian in Virginia...* (Charlottesville, Va., 1910), pp. 79 f.

The planters of Virginia had their saving graces. Elegant manners, a sense of honor, a spirit of public service, and of *noblesse oblige* characterized the better ones. The leisure time of such planters was devoted not only to sensual pleasures, but also to the development of the intellect. Where, but in the Virginia of the Golden Age, could a Thomas Jefferson have flourished? Steeped in classical and modern culture, they concentrated on law and politics.

Lords of many acres, owners of Negroes who were their slaves, the Virginia rural aristocracy developed a pride that is usually the inevitable concomitant of virtually autocratic power.[37] Their authority not being subject to questioning by their dependents, they would brook no interference with their actions in the political sphere. Like the lords of the feudal age, they felt almost instinctively that men, that is, aristocrats, had certain rights which governments could not infringe. Edmund Burke had early observed this feature of slavery in his speech on conciliation with America:

> There is . . . a circumstance attending these colonies [southern] which . . . makes the spirit of liberty still more high and haughty than in those to the northward. It is, that in Virginia and the Carolinas they have a vast multitude of slaves. Where this is the case in any part of the world, those who are free are by far the most proud and jealous of their freedom. Freedom is to them not only an enjoyment, but a kind of rank and privilege.[38]

Is it any wonder that, when the French people revolted in the name of the rights of man, the planters of the Old Dominion should applaud enthusiastically? Did not the French Revolution confirm the principles for which they were struggling in

37 *V., e.g.*, Fillmore Norflett, "Norfolk, Portsmouth, and Gosport As Seen By Moreau de Saint-Mery in March, April, And May, 1794," *Virginia Magazine Of History And Biography*, vol. XLVIII, no. 3 (July, 1940), *p.* 259.

38 *Burke's Speech On Conciliation With America*, Hammond Lamont, ed. (Boston, 1898), p. 22.

the United States against the encroachments of a newly-established federal government? Was not the revolution in France led at first by liberal aristocrats, like the famous soldier of the American Revolution, the Marquis de Lafayette?

Soon, however, deep in the bowels of the rural society of the West Indies and of Virginia rumblings were heard. The slaves had hearkened to the magic words "Liberty, Equality, and Fraternity" that wafted across the Atlantic. San Domingo was in the van of the movement. Gabriel's abortive rising in the vicinity of Richmond in 1800 was the most serious in the United States during the Napoleonic era. Revelations and rumors were rife thereafter in Virginia, even though there was no major occurrence again until 1816.

Some aristocrats of Virginia, frightened by the holocaust which had been let loose, drew back aghast. Reënforced by the consolidation of slavery in the cotton plantations farther south, emancipation ideas were gradually forgotten. Class and race consciousness increased. Now that the slaves were trying to apply the principles of the French Revolution, the latter seemed to foster some subversive ideas. John Randolph of Roanoke became the arch-exponent of the emerging conservative views on slavery that were to become prevalent in the ante-bellum South. When restrictions on the domestic slave trade were proposed in the second session of the Ninth Congress, he saw "red" and declamed excitedly about the rights of property.[39] Yet this was the man who could write in his private letters about "the curse of slavery" and who was to manumit his own slaves by will. Such was the ambivalence of many a planter's attitude on slavery and freedom in the Napoleonic era. Governmental action was one thing; but action by the lord and master was his prerogative. The libertarian ideas of the American and French Revolutions still held an appeal for such Virginian aristocrats—up to a point.

39 See his speeches in the House of Representatives on February 18 and 26, 1807. *Annals of Congress*, 9th Cong., 2nd Sess., 528, 626 f.

Although the agricultural economy of much of Virginia—particularly east of the Blue Ridge—was on the decline in the late eighteenth and early nineteenth centuries, commerce and industry in the state were prospering. Norfolk [40] was an example of the commercial growth. Before the close of the eighteenth century, because of the increasing size of ocean-going ships, Richmond and Petersburg began to lose their direct trade with Europe and to make shipments and receive supplies through Norfolk. According to the careful French observer the Duc de la Rochefoucauld-Liancourt, in 1796, the Richmond merchants sent the grain, flour, and tobacco of the back-country down in lighters to Norfolk, where they kept their ships, and where they completed their cargo. Norfolk thus carried on almost all the external commerce of Virginia south of the Rappahannock and of North Carolina far beyond the Roanoke.[41] Trade with the Antilles grew rapidly. Norfolk also participated in the tremendous growth of the carrying trade, which the United States virtually controlled during the Napoleonic wars. Exports from the town rose in value from a little over a million dollars in 1792 to seven millions in 1807.[42]

While the years of commercial restrictions and the war with England checked Virginia's commercial expansion, its industrial growth was generally unhindered, if not fostered, by the developments of the Napoleonic era. The Old Dominion ranked fourth in the industrial production of the United States in 1810.[43]

40 Compared with the North, Virginian towns were insignificant. Norfolk, the largest in the state in 1800, had a population of 6,926 (of which only 3,850 were whites), while New York City and County had 60,489. *Second Census Of The United States.*

41 La Rochefoucault Liancourt, *Travels*, II, 7, 33.

42 Thomas J. Wertenbaker, *Norfolk, Historic Southern Port* (Durham, 1931), pp. 93-4.

43 Among the products of Virginia were coal, iron, snuff, tobacco, and salt. *Vide* Tench Coxe, *A Statement Of The Arts And Manufactures Of The United States Of America, For The Year 1810* (Philadelphia, 1814).

Little of the capital that was invested in this commercial and industrial expansion was native. After all, this was a new country. The United States was still economically a colony of Great Britain. In 1790, nearly one-half of the exports of the nation went to the British Empire, while the latter was the source of over three-fourths of the imports. Within a few years of the close of the American Revolution, the British mercantile interest had again become firmly entrenched. La Rochefoucauld stated in 1796 that the generality of the Richmond merchants were agents or partners of British houses.[44] Increasing numbers of merchants in Virginia, as elsewhere, were probably American. But among these were to be found former agents of British firms, who had been ordered by the concern at home to become naturalized citizens in order to obtain the benefit of the laws on debt collection.[45] Whether factitious citizens, as Jefferson described such, or true citizens, the American merchants were still largely dependent on British capital. Since many of the small merchants of the Virginia back-country were dependent on the credit, supplies, and purchases of the merchants to the eastward, at Philadelphia, Baltimore, Alexandria, Richmond, etc., they became subjects of the latter.

Is it so remarkable, then, that the bourgeoisie in Virginia, as elsewhere in the United States, in the main preserved its attachment to "mother England"?[46] Is it any wonder that an enemy of England tended to become its enemy as well?

Lawyers who lived on the legal squabbles of such merchants would be likely to mirror the views of their employers. Sometimes, the attorneys themselves engaged in economic ventures which bound them still more closely to the merchants. There is the case of the young frontiersman, soldier, and lawyer, John

44 La Rochefoucault Liancourt, II, 33.

45 Edward Thornton, the British chargé d'affaires at Washington, to Grenville, March 28, 1801. *Great Britain. Public Record Office. London. Foreign Office 5* [hereafter: *Great Britain, F. O. 5*] (Transcripts and Photostats, LC), vol. XXXII, p. 78.

46 *Id.* See also Jefferson to Elbridge Gerry, May 13, 1797; *Jefferson Writings*, Washington ed., IV, 173.

Marshall.[47] Practicing in Richmond in the 1780's and 1790's, he found that most of his best clients came from the commercial classes. He made repeated purchases of " military certificates," which were redeemable in land, and invested in various river improvement companies. In 1793 or 1794, he, his brother, James M. Marshall, his brother-in-law, Rawleigh Colston, and Light-Horse Harry Lee became members of a syndicate to purchase the remnant of the great Fairfax estate in the Northern Neck.[48] The money was advanced by the financial " tycoon," Robert Morris. In 1795, James married Morris's sister. Connected socially and economically with commercial and financial circles, John Marshall could hardly fail to develop similar likes and dislikes. These included the attitudes toward the developments in France.

Forces for the weakening of the Anglo-American economic bonds were, however, emerging. Native capital was accumulating in Virginia as in the rest of the United States. The *Norfolk Gazette and Publick Ledger* could write on November 25, 1805, that extensive British credits for goods imported directly from Great Britain were not as common as previously. By 1815, Virginia had two state banks, with numerous branches. True American merchants, trading on American capital, began to appear on the scene. If, to climax it, their trade was with France or the French West Indies, or both, they would be likely to react vigorously against the genuflections of the other merchants toward Westminster. Native Virginian producers of manufactured commodities, relying on their own resources, and making articles which competed with the British, *e.g.*, iron implements, would also, if guided by their economic interests, tend to take an anti-English interpretation of world events.

. . . .

47 *V.* Albert J. Beveridge, *The Life Of John Marshall,* 4 vols. (Boston, 1916-1919) ; and Edward S. Corwin's biography in *Dictionary of American Biography*, Allen Johnson and Dumas Malone, eds., XII.

48 The Northern Neck is that long narrow peninsula bounded by the Potomac and the Rappahannock and a straight line connecting their sources.

In the complex of society from which Virginian opinion of France emanated, political and cultural factors were very significant.

The constitution of the predominantly agrarian Old Dominion lodged power in the hands of the substantial landholders.[49] Various factors—*e. g.*, property qualifications for voting and holding office, the control of the Justices of the Peace over elections,[50] and the overrepresentation of the territory east of the Blue Ridge, especially the Tidewater, in the General Assembly [51]—insured the control of the larger planters. Attempts to democratize the franchise were unavailing. The demand of the back-country for representation according to population was, however, partly satisfied by the creation of new counties from time to time.

The character and philosophy of each political party in the state was of great moment in the formation of attitudes toward the French Revolution and Napoleon. The division of opinion concerning the happenings in France on the whole followed party alignments.

From the outset, the Federalist party had not a chance to control the politics of the Old Dominion. It was constantly in the minority, throughout the period 1789-1815, both in the General Assembly and in the delegation to the federal Congress. Its policies and philosophy ran counter in many ways to the needs and beliefs of the average planter. The backbone of the party was composed of the merchants dependent on British capital, directly or indirectly, lawyers entangled in the mesh of their bickerings, and some planters relying on merchant or British capital for land or other speculation. It also drew recruits in the 1790's from farmers west of the Blue Ridge.

49 *Vide* John Randolph to Thomas M. Forman, October 26, 1813; Box of Letters of John Randolph to T. M. Forman and T. F. Bryan (MSS., LC).

50 *Vide* Isabel Ferguson, "County Court In Virginia, 1700-1830," *North Carolina Historical Review*, vol. VIII, no. 1 (January, 1931), pp. 14-40.

51 The legislature, composed of the House of Delegates and the Senate, was so denominated.

Numerous factors operated to make it possible for many farmers of the Valley and Trans-Alleghany to vote Federalist. With markets in eastern cities, with few or no slaves, with dislike of the eastern aristocrats in control of the state, in need of a strong national government to protect the frontier against the incursions of Indians and foreign powers, and, if Presbyterian in particular, aroused by their clergy to oppose the "infidel" Jefferson [52]—their opposition to the Republicans was not surprising.

In the presidential election of 1800, John Adams was beaten disastrously in Virginia, receiving only 6,224 out of a total of 27,335 votes in nearly complete returns.[53] The Federalist candidate was strong only in the commercial towns, in some counties of the Tidewater, and in the northern Piedmont, the Valley, and the Trans-Alleghany. Relative prosperity and a successful western policy on the part of the Jefferson administration weaned the back-country of much of its Federalism. The Federalist party was so weak during certain periods of the Jefferson administration as to return only one federal representative in the elections of 1801, 1805, and 1807, respectively. Hard times after 1807, which were attributed to the policy of commercial restrictions, revived the Federalists and nourished the new opposition group, the Quids. In the latter half of the Napoleonic era, the Federalist party retained its influence in the commercial towns, consolidated its control of the congressional district composed of the counties of Loudoun, Fairfax, and Prince William, and welcomed parts of the Valley and Trans-Alleghany back to the fold.

Eminent Federalists were inevitably few in the Old Dominion. John Marshall had become the acknowledged leader of the party

52 Jefferson frequently compared the attitude of the Presbyterian clergy of the Valley of Virginia with that of the New England clergy. See, *e. g.*, Jefferson to Gideon Granger, May 20, 1803; *Jefferson Writings*, Ford ed., VIII, 233.

53 See Maude H. Woodfin, "Contemporary Opinion in Virginia of Thomas Jefferson," in *Essays In Honor of William E. Dodd . . .*, ed. by Avery Craven (Chicago, 1935), p. 61.

in Virginia by the late nineties. But a President grateful for his loyalty in a period of serious party rifts promoted him to the highest judicial post in the land, and thereby withdrew him from the local political scene. The state was to remain thereafter without a prominent Federalist leader.

"In Commercial Cities the deformities of federalism are greatest," wrote the Republican Representative Thomas Newton, Jr., of Norfolk, in 1813.[54] The economically dependent and weak commercial capitalists—the nucleus of the Federalist party—shaped whatever political philosophy it developed. The Federalist party was essentially the party of political conservatism, though economically it represented the forces of change. It wished to maintain the political institutions of the time, crowned by the new federal constitution. It praised Alexander Hamilton's financial system, which implemented the constitutional structure by providing it with a solid financial base. Many Republicans sincerely felt that the leaders of the Federalists, in particular, were plotting to establish a monarchy in the United States modeled on that of Great Britain.[55]

In the presence of an overwhelming agricultural population, which had—so the Federalist leaders felt—endangered the security of property and contracts in the 1780's, and might do so again, they became secretly, if not always publicly, fearful of popular government. George Washington wrote in 1786 that "mankind, when left to themselves, are unfit for their own government." [56] In 1787 John Marshall declared, "I fear, and there is no opinion more degrading to the dignity of man, that these have truth on their side who say that man is incapable of governing himself." [57] These fears about the common man

54 To President Madison, December 29, 1813. *Papers of James Madison* (MSS., LC), vol. LIV, no. 5.

55 *E.g.*, *v.* Madison to Jefferson, December 25, 1797; *ibid.*, vol. XX, no. 74. Jefferson to Charles Pinckney, October 29, 1799; *Jefferson Papers*, LC, vol. CV, p. 18078.

56 Quoted in Beveridge, *John Marshall*, I, 301.

57 Marshall to Gen. Wilkinson, January 5, 1787; John E. Oster, *The Political and Economic Doctrines of John Marshall*... (New York, 1914), p. 90.

—and the concomitant belief in government by the few or well-born—were retained in the succeeding decades and reënforced by the events of the French Revolution.

As the Federalist leaders saw the tide turn against them in national politics, as the chances for a return to power receded to a remote and unattainable distance, their wrath knew no bounds, and their venom increased until they virtually frothed at the mouth. They raved and ranted about "real Americanism," which was, in their minds, identical with Federalism.[58] They did not consider as real Americans those Irish or English who had escaped from political persecution to seek refuge in the United States.[59] In other words, they gave nationalism a party label. They saw only the work of atheistic, anarchic, Jacobinical, French democrats in the policies and achievements of the Republican administrations. The leaders of the Federalists and those who continued to follow them ended in a frustrated dream-world of hatred and unhappiness.

Meanwhile, the Republicans ruled the land. They represented the majority of Virginians, as well as of Americans, throughout the Napoleonic era. In the Old Dominion they received the support of most planters, many farmers, American commercial capitalists independent of British capital, lawyers affiliated with either of the previous categories, and mechanics. The planters formed the nucleus.

The philosophy of the Republican party developed in the matrix of an agricultural society. In its most influential form, it was excogitated by Thomas Jefferson, planter of Albemarle County, Virginia. Imbued with a deep humanitarianism, an unbounded curiosity for knowledge, a truly scientific spirit, the author of the Declaration of Independence was recognized by the philosophers of Europe, after the death of Franklin, as the

58 Marshall to Harrison Gray Otis, August 5(?), 1800; John Marshall Papers (Transcripts and Photostats, LC), vol. I.

59 But those Britishers who came here with property and of their own choice—*viz.*, the merchants—were welcome. *V.* the Federalist *Norfolk Gazette and Publick Ledger* of August 21, 1809, and August 16, 1811.

leading American figure of the Age of Enlightenment. Although a facile conversationalist with a vast stock of information, he shunned crowds and did not like to speak at a public meeting. Yet Thomas Jefferson expressed most pointedly the aspirations of the common man of the young agrarian Republic and became the spiritual founder of American liberalism.

His ideas, primarily created by the practical needs of the moment, were never fused into a coherent philosophical treatise, unless his *Notes on Virginia* be considered as a partial attempt at a *summa* in his earlier days. Instead, Jefferson's beliefs were modified and altered as conditions changed. Incongruities and lacunae there were. Every human being has his frailties. But there was a fundamental strain in his thought—that is the enduring thing—which was gradually developed and matured.

Thomas Jefferson reasoned that, since man was a social animal, and since no society could exist without the practice of morality, nature or the Creator must have implanted in man a primordial moral sense, a love of others, a sense of duty to them.[60] Virtue was founded on utility. As with other characteristics, mental or physical, not every human being had the same degree of propensity for virtuous action. Where the moral sense was wanting, education and reason might supply the deficiency. A proper environment nourished morality. " Those who labor in the earth," exclaimed Jefferson in his *Notes on Virginia* in the 1780's " are the chosen people of God, if ever he had a chosen people, whose breasts he has made his peculiar deposit for substantial and genuine virtue." Cities, however, were " pestilential to the morals, the health and the liberties of man." [61]

The Virginian's faith in human nature varied with events, tending to increase after the successful " Revolution of 1800." The fundamental strain in his philosophy was, undoubtedly,

60 To Thomas Law, June 13, 1814; *Jefferson Writings,* Washington ed., VI, 350. To Francis W. Gilmer, June 7, 1816; *Jefferson Writings,* Ford ed., X, 32.

61 To Dr. Benjamin Rush, September 23, 1800; *Jefferson Papers,* LC, vol. CVII, p. 18380.

optimistic. This was a good world on the whole. The possibility of progress was indefinite, though not infinite.

Jefferson's belief in the goodness, reasonableness, and dignity of man—especially of the rural American—was the cornerstone of his political philosophy. Men, being created equal, are thereby endowed with certain inalienable natural rights. Governments are instituted among men for the purpose of securing these reserved rights. They are the right to live, to sustain life, to move about freely (the right of expatriation), and, above all, to think, speak, and write with freedom.

Government, therefore, derives its power from the consent of the governed. The best form of government is republicanism. Republican government is antithetical to barbarism, bigotry, and despotism. It is based on reason, justice, and the free consent of the majority, while monarchy is grounded in compulsion and bolstered by aristocratic and clerical privilege. The ideal citizen of a republic is rational and virtuous, glorying in his freedom and respecting the freedom of his neighbors. A republican government protects these freedoms; maintains order by means of a militia, a citizen army,[62] not a standing army, which is a threat to free government; provides equal justice to all; and performs these functions in the most frugal manner.[63] The foreign policy of a republic is rational and peace-

62 One of the basic ideas of the Republican party of Virginia was a firm belief in the militia, which was so essential for the maintenance of the authority of slave-owners over their human chattels. See Representative Matthew Clay's address in the House, January 19, 1808; *Annals of Congress,* 10th Cong., 1st Sess., II, 1474.

63 Republican government would not interfere with the economic activities of the individual. Did the self-reliant farmer or planter require assistance? Laisser-faire, in general, was the password of Thomas Jefferson in economics. Later, however, during the period of a foreign policy of commercial restrictions, he saw an advantage in the protective wall established thereby for American manufactures. Having recognized from the beginning the visionary character of his hope that America would remain purely an agricultural nation, he did not find it too difficult to reach a fuller conception of economic activity in those years. Jefferson then favored an equilibrium between agriculture, industry, and commerce in the United States. Industry was merely to use the raw materials of the American farmer and manu-

ful. War brings in its train dangers to republicanism. A republic, consequently, abides by international law, which is natural and reasonable law.

By republican government Thomas Jefferson meant popular government. During his active political career, which covered most of his life, he did not implement republicanism in a truly democratic fashion. True, the suffrage he had proposed for Virginia at various times, even prior to 1809, had been practically universal for adult males.[64] But he had dreaded the tyranny of the legislature, as of the other branches of government. His unfortunate experiences as governor of Virginia from 1779 to 1781 had left an almost indelible impression on his mind. Consequently, among other tenets, he had believed in checks and balances, and had leaned to the concept of an upper house selected in an undemocratic fashion as against a popularly elected lower house. Jefferson's own rational mind, however, was educated by experience. Particularly after his retirement, the sage of Monticello arrived at democracy—the logical inference from his belief in the dignity of man.[65] But

---

facture only enough for American consumption, and commerce would simply carry the surplus produce of agriculture to foreign countries in exchange for articles not grown or manufactured in the United States. *Vid., e. g.*, the letter to James Jay, April 7, 1809; *Jefferson Papers*, LC, vol. CLXXXVII, p. 33246.

64 That was so even in the earliest plan, the proposed constitution of 1776. Although land or taxes was made the basis of its franchise, he provided that the state government should grant adults not meeting the qualifications a small parcel of land which would be more than sufficient to satisfy the voting requirements.

65 In a famous letter to Samuel Kercheval (July 12, 1816; *Jefferson Papers*, LC, vol. CCVII, pp. 36948-51) he admitted that he had not originally, but that he had finally, penetrated the basic principle of republicanism, that "'governments are republican only in proportion as they embody the will of their people, and execute it.'" Hence, besides a general suffrage, he proposed for Virginia direct elections, equal representation, and a popularly elected governor and judiciary as well as a legislature. He wanted to increase the participation of the citizens in government through the division of counties into small units of local government (wards). Finally, he favored periodical amendments to the constitution, since laws and institutions must advance *pari passu* with the progress of the human mind. He might have added another reason, which he had used on previous occasions, *viz.*, that the earth belongs to the living.

even his democracy was nourished by a fear of the concentration of power.[66]

The United States, in his opinion, was best suited for the great republican experiment.

> Never was a finer canvas presented to work on than our countrymen. All of them engaged in agriculture or the pursuits of honest industry, independent in their circumstances, enlightened as to their rights, and firm in their habits of order and obedience to the laws. . . . If ever the morals of a people could be made the basis of their own government, it is our case. . . .[67]

Unfortunately, this could not last forever. Merchants were already a source of avarice and corruption. Jefferson felt so, especially after the opposition of New England to the embargo. He believed that when the vacant lands had been occupied, and the safety-valve closed, the mechanics would be reduced to the minimum of subsistence and, hence, to depravity, like the pauperized laboring population of European cities.[68] Eventually, Americans would be concentrated in large cities, and become as corrupt as Europeans. But the benevolent sage did not usually think about the ultimate degeneracy of American society. It was too far off in the distant future. America was still an agricultural nation.[69]

66 See his letter to Joseph C. Cabell, February 2, 1816; *Jefferson Writings,* Washington ed., VI, 543-4.

67 Jefferson to Vice-President Adams, February 28, 1796; *Jefferson Papers,* LC, vol. XCIX, p. 17036. The first letter of each sentence quoted from Jefferson's manuscripts has been capitalized in the text, although Jefferson did not usually do so.

68 Jefferson to J. Lithgow, January 4, 1805. *Jefferson Papers, 1801-1808, Not printed by P. L. Ford in his Writings of Thomas Jefferson* (MSS., Massachusetts Historical Society: hereafter, MHS). Incorrectly listed: to "Mr. Lithson," in *Jefferson Writings,* Washington ed., IV, 563. Note Jefferson's recognition of the important rôle of the frontier in American history.

69 Since Jefferson believed that education as well as independence of circumstances was essential to render the people safe depositaries of government, he asserted that it was the function of a republican government to provide free education. The common man merely required a limited education

Other countries, lacking the necessary prerequisites, were not as yet prepared for such a degree of popular government as was America. A people had to be ready for self-government. Otherwise, it would end in the "tyranny . . . of the many, the few, or the one." [70] The excellence of every government was its adaptation to the state of those to be governed by it. Through the progress of knowledge and habituation to independent circumstances, a people would become capable of estimating the true value of freedom and the principle of majority rule upon which it rested. A progressive extension of popular government would thus follow the progress of the individual.

Thomas Jefferson frequently reiterated in his numerous letters that the Republican party was the party of the agricultural interests as opposed to the Federalist party of merchants, financiers, and stock-jobbers. It was the agrarian character of the Republican party that attracted the average planter of the Old Dominion. The paradox of conservative-minded individuals, like Edmund Pendleton, in a party led by Jefferson thus becomes comprehensible. As in other movements or parties in history, the leader found that he had a diversity of followers. Many agreed with the fundamental features of his philosophy, a considerable number were more conservative, and some were more radical. It might be said that Jefferson was "a little left of center."

Republican politicians in Congress defended the liberal principles of government by the people (though usually meaning property-owners),[71] majority rule, civil liberties, and a citizen

---

to enlighten him concerning the dangers of government degenerating into tyranny and to prepare him for active citizenship. The educational system, however, must also select the most promising students, regardless of wealth or birth, for further training to become "the aristocracy of virtue and talents." This "aristocracy" would rule the republic. *Vide* the preamble to Jefferson's "Bill for the more General Diffusion of Knowledge," 1779, *Jefferson Writings*, Ford ed., II, 221; and the letter to John Adams, October 28, 1813, *Jefferson Writings*, Washington ed., VI, 221 f.

70 To Lafayette, February 14, 1815; *Jefferson Papers*, LC, vol. CCIII, p. 36140.

71 There was, however, an important left-wing of the party to whom "the people" signified all, or practically all, adult males. Among those actively

army. They bitterly opposed strong governments, standing armies and navies, and onerous taxes. They accused the Federalists of pursuing such policies in the 1790's and, thereby, following the practices of the British monarchy. Republicans were vitriolic against the British and other monarchies. The "paper-men," they expostulated, were aristocrats and monocrats.

During the 1790's, the decade of adversity for Republicans in the federal government and of enthusiasm for the French Revolution, there was an emotionalism and a romanticism in Republican terminology. These qualities were stimulated by various individuals. There was, as an example, the young Irish revolutionist, refugee, and writer, John Daly Burk. Editor of newspapers in Boston and New York, he was adversely affected by the operation of the Alien and Sedition Acts, and fled to Petersburg, Virginia. While his heart remained in Ireland, he wrote plays glorifying the American Revolution and expressing passionately the romantic libertarianism of the period. He breathed hatred of kings and love of liberty and equality.[72] To him Jefferson's election to the presidency marked the birth of a new world of freedom for man.[73]

Bishop James Madison, cousin of the Madison who was to become president of the United States, did his share. The first

---

championing, at one time or another, the extension of the suffrage and other democratic reforms in the state of Virginia, were, in addition to Jefferson, William A. Burwell, warm friend of President Jefferson, his private secretary during the first term, and Congressman from 1806; and William Munford, poet, dramatist, and reporter of the decisions of the state Supreme Court of Appeals. Some newspapers, on occasions, also supported reform: for example, the influential Richmond *Virginia Argus*, published by Samuel Pleasants, Jr., on December 29, 1801, and the Petersburg *Republican*, published by Edward Pescud, on December 1, 1806.

72 See, for example, his *Bunker-Hill; Or The Death Of General Warren* (New York, 1797); and *Female Patriotism, Or The Death Of Joan D'Arc* (New York, 1798).

73 *An Oration, Delivered On The Fourth Of March, 1803, At The Court-House, In Petersburg: To Celebrate The Election Of Thomas Jefferson And The Triumph Of Republicanism* (T. Field, Printer).

bishop of the Protestant Episcopal Church of Virginia and President of the College of William and Mary was a scientist, cartographer, and true *philosophe*. Bishop Madison developed a republican interpretation of Christianity. He wrote to Jefferson in 1800 that the Christian religion, correctly understood and carried into full effect, would establish "a pure Democracy" throughout the world. "Its [*i. e.,* Christianity's] main Pillars are Equality, Fraternity, Justice, Universal Benevolence. . . . The true X^{n} [*sic,* for Christian] must be a good Democrat." [74] Is it any wonder that the College of William and Mary was a hot-bed of libertarian doctrines in the late eighteenth century? Joseph C. Cabell, later the principal coadjutor of Jefferson in the founding of the University of Virginia, then a student at the College, stated in 1798 that Rousseau seemed to be the standard authority on politics for the students, and that democrats were in abundance, "some moderate, some warm, some red hot." [75]

However, as the Republicans consolidated their power in the national theatre, as their accomplishments fell short of the liberal expressions of their leader, and as popular government in France was replaced by one-man government, the romantic revolutionary idealism of the last decade of the eighteenth century waned. The emotional development of the American and French people during the Napoleonic era was thus strikingly similar.

Symptomatic of this illiberal trend was the emergence after 1805 of the Tertium Quids, predominantly a group of Republican politicians of Virginia. Power for the Republican party brought in its train internal disputes and dissent. The Tertium Quids became the chief faction of opposition Republicans in the Old Dominion. Though personal factors played their part

74 Bishop Madison to Jefferson, February 11, 1800; *Jefferson Papers*, LC, vol. CVI, p. 18180. The term "democracy" was frequently used loosely as equivalent to republicanism.

75 Cabell to David Watson, March 4, 1798. Garret Minor-David Watson Correspondence (MSS., LC).

in precipitating the rupture with the administration, the Quids differed from the majority Republicans on fundamental domestic and foreign issues. The height of their influence was reached in the abortive attempt in 1808 to elect as successor to Jefferson the disgruntled and ambitious minister plenipotentiary and extraordinary, James Monroe. His strength, the election proved, lay chiefly in the Tidewater. The Monroe ticket, however, received only 2,770 votes in the entire state as against Madison's 12,451, in practically complete returns.[76]

The leader of the Quids—in so far as such an amorphous faction could have a leader—was John Randolph, the baron of Roanoke. Emotionally hypersensitive, he suffered—or imagined he did—from a variety of physical illnesses. When not in Congress or at the races, the bachelor, dejected and despondent, lived a life of solitude on his large plantation. He yearned for mental peace, eventually turning to emotional religion for solace in the last years of the Napoleonic era. He was proud, haughty, vain, egotistical, ambitious. Booted and spurred, with whip in hand, the "pale, meagre, ghostly man,"[77] swaggered about the House of Representatives. He led the administration majority during Jefferson's first term with ability, but in 1806 went over to the opposition. He was a preëminent orator, despite the rambling, incoherent, and repetitious character of many of his extemporaneous speeches. Randolph was acrid and intemperate in debate, the scourge of anyone who disagreed with him. "For hours on end his shrill but flute-like voice irritated and fascinated, pouring upon his audience shafts of biting wit, literary allusions, epigrams, parables, and figures of speech redolent of the countryside."[78]

76 Charles H. Ambler, *Sectionalism in Virginia from 1776 to 1861* (Chicago, 1910), pp. 89-90. Many Federalists voted for Monroe in the election.

77 The description of Senator William Plumer of New Hampshire; quoted in William C. Bruce, *John Randolph of Roanoke, 1773-1833 . . .* (New York, 1922), I, 175.

78 Dumas Malone's biographical article on John Randolph in the *Dictionary of American Biography*, XV, 366.

While Randolph might be considered the political chieftain, John Taylor of Caroline, on the outer fringes of the faction, was the philosopher. Taylor was a wealthy planter and occasional United States senator who championed scientific agriculture and wrote voluminous abstruse works on political philosophy. Other prominent Virginia Quids were James Mercer Garnett, gentleman farmer and congressman; Benjamin Watkins Leigh, a promising young Petersburg lawyer; George Hay, who was with the group until his father-in-law, Monroe, as Secretary of State under President Madison, accepted the administration policy; and Representative Edwin Gray.[79]

Those who were consistently Quids criticized virtually the entire foreign policy of the Jefferson and Madison administrations, beginning with the Florida appropriation and the Non-Importation Act of 1806. Their attitudes on foreign relations and Napoleon I brought them close to the Federalists, whom they considered their enemies.

After all, the Quids maintained that the Republican administrations were betraying *the cause*. Entrapped by power and the capitalistic interests—*i.e.*, non-agricultural capitalism—the Republican party, they insisted, was adopting Hamilton's program of fostering finance, commerce, and industry at the expense of the agricultural classes of America. The Quids wanted to transform the Republican party into a one hundred per cent Southern planters' party, exclusively concerned with the preservation of the landed order. They harped on the program of the 1790's as the only true program of the Republicans—opposition to strong government, standing armies, navies, and federal taxation. Though they had supported the Louisiana Purchase while Republicans, they now, being in the opposi-

79 Mr. Ambler is incorrect (*Sectionalism*, p. 87) in including Matthew Clay, uncle of Henry Clay, among the Quids. Clay in his votes and actions was generally an administration man. He supported the embargo, tried to dissuade Monroe from running against Madison in 1808 (letter to Monroe, February 29, 1808; *Papers of James Monroe*, MSS., LC, vol. XVI, p. 2816), and, although not present when the vote for war against Great Britain was taken, he supported it.

tion, again clamored for state rights as in the Virginia and Kentucky Resolutions. They became the champions of Southern sectionalism.[80]

Embittered John Randolph—delivering one philippic after another against the "dictatorship" of "St Thomas of *Cantingbury*"[81] and his successor—gave the arch-agrarianism of the Quids, especially in the last years of the Napoleonic era, a truly aristocratic and conservative flavor. His hypersensitivity concerning the rights of the master over his slaves has already been indicated.[82] Randolph was also at the head of other conservative currents in early nineteenth-century Virginia. He ridiculed the "Utopian idea of human excellence,"[83] vigorously resisted any talk of universal suffrage, and wished to keep America for Americans by opposing immigration. Thomas Paine was to him but an irreligious staymaker. Randolph was "no man for a Government of mobs, but of order, law, and religion. . . ."[84] A conception of an Anglo-Saxon Christian

80 John Taylor, in *Arator*, a treatise on scientific agriculture and agrarian politics, and in *An Inquiry Into The Principles And Policy Of The Government Of The United States,* developed the philosophy of agrarianism which was inherent in the Republican party. The basis of republicanism, he maintained, was the landed interest. The real source of danger to republicanism in America was a capitalistic aristocracy of "paper and patronage." Banks, tariffs, and the other paraphernalia of capitalism exploited and ruined agriculture. A republican government, therefore, must adhere unswervingly to a policy of laisser-faire, and abolish all special privileges for capitalism, whether in the form of charters or tariffs. (*Arator*, originally published as a series of essays in a Georgetown newspaper in 1803, was reprinted in book form a decade later. I have used the 2nd ed., revised and enlarged, Georgetown, D. C., 1814. *An Inquiry*... ; Fredericksburg, 1814. Taylor had broached these ideas in a number of pamphlets in the 1790's.)

81 So Randolph called Jefferson; see the letter of Randolph to Garnett, August 14, 1810; *Letters of John Randolph of Roanoke, Charlotte County, Va., and James M. Garnett of Elmwood, Essex County, Va., 1806-1832* (Transcripts, LC), p. 124.

82 *Supra,* p. 23.

83 Letter of Randolph to Josiah Quincy, October 18, 1813. *Life of Josiah Quincy of Massachusetts* by his son, Edmund Quincy (Boston, 1867), p. 337.

84 Speech of January 10, 1816, in the House; *Annals of Congress,* 14th Cong., 1st Sess., 590.

America was emerging. Under the circumstances, Protestant England became especially attractive. John Randolph of Roanoke thus became the harbinger of the conservative South of ante-bellum days.

In the field of culture as well as of politics the period of the French Revolution and Napoleon was an age of transition for Virginia—and the United States. On the one hand, were the representatives of the Age of Enlightenment, led by Thomas Jefferson, president of the American Philosophical Society from 1797 to 1815. Cultured, widely read, versatile, inquisitive, curious about all knowledge; with a scientific spirit, skeptical, critical, questioning all authority; cosmopolitan[85]—they were the American products of the Age of Reason. In religion their norm was deism, or " rational " religion. Church dogmas were to them the children of superstition, and of conniving priests and kings greedy for power.[86] On the other hand, were the religious awakening and the increasingly successful crusade against " infidelity " especially by the Presbyterian, Methodist, and Baptist churches. Small back-country farmers and aristocratic planters, like John Randolph, were swept up by the revivalist tide.

Still predominantly English in culture, the Virginian and American mind had been modified by local, national, and French influences in the late eighteenth century. Among the more ardent patriots, the American Revolution had left a legacy of dislike for things British. A consciousness of national independence, a desire to be free of England, culturally as well as politically, stirred them. Interest and affection were turned in the direction of France, the great ally in the war for liberty. For example, Jefferson's " Romanism " in architecture—strengthened by a feeling of nationalism—was matured during his stay

85 Note Jefferson's frequent references to the cosmopolitan character of scientists; *e. g.*, Jefferson to Dr. Wistar, December 16, 1800; *Jefferson Papers*, LC, vol. CVIII, p. 18498.

86 *V.*, *e. g.*, Jefferson to Samuel Kercheval, January 19, 1810; *Jefferson Writings*, Washington ed., V, 492.

in France.[87] The French Revolution had further stimulated interest in the French language, manners, fashions, art, philosophy, and religion. But during the Martian era of Napoleon, the cultural influence of France waned.[88] Thomas Jefferson, nevertheless, continued to maintain contact with his intellectual French friends despite international complications.

The press of Virginia mirrored the political and cultural development of the state and the nation. Newspapers were quite important in the early republic. The French ambassador Turreau implied that the Americans were distinctive. "... *L'on sait*," he reported to his government, "*que les Américains se levent et se couchent, leurs Journaux à la main.*" [89] Since the electorate was relatively small and generally literate, it is not surprising that the leading politicians among Federalists, Republicans, and Quids attested to the great influence of the newspapers. Though their circulation was limited, a single copy passed through many hands.

Most newspapers in Virginia during the Napoleonic period appeared once, twice, or at the most, thrice a week. Dailies were few. The papers now had a four-page format, but the more important ones enlarged their pages to accommodate six or seven wide columns.

During the Napoleonic period, as before, foreign news was generally of greater importance than domestic news. This was natural, since the United States was virtually a part of Europe and buffeted by the domestic and international storms on the other side of the Atlantic. Being predominantly English in culture, the American press relied upon English papers, both Tory and Whig, for the major source of its news. Private

87 In harmony with the classical spirit Jefferson designed the capitol of Virginia, the great country house at Monticello, and later the University of Virginia.

88 See Howard Mumford Jones, *America and French Culture, 1750-1848* (Chapel Hill, 1927).

89 Turreau to Talleyrand, 29 *Frimaire, an* 13; *Affaires Étrangères, États-Unis*, LC, vol. LVII, pt. 6, fol. 438.

letters of merchants and continental papers supplemented the information.

It took from six to ten weeks for news from France to reach the Old Dominion. The lack of a proper system of news gathering made for much more reliance on rumors than nowadays. Spurious documents as well as events in Bonaparte's life were frequently reported.

In a majority of papers the editor was the printer and publisher as well. In the Napoleonic era, editorial columns began to appear, almost regularly, under the local heading on the second or third page. As an editor, the printer's chief implements were frequently scissors and pot-paste, lifting comments from other papers—North and South—freely. Haphazardly, this gave the local newspaper a national tone. Another means of expressing opinion was the publication of " letters "—sometimes in the editorial column—submitted by private individuals, under fanciful pen-names, or occasionally written by the editor himself. Some Virginians—*e. g.*, Henry Banks of Richmond—became prolific contributors of such articles to the local press. In the late eighteenth and early nineteenth centuries the major newspapers of the state began to publish original editorials. The specialized editor appeared upon the scene.

The one to become most famous as an early editor was Thomas Ritchie. Ritchie was the son of a wealthy colonial merchant, who died when Thomas was a child. His cousin Spencer Roane, who became a leading Republican politician and judge of the state Supreme Court of Appeals, guided him in his early youth. After essaying several professions, he became an owner of a small book store in Richmond in 1803. He was only twenty-five years of age when he became the editor of the newly-established Richmond *Enquirer* in 1804. The *Enquirer* was to become the greatest journal in the South.[90]

90 Frank L. Mott, *American Journalism, A History Of Newspapers In The United States Through 250 Years, 1690 to 1940* (New York, 1941), p. 188.

A newspaper editor was influenced in his opinions by various factors connected with his business. A state printing contract, legal publications for the federal government, or the position of postmaster would develop predilections, if he did not already have them, toward the party in power. On the other hand, since subscriptions were usually inadequate and subscribers delinquent in their payments, a newspaper without government support had to rely mainly on advertisements for its existence. An advertising clientele of British-minded merchants would create a Federalist paper. As Jefferson neatly expressed it, "the editors are but cooks who must consult the palates of their customers." [91]

The newspapers were primarily political journals, published in urban areas. Some Virginia newspapers in the 1790's strove for impartiality between Federalists and Republicans. By the last years of the decade, however, practically all journals began to affiliate with one or the other party. The newspapers were founded more and more often as spokesmen of political parties, instead of, as previously, being set up as auxiliaries of a printing establishment. For example, the need for a Republican paper in Richmond in 1804 led to the establishment of the *Enquirer,* sponsored by Judge Roane and encouraged by President Jefferson.[92] Official patronage nourished the paper.

Paralleling public opinion in the Old Dominion, Republican newspapers outnumbered Federalist throughout the Napoleonic period. A Republican journal like the *Enquirer* stressed its

91 To William Short, November 10, 1804; *Jefferson Papers,* LC, vol. CXLIV, between pp. 25125 and 25126.

92 C. C. Pearson, in his biographical article on Roane in the *Dictionary of American Biography,* XV, 642, states that Roane founded the *Enquirer,* but in his article on Ritchie, *ibid.,* 628, Roane's connection with the establishment of that newspaper is not clearly defined. Charles H. Ambler in *Thomas Ritchie, A Study in Virginia Politics* (Richmond, 1913), does not even mention Roane in that connection (p. 19). Rex Beach attributes its founding to Roane; "Spencer Roane and the Richmond Junto," *William and Mary College Quarterly Historical Magazine,* ser. 2, vol. XXII, no. 1 (January, 1942), pp. 1-2.

liberalism,[93] and, when occasion warranted, lauded the agriculturist as against the merchant.[94] On the other hand, a Federalist journal like the *Norfolk Gazette and Publick Ledger,* "whose chief dependence was on advertising custom," [95] declared in its prospectus in 1804: "Our country may well be said to exist by Commerce; as all its fiscal resources are derived from thence. The exertions of every person in the state, ought, therefore, to be directed to the advancement of the interests of the merchant. . . . The Editors of this Gazette will endeavour to discharge this duty." [96] This Norfolk paper frequently insisted that the United States was a representative republic and that it must not become an anarchical Jacobinical democracy.[97] Its tone throughout was conservative.[98]

In accord with the emotionalism of American politics at the time, the press reached the height of blatancy and scurrility. Jefferson was the chief sufferer of the vulgar attacks on personal character. Most infamous in this connection, belying the implications of its original title, was the Richmond *Recorder; or, Lady's and Gentleman's Miscellany.* Through the medium of its columns, one of the publishers, the inebriate, though able, emigrant Scot, James Thomson Callender, spewed forth most furious and billingsgate paragraphs against his former patron. No wonder that the venerable republican sage Chancellor Wythe is alleged to have remarked in 1802 that "the occupation of newspaper editors had become lower than that of scavengers; the former brought filth into our streets, the latter cleansed them." [99]

93 See, *e.g.*, the editorial of June 14, 1805; note its great similarity to Jefferson's views.

94 *E. g.*, *v.* the editorial of December 10, 1812.

95 Editorial of July 18, 1808.

96 Issue of July 17, 1804.

97 *E. g.*, a series of reprints from a non-Virginia paper in September and October, 1805.

98 *V. s.*, p. 30 and n. 59.

99 Quoted in Samuel Mordecai, *Virginia, Especially Richmond, In By-Gone Days . . .* (2nd ed., with many corrections and additions; Richmond, 1860), footnote on p. 229.

The Old Dominion was thus in an age of transition in the late eighteenth and early nineteenth centuries. While the plantation system was declining, commerce and industry—though largely dependent—were prospering. In politics and culture there was an increasingly bitter, many-sided contest between liberalism and traditionalism.

Many aspects of this local environment directly influenced the attitudes toward France or Great Britain. They included the problem of slavery; the market for agricultural produce; the relation between agriculturist and middleman; the sources of capital for commerce and industry; and the character and philosophy of political parties and of the press.

But Virginians were Americans. The developments in the national arena added to the complexity of forces which molded the opinions of the Old Dominion in the Golden Age.

Thus the Virginians, with their diverse personalities, faced the challenge of a Europe in turmoil.

CHAPTER II

INTELLECTUAL AND DIPLOMATIC CHALLENGES—THE FRENCH REVOLUTION AND GENERAL BONAPARTE (1789-1799)

THE early phase of the struggle for a better life in France was generally hailed with enthusiasm in Virginia as in the rest of the United States. The American Revolution was considered by many as the mother of the French Revolution.[1] Admiration of one's offspring was inevitable.

The virtually unanimous approval of the French Revolution, however, did not last long. A host of forces cut a swath across Virginian—and other American—attitudes toward the revolution. As the division of opinion became clear-cut, passions rose to white heat.

Developments in France, the rest of Europe, and the United States coalesced to produce the change. The control of the revolution fell into more and more radical hands. Externally, the French found themselves at war with Europe. And Great Britain was one of the enemies. Great Britain, the European country which aroused such profound and mixed feelings in Americans, became the vanguard of the coalitions against France. The repercussions of the European conflict reached the American shore. The young republic, ostrich-like, tried to bury its head. President Washington issued the Neutrality Proclamation.

Americans, meanwhile, were dividing over domestic issues. Led by Thomas Jefferson, the Republican party emerged as a protest of planters and farmers against the financial policies of Alexander Hamilton. Jefferson's retirement from the ad-

1 *Cf.*, *e. g.*, Madison to Edmund Randolph, October 17, 1788; Gaillard Hunt, ed., *The Writings of James Madison*... (New York, 1900), V, 276. Jefferson to Dr. Price, January 8, 1789; *Jefferson Writings*, Washington ed., II, 553-4.

ministration at the close of 1793 marked the definitive schism between Republicans and Federalists. French developments confirmed and intensified partisan beliefs.

The division of opinion concerning the French Revolution coincided, in general, with the party alignment. Federalists turned against it; Republicans continued to espouse its cause. Complete uniformity within each group did not exist; but there was agreement on fundamental ideas. By 1793 the French Revolution had become a party issue. Republican politicians tested party loyalty by the constancy of one's adherence to the revolution in France.[2]

Virginia Federalists began to criticize the happenings on the other side of the Atlantic. Essentially conservative, they disapproved of the increasing signs of a radical transformation of the French Revolution. The outbreak of war between France and Great Britain transferred the revolution from the realm of ideas to the arena of practical politics. Those elements of Virginia society—and their dependents—who were fastened by bonds of trade and finance to London and Glasgow tended to rally to the cause of " mother England." The admirable British constitution and government, they felt, had to be defended. To paraphrase,—in the eyes of extremists,—France now could do no right.

On the other hand, proud planters of the Old Dominion—and their allies—saw in the struggles of the French republicans a striking similarity to their own domestic contention with British-loving monocratic Federalists. To Jeffersonian liberals the French were still striving for freedom and rational government. The Anglo-French war aroused the planters still more. " Perfidious Albion," they felt, was again trying to destroy liberty, as previously in America. Cornwallis had ravaged plantations and carried off about thirty thousand slaves from Virginia.[3] The British had never paid any compensation, but

2 *Cf.* Madison's letters of 1793. *E. g.*, to Jefferson, July 22, 1793; *Madison Writings*, VI, 136.

3 According to Jefferson, in a letter to Dr. Gordon, July 16, 1788; *Jefferson Writings*, Washington ed., II, 426-7.

they were rigorously trying to recover their "unjust" pre-revolutionary debts. As the Virginia squires interpreted it, the British capitalists formed an interlocking directorate with the enemy of agriculture, the merchant capitalists who dictated Federalist policies. England, moreover, was attempting to restrict the economic activities of its former colony—witness the experience of Jefferson as nail producer. On the other hand, France in the 1790's was a market not only for tobacco but also for some wheat. Merchants independent of British capital and trading with the French West Indies reënforced the ranks of Republicans and admirers of France.

. . . .

French domestic developments were now generally interpreted unfavorably by the Federalists. Conservative Federalists looked with dismay upon the course of events in France. They were loud in condemning the execution of Louis XVI and the steady fall and rise of the blade of the guillotine that soon followed. The religious experiments of the French were in the eyes of many but expressions of vice and depravity. Horrible anarchy had reared its head. "Jacobin" became a term of the vilest opprobrium.[4]

Criticism by Federalists of the more conservative Directory was at the beginning occasionally tempered with some favorable opinion.[5] But the XYZ affair and the apparent preparation of the victorious French government to invade England roused the Federalists to a frenzy of hatred against the Gallic power and the principles it embodied. John Marshall,—a mem-

4 *Cf.* Chief Justice Marshall's eulogy more than a decade later of Gouverneur Morris's opinion of the radical phase of the revolution. John Marshall, *The Life of George Washington...*, vol. V (Philadelphia, 1807), appendix, p. 26, n. XIII.

5 *E. g.*, they approved the suppression of the Babouvist conspiracy of 1796 and referred to the supporters of the French government as the true friends of liberty. *Cf.* the Richmond *Virginia Gazette and General Advertiser*, August 17, 1796. John Marshall expressed some approval of the form of government. Marshall to George Washington, September 15, 1797; Marshall MSS. in the Sparks MSS. (Harvard University Library), vol. LXVI.

ber of the mission to France,—humiliated by the Directory, returned to the United States in a rage. At a dinner in his honor at Richmond on August 11, 1798, he gave vent to a blistering attack on the French state and its policies. He described the government of that country as a despotism, " borrowing the garb and usurping the name of freedom." [6]

No epithet was now strong enough for Federalists to express their detestation of the French régime. The Jacobinical French Republic ruled by " the five-headed monster " was the epitome of all evil: barbarism, mad democracy, despotism, anarchy, atheism.

Appraising the vicissitudes in the history of France in the past decade, the Federalist Fredericksburg *Virginia Herald,* published by Timothy Green IV, of the distinguished American family of printers, stated on October 15, 1799:

> Her various constitutions, her principles of representation, reared upon the cadaverous pile of thousands of her citizens, and cemented with the most generous, enthusiastic blood of the nation, are totally buried under the chaos of anarchy and confusion; and Jacobinism, that rare fungus of the body politic and the bane of social compact, is upon the rubbish rearing its Gothic temples, where every director, not even BARRAS excepted may find his name enrolled on the register of denunciation. Certainly this nation must have reached the acme of wickedness, where from the year 1, to the present day, every man entrusted with the affairs of the people, has proved himself a villain! [7]

The successive purges in France, and the denunciation by sectarian revolutionists of their predecessors as the embodiment of all evil—a fundamental trait of cataclysmic revolutions—had undoubtedly reënforced the conclusion that France itself was then fundamentally wicked.

The administration press in Virginia was beginning to show a little sympathy for France in the latter part of 1799. Presi-

6 See the Fredericksburg *Virginia Herald* for August 24, 1798.

7 Reprinted from the Baltimore *Federal Gazette.*

dent Adams, upon being assured that the special American delegation would be received by the French government, had directed it to proceed. Some Federalist newspapers, thereupon, could state that, despite all the outrages and vices of the French, Americans still hoped that they would find happiness in a government of their choice, a well-regulated republic and not a monarchy. The President's action might infuse a new spirit into the French nation.[8]

Federalists were not only interested in the domestic developments in France *per se*. The international implications of the French Revolution had worried them for some time. They pointed to San Domingo,[9] warning Virginia slave-owners of the danger of espousing French ideas.[10] The revolution was international.[11]

What made matters even worse for Federalists was their belief that the French government used the subversive principles of the revolution, *e.g.*, equality, as an instrument of foreign policy. They claimed that France attempted everywhere to detach the people from their established government—witness Genêt. Divide and conquer was the policy. The Richmond federal postmaster, Augustine Davis, using the scissors as his editorial tool, selected an alarming item from a New York newspaper for insertion in his *Virginia Gazette and General Advertiser* of May 24, 1799. The editorial described French

8 Editorial in the two Federalist papers of Richmond, the *Virginia Federalist* and the *Virginia Gazette and General Advertiser*. Quoted in the Alexandria *Times; and District of Columbia Daily Advertiser* for November 21, 1799.

9 *Cf.* John Marshall, *Life of George Washington*, V, 367-8.

10 *E. g.*, the speech of George Keith Taylor, a brother-in-law of John Marshall, in the House of Delegates, session of 1798-1799; in Ambler, *Sectionalism in Virginia*, p. 69.

11 Some extreme conservatives, particularly among the Northern clergy, interpreted the whole era as an international conspiracy of Freemasons and Illuminati against governments and religions. See Jefferson's brilliant analysis of this historical myth in a letter to Bishop Madison, January 31, 1800; *Coolidge Collection* of *Jefferson Papers* (MSS., MHS).

agents as successfully propagating the pestiferous spirit of discontent in Europe, stirring up the poor against the rich, and instigating desertions from the armies of the coalition. News of the arrival of a number of French citizens at New York, with a M. Du Pont at the head, induced the shivers—or so it was pretended—in a writer using the unconvincing pseudonym "Veritas" in the Fredericksburg *Virginia Herald.*[12] In an article dated January 31, 1800,[13] "Veritas" warned all Federalists and Christians—terms inextricably intertwined in his language—to beware of this group of Frenchmen. They had been sent to the United States by their government and their atheistic Society of the Propaganda [14] to sow dissension and pave the way for French conquest. The only hope was that good Christians would vote Federalist.

In every country, the Federalists maintained, the French had their supporters. The "French party" in the United States was the Republican. True to type, the Republicans were opposed to preparations for defense, no matter what France did to American rights and interests. John Marshall, writing to his brother James on December 16, 1799, concluded that it seemed as if the democrats—a term of opprobrium in the Federalist dictionary applied to Republicans—wanted to push the United States into a war with Britain and to have our country embraced by France.[15] Representative Leven Powell, retired merchant and a Federalist leader in Loudoun County, wrote on December 25, 1799, that he was certain that there were people in the United States who, rather than not rule at

12 The Du Pont was probably Pierre-Samuel du Pont de Nemours and his relatives. Did "Veritas" know that Du Pont was on intimate terms with Jefferson?

13 In the *Virginia Herald* of February 18, 1800. Though this is shortly after the coup of Brumaire became known in Virginia, the ideas in the article were especially relevant for the pre-Napoleonic period.

14 This was a figment of the imagination.

15 Box of John Marshall MSS., LC.

all, would willingly do so with the aid of France, even if it involved the surrender of American independence.[16] In Federalist propaganda, a Republican was a Jacobin, with all the allegedly horrible implications of the appellation.

Even regardless of the alleged Republican intrigue, the wars of the French Republic with the crowned heads of Europe ultimately evoked strong emotional reactions from Federalists. They sympathized with Great Britain and, hence, eventually with its allies in the struggle against the subversive revolution.

As French arms established the victorious tricolor on one rampart after another, and as Franco-American relations became more and more strained, Federalists began by 1795 to talk of the secret and hostile ambition of France against the United States.[17]

The XYZ incident and French violations of American neutral rights—a harbinger of the Napoleonic period—coincided with the danger of a French invasion of "the seagirt isles." Federalists of the Old Dominion, led by John Marshall, believed that the world was at the crossroads. The independence of Europe and America, wrote Marshall from Paris, March 8, 1798, hung on the outcome. If France won, England would become another vassal state, with its fleet at the disposal of the French government.[18] Great Britain with its navy thus became for Federalists the bulwark of the United States against the anarchical French Republic.

After his return to the United States in mid-1798, Marshall clamored for war. Peace could be purchased only by submitting to the yoke of France. Even then peace could only be of short duration, for America would soon be embroiled in the quarrels

16 To Major Burr Powell. "The Leven Powell Correspondence," *The John P. Branch Historical Papers of Randolph-Macon College,* vol. I, no. 3, 1901, p. 237.

17 *Cf.* an essay by James Madison, April 20, 1795; in *Letters And Other Writings Of James Madison...,* Published By Order Of Congress (New York, 1884), IV, 496.

18 To Washington; Sparks MSS., vol. LXVI, Harvard.

of its master.[19] Frenchmen could not be trusted, he wrote.[20] He insisted that whenever France exhibited a disposition to deal justly with the United States, it was trying to ensnare the American Republic into fighting on its side as a dependent nation. If France continued to wage "an unprovoked war" against the United States while the Anglo-French struggle was on, it would be folly for America not to form a temporary alliance with England. The British navy, Marshall pointed out, would then protect the United States against an invasion.[21]

The war hysteria spread. Youths with large black cockades in their hats marched through the little Virginia towns declaiming about patriotism and demanding war against the detestable French Republic.[22]

Federalists and their supporters—reviving a concept of the colonial era [23] and presaging a major charge against Napoleon —warned Americans of the ambition of France to enslave and rule the world. The renegade Republican Josiah Parker, representing the Norfolk electoral area in Congress, stated positively to the House on February 11, 1799, that the goal of the French was universal dominion. This insatiable ambition seemed to be a fundamental national trait, for, according to Parker, its origins were pre-revolutionary.

> This effort [at world rule] was feebly made by Louis XIV.; but as the energies of that nation are now in action, and supported by military enthusiasm, they have advanced, unhappily,

19 Speech at the Richmond dinner of August 11, 1798, in his honor; Fredericksburg *Virginia Herald,* August 24, 1798.

20 To Pickering, August 25, 1799. *T. Pickering MSS., Letters From Correspondents, July-December, 1799,* XXV, 113; MHS.

21 Answer to a set of queries, September 20, 1798; in the Alexandria *Columbian Mirror and Alexandria Gazette,* October 9, 1798.

22 *Cf.* the Republican Alexandria *Times and Alexandria Advertiser,* July 6, 1798.

23 *V.* Max Savelle, "The Appearance of an American Attitude toward External Affairs, 1750-1775," *American Historical Review,* vol. LII, no. 4 (July, 1947), 658 f.

> too far in this career; a great part of Europe and Italy have either been conquered or revolutionized, and the rest paralyzed. Africa now bends under its weight, and Asia is threatened, and trembles for its fate; and, after having extended their arms to every other quarter, if they could get together a navy for the purpose, he [Parker] should expect them to make the attempt upon us.[24]

From 1798 on much talk was heard in Federalist circles of the imminence of a French invasion. After all, the United States was virtually at war with that country. General Washington, however, called from retirement to command the army, wrote more soberly to Timothy Pickering on October 18, 1798. He did not think a formidable invasion of the United States was possible so long as France was embroiled with England. France would willingly attempt it; but the British blockade prevented any transport of troops and munitions across the Atlantic.[25]

England's allies now likewise held a central position in the Federalist picture of the world. Were not the handsome Cossacks and the pious Russian commander Suvarov fighting a holy war for established governments, religion, and the balance of power?[26] Did not the Frenchmen commit unheard-of atrocities? French defeats in 1799, consequently, rejoiced Federalist hearts. The safety of the world, including that of the United States, depended on such events. The venerable Washington, however, again introduced a note of caution. Though pleased with the allied victories, he hoped that the coalition would be wise enough to know at what point to sheathe the sword so that a firm peace could be established.[27]

24 *Annals of Congress*, 5th Cong., III, 3rd Sess., 2872. *Cf.* with James A. Bayard's speech of January 17, 1799; *ib.*, 2712.

25 Worthington C. Ford, ed., *The Writings of George Washington* (New York, 1891), XIV, 109.

26 *Cf.*, *e. g.*, the Republican Richmond *Examiner*, July 12, 1799; and the Federalist Richmond *Virginia Gazette and General Advertiser*, November 3, 1799.

27 To William Vans Murray, October 26, 1799; *Washington Writings*, Ford ed., XIV, 213-214.

John Adams knew when to sheathe the sword. His decision in 1799 to resume negotiations with France opened up the possibility of peace. Administration supporters began to moderate their tone. It was the President's duty to meet the advances of the Directory, wrote Leven Powell on December 11, 1799.[28] True, those people could not be trusted; but if we were not to negotiate with them until they became virtuous, a perpetual state of warfare could be expected. Some thought, he continued, that the administration's action would produce a rupture with Great Britain. The latter could injure us more than France could. If the United States had to be at war, it would be better to fight with France. But, he concluded, he did not believe England would act in such a fashion, and even if it did, he would not ask permission from one nation to settle our differences with another amicably.[29] The opinion of administration supporters moved closer to impartiality late in 1799.

While the French Revolution thus, in general, appeared to Virginia Federalists as the darkest of nights in the history of man, for Republicans of the Old Dominion it marked the dawn of a bright new era. Republicans continued to equate the principles of the American and French Revolutions, of the parent and the child. The establishment of republican government in France intensified their zeal for the cause. Our French friends were trying to emancipate themselves from the oppressions of a king, a privileged aristocracy, and a privileged priesthood. They were striving for liberty, the rights of man, and rational government. What could be more glorious?

The revolution, however, took a circuitous path. For Republicans the Reign of Terror was a necessary, though deplorable, phase of man's struggle for freedom.[30] The ensuing events were more promising. Through the instrumentality of

28 To Major Burr Powell; "The Leven Powell Correspondence," *Branch Historical Papers,* I, no. 3, 232.

29 *Cf.* the *Norfolk Herald,* October 29, 1799.

30 *V., e. g.,* Jefferson to M. d'Ivernois, February 6, 1795; *Jefferson Writings,* Washington ed., IV, 115.

James Monroe, young friend of Thomas Jefferson and minister to the French Republic, the Thermidorians transmitted an encomium of themselves along with a denunciation of their predecessor, "the monster Robespierre," to sympathizing Republican leaders in Virginia. The centrist political views of those Frenchmen harmonized with the moderate republicanism which characterized many Virginians.[31] The government of the Directory was consequently greatly admired by many Republicans, though Jefferson had his doubts concerning the practicality of an executive committee.[32] The experiences of America under the Articles of Confederation had left a deep impress on him.

Monroe was writing home gleefully about the similarity—unfortunately not yet complete—between the American and French governments and the great spirit of contentment that was allegedly discernible among all. Party newspapers echoed these views. The *Richmond and Manchester Advertiser,* the future *Virginia Argus,* published by the Quaker Samuel Pleasants, Jr., praised the new French constitution on February 20, 1796. After many vicissitudes, the editorial stated, the French have finally established a government which agrees in the main with American principles: the abolition of hereditary power, of titles and rank; the popular basis of government; separation of powers; bicameral legislature; subordination of the military to the civil authority; trial by jury, etc. The belief that the Directory had a horror of banks and of funding systems[33] enhanced its merit for Monroe and his Hamilton-hating rural friends in the Old Dominion.

The régime of the Directory was defended by Republicans against Federalist torrents of abuse even during the years of de facto Franco-American war. The editorial in the Richmond

31 *E. g.*, the belief that property should be the basis of the franchise.

32 To John Adams, February 28, 1796; *Jefferson Papers*, LC, vol. XCIX, pp. 17036-7.

33 Monroe to Jefferson, July 30, 1796; Stanislaus M. Hamilton, ed., *The Writings of James Monroe*... (New York, 1898 f.) III, 45.

Virginia Argus of September 6, 1799, is a case in point. It concerned London reports which expected a coup d'état in Paris because the Council of Five Hundred had remonstrated with the Directory. The editorial interpreted the situation favorably:

> This is a proof that the accusations daily uttered here against the directory are false. We have heard much nonsense about the Five Headed Monster, and of that tyranny it exercises over the nation; but we do not see in the proceedings of the legislative body any symptoms of a base or servile submission in its members. The necessary jealousy concerning the management of their finances is preserved, and the council fears not to adopt a firm and energetic language in their communications with the executive.
>
> 'Tis folly for the royalists to expect any thing favorable from a convulsion at Paris. Hitherto the elevation of one party over another, has been the prelude to greater exertion and energy on the part of the Republic; if therefore any change should happen, it would most likely be injurious to the cause of monarchy and slavery.[34]

Though the internal developments of the French Revolution aroused much fervor in Republicans, its international potentialities and significance perhaps stirred their greatest interest and enthusiasm.

The success of that revolution, Jefferson had written as early as February 4, 1791, was necessary not only to ensure the progress of liberty in Europe but also to bolster popular government in the United States against the attempts of stock-jobbing Hamiltonians to establish that " Half-way house," the English form of government.[35]

The establishment of the French Republic reënforced Jefferson's concept of the interdependence of America and France.

34 Reprinted from the *New York Argus.*

35 To George Mason; *Jefferson Writings,* Ford ed., V, 274-5.

Republicanism was a new force in the politics of western civilization. The American Republic felt isolated in a world of monarchies. How much safer it would be for the United States to have a major European state adopt a similar form of government! The Virginia philosopher could, therefore, declare in an impassioned letter on January 3, 1793, that "the liberty of the whole earth was depending on the issue of the contest" in France.[36] He was prone to exaggerate when transported by emotion. In a calmer mood he admitted that the success of the American Republic was dependent only in part on the outcome of the revolution across the Atlantic. A failure there would provide a strong argument for the apostles of "English despotism" to prove that the American experiment had to fail also. But we would still remain free.[37] Nevertheless, the international character of republicanism and the interdependence of the American and French Republics became the stock in trade of Thomas Jefferson and the Virginia Republicans throughout the French Revolution.

To them the conflict between France and the other European powers, led by "perfidious Albion," was the product of a conspiracy of princes against human liberty. The combined despots of Europe were trying to prevent the French people from choosing their own form of government. The monarchs feared that a successful revolution in France would influence their own enslaved peoples to raise their heads and insist upon the rights of man. The European war was thus a struggle between the privileged orders and the people, between despotism and liberty, between superstition and reason.

Could American republicans remain aloof from such a cause? Our fate was tied up ideologically with that of France. Moreover, once the crowned tyrants had defeated the French Republic, annexed parts of it (if not the whole), and reëstablished despotism in the remainder, might they not pursue liberty to

36 To Short; *ib.*, VI, 154.

37 To Brissot de Warville, May 8, 1793; *ib.*, VI, 249.

its native clime and attempt to destroy it here also?[38] France was our bulwark.

Republicans aped French revolutionary fashions, hailed each other as Citizen,' wore red caps of liberty or mounted the tricolor cockade, and dated their letters from Year I of the French Republic.[39] Many newly-founded Democratic Societies advocated war in behalf of France.[40] The Martinsburg *Potowmac* [*sic*] *Guardian, and Berkeley Advertiser* blazoned as its motto "Where Liberty Dwells, There Is My Country. *Franklin*." Youthful William Munford, in an oration at William and Mary on the seventeenth anniversary of the American Republic, depicted a glorious vista for mankind. Republican France was on the march! Victory had to attend those who fought for liberty. Once France was free, all of Europe would follow the example.

> Then, at the call of reason and philosophy, mankind will throw away the weapons of death, and embrace in friendship. The land, cultivated by free men, will yield a sufficient produce for its numerous inhabitants: the same hand that sowed shall reap the grain. . . . Vanity and ambition will desolate the world no more, no more will ardent warriors meet in battle. No more will the ship intended for commerce, carry in its bosom the thunder of war, but all nations will form one

38 *Vid., e.g.*, Monroe's *A View of the Conduct of the Executive, in the Foreign Affairs of the United States connected with the mission to the French Republic during the years 1794, 1795, and 1796* (1797), in *Monroe Writings*, Hamilton ed., III, appendix, p. 453; and a draft of his essay in answer to criticisms of the *View* (1798), in *Papers of James Monroe*, LC, vol. V, p. 906.

39 *V., e.g.*, the entry in the journal of the émigré Moreau de Saint-Mery for May, 1794, concerning Norfolk opinion; in Norflett, "Norfolk... As Seen By Moreau de Saint-Mery...," *Virginia Magazine Of History And Biography*, vol. XLVIII, no. 3 (July, 1940), p. 255.

40 See, for example, the "Address to the People of the United States" by the Democratic Society of Wythe County; quoted in Charles D. Hazen, *Contemporary American Opinion of the French Revolution* (Johns Hopkins University Studies in History and Political Science, Extra vol. XVI; Baltimore, 1897), p. 202.

vast society of brethren. Then, over all the earth perpetual peace will diffuse her heavenly joys, and all grief and mourning will be buried in endless oblivion.[41]

French conquests in the succeeding years did not daunt Republicans. They could not believe that France, as a republic, could be imbued with a lust for domination, as the Federalists charged. Indeed, by overthrowing such governments as those of Holland, Switzerland, and the Papal States, France was liberating oppressed peoples. The tribute levied by France on the defeated peoples was small in contrast to taxes in Great Britain.[42] France could not be upsetting the balance of power, because such a balance was a mere figment of the imagination.[43] Stories of French atrocities, Republicans insisted, were concocted by the enemies of the revolution in Great Britain and the United States. Federalist glorification of the Russians was answered by Meriwether Jones, publisher of the *Examiner,* the leading Republican newspaper in Richmond during the Adams administration.[44] The issue of July 12, 1799, stated: "All mankind know that the Russian Cossacks are ugly to a proverb, and that their manners are as barbarous as barbarity itself." Suvarov was described as "the most detested butcher in Europe."

The British government, leader of the coalitions against France, received its due share of Republican invective. England was uniformly considered as the aggressor. It was moti-

41 William Munford, *Poems, And Compositions In Prose On Several Occasions* (Richmond, 1798), 2nd ed., p. 162. Middle-aged Tom Jefferson could easily match this fervent bit of libertarianism. To Tench Coxe, May 1, 1794; *Jefferson Writings,* Washington ed., IV, 104.

42 *The Times and Alexandria Advertiser* of August 29, 1798. The title of the paper was altered on April 17, 1799, to *The Times; and District of Columbia Daily Advertiser.*

43 William B. Giles in the House of Representatives, March 29, 1798; *Annals of Congress,* 5th Cong., II, 2nd Sess., 1349.

44 According to the obituary in the Richmond *Enquirer* of August 22, 1806, Jones in 1799 frequently superintended his press with his pistols within reach.

vated, they said, by the same prime reason as the continental powers, namely, to destroy liberty in France and then in the United States. Did not Britain oppress the Irish? Did not Federalist monocrats pray for a British victory to aid them in establishing a monarchy in the United States? Why, some of the influential Anglo-aristocrats were even dreaming of the restoration of "his most gracious Majesty George the Third"![45] British machinations, some Republicans claimed, were responsible for the continued shedding of blood by the continent to protect the island kingdom against the invasion with which a rejuvenated France now threatened it.[46]

Virginia Republicans fervently hoped for the establishment of a republican government in Great Britain. They thought they saw conditions in that kingdom which would produce a revolution: an oppressive government, a staggering national debt, a ruined commerce. If internal conditions were not ripe enough, England's defeat by France should lead to the desired result. Why should not France, especially when freed of its continental foes, be able to succeed? France, with its superior resources, population, and military skill, had to win. The French justly hated the British despotism. They would not desist until victory had been achieved.[47] Most Republicans in their calmer moments probably did not desire that England be subjugated by France but that it should merely be republicanized.[48]

Republicans of the Old Dominion generally insisted that French successes, if not ultimate victory over Britain, would redound to the direct benefit of the republican United States.

45 Jefferson to S. T. Mason, October 11, 1798; *Jefferson Writings,* Washington ed., IV, 258.

46 *Virginia Argus,* April 11, 1797.

47 *E.g.,* John Clopton to his constituents, February 22, 1796; in the *Richmond and Manchester Advertiser,* March 12, 1796. Giles in the House of Representatives, March 29, 1798; *Annals of Congress,* 5th Cong., II, 2nd Sess., 1351-2.

48 *V., e.g.,* Jefferson to P. Fitzhugh, February 23, 1798; *Jefferson Writings,* Washington ed., IV, 217-8.

English defeats would compel that government to curtail its aggressions against us. Federalists would hesitate in their drive for war with France. And if Great Britain could be republicanized, the American form of government would be safe.[49]

The attitude of the Virginia Republicans toward the foreign policy of the United States was, consequently, militantly anti-British throughout the period of the French Revolution. England was our natural enemy; France, our natural ally. Though, in general, the leaders of the party favored American neutrality in the European war, they had criticized Washington's method of implementing this policy as "Anglomany." [50] Jay's treaty aroused a storm of indignation. John Nicholas of Albemarle County expressed this feeling in the House of Representatives on April 16, 1796, by declaring that the people of the United States would not transfer their alliance from France to England.[51]

French depredations on American commerce complicated matters. Federalists began to talk of war with France. Republicans, however, continued to insist upon neutrality as the only correct course to pursue between the Scylla and Charybdis of the European war. The hostility of France was comprehensible, they said. It was the fruit of the Jay Treaty.[52] Besides, England also injured our commerce; in fact, it had been the first to do so. France had been sympathetic to our commercial activity, Jefferson claimed in a letter of February 21, 1798, until she realized that the United States was throwing its weight into the scale of her enemies. Hence France, like Britain earlier, had decided to exclude America from the

49 *E. g.*, Jefferson to Thomas Mann Randolph, January 11, 1798; *Jefferson Papers*, LC, vol. CII, p. 17554.

50 The leaders, however, did not approve of "the indiscretions" of the French minister Genêt. *E. g.*, Monroe to John Breckenridge, August 23, 1793; *Monroe Writings*, Hamilton ed., I, 272.

51 *Annals of Congress*, 4th Cong., 1st Sess., 1014.

52 James Madison to J. Madison, Sr., March 12, 1797; *Madison Writings*, Hunt ed., VI, 309.

ocean. But the lord of Monticello concluded on an optimistic note: " How far it may lessen our happiness to be rendered merely agricultural, how far that state is more friendly to principles of virtue & liberty, are questions yet to be solved. . . ." [53]

Republican France, Jefferson and his followers agreed, could not desire war with the American Republic. Nor could the United States fight a government based on the principle of freedom. Republicans, furthermore, declared that mere talk of war caused suffering for farmers as agricultural prices dropped. Neutrality was, for all of these reasons, the only policy. John Taylor of Caroline hinted that the South might find it to its interest to secede in case of war and the resultant " immovable fixation of our monarchy." [54]

The XYZ affair, however, and the war hysteria it occasioned, found Republicans completely on the defensive. Some Virginia congressmen abstained from voting on the war measures. Josiah Parker joined the war party. The party line, however, continued to adhere to peace, while stanch Republicans attempted to hamstring the Federalist preparations for war. After studying the documents on the XYZ incident, Thomas Jefferson decided that the Directory had no connection with the mysterious individuals who approached the American commissioners. By January 29, 1799, he was describing it as a " dish cooked up by Marshall, where the swindlers are made to appear as the French government." [55]

That was sufficient proof for Republicans that the Anglomonocrats were determined to engage in war on the side of Great Britain. Thereby they could consummate their nefarious plans for the annihilation of the American Republic. Was there, consequently, any wonder at French hostility toward the ad-

53 To Gen. Gates, February 21, 1798; *Jefferson Papers*, LC, vol. CIII, pp. 17594-5.

54 To Henry Tazewell, June 13, 1797. Summarized in Henry H. Simms, *Life of John Taylor*... (Richmond, 1932), p. 69.

55 To Edmund Pendleton, January 29, 1799. *Washburn Papers* (MSS., MHS), vol. II (*Jefferson Papers*), no. 19.

ministration? The only hope for peace, Republicans felt, lay in French victories in Europe that would frighten the Federalist warmongers. The publication of Elbridge Gerry's correspondence convinced Jefferson and his followers that the Directory wanted peace despite the anti-French policy of the administration. Moreover, Jefferson claimed on February 11, 1799, that English captures of American vessels had greatly exceeded the French duing the preceding six months.[56] If a war had to be fought, wrote Edmund Pendleton in a campaign document of 1799, it ought to be against the British rather than the French. He maintained, however, that there was no real cause for fighting either.[57] Republicans, therefore, asked the administration to attempt to establish peace with France.

Federalist charges of French influence upon the Republican party were vigorously denied. A typical reply was included in John Page's circular of November 16, 1798, soliciting election to the House of Representatives.[58] Page, a life-long friend of Thomas Jefferson, explained that as a citizen of a republic, which had been enabled to attain its freedom with the assistance of France,—now also a republic,—he had thought it just and politic to cherish the good-will of that country. The American people should be on guard against the wiles of the British monarchy to subvert our government in order to replace it with a monarchy, establish commercial control over us, or even reconquer us. An alliance with Great Britain would, therefore, be dangerous to our liberties. But a close connection with France, he had felt, would give us security against the English. Peace with both was, nevertheless, his wish. Page deplored the

56 To Monroe; *Jefferson Writings*, Washington ed., IV, 283.

57 The pamphlet written by the aged leader of the moderates in Virginia during the American Revolution was in response to an urgent plea from the party chieftain, Jefferson. The Republican party on the defensive was marshaling all its forces. For a summary of the address see Robert L. Hilldrup, *The Life and Times of Edmund Pendleton* (Chapel Hill, 1939), pp. 313 f.

58 John Page, *To the Citizens of Accomack* [*sic*], *Northampton, Elizabeth-City, Warwick, and York.* Rosewell, November 6, 1798 (Broadsides, LC).

then unhappy state of affairs with France, but declared that he would be bound by the will of the majority and support only American interests. Though John Page did not at this time specifically accuse the Federalists of being pro-British, the cry of "British faction" was common in Republican recrimination.

Federalist alarm at the danger of a French invasion was ridiculed by the opposition. Representative Richard Brent, arguing on May 8, 1798, against a bill to enlarge the army, attempted to demolish the chief reason offered for its necessity —invasion. "... It is a mere bugbear. Gentlemen who speak of this have surely forgotten the immense ocean which happily separates us from Europe, as well as the immense militia of the country." The French, he continued, had no means of transporting a large army to the United States unless they used balloons. France, moreover, had no desire to invade our country. Even if she was imbued with that spirit of domination of which Federalists spoke, she did not have to cross a tempestuous ocean to exercise it. There were better opportunities nearer home. Brent, therefore, concluded that there was no danger of an invasion from France.[59]

After President Adams had sent another commission to France in 1799, the Republicans attempted to have the law of July, 1798, prohibiting commercial intercourse with France, modified. In a speech in the Virginia House of Delegates on January 8, 1800, in favor of an instruction to that effect to the state's senators at Philadelphia, William B. Giles affirmed that the law had given the British a monopoly of tobacco. By the other war measures Virginia had been excluded from the markets of several continental nations besides France. Tobacco, he stated, had, therefore, fallen from a mean of $10/cwt. to $3.33, the difference being taken from the pocket of the Virginia planter and put into that of the British merchant.[60] Madison reported to Jefferson on January 12 that the

59 *Annals of Congress*, 5th Cong., II, 2nd Sess., 1640-1641.

60 Reported in the Richmond *Examiner*, January 10, 1800.

resolution had passed the Virginia House without a count or division. On January 17, from Philadelphia, Jefferson informed his daughter Maria Eppes that the Northern members were about to renew the law for non-intercourse with France. By that law, he asserted, the North (meaning the commercial interests) planned to prohibit the exportation of tobacco and to reduce the tobacco states to passive obedience by poverty.[61]

. . . .

The appearance of General Napoleon Bonaparte upon the stage of history did not alter by a tittle the Janus-faced interpretation of the French Revolution which Virginians had elaborated. The general merely stepped into the appropriate niche and, it appears, remained there until the events of Brumaire awakened the Old Dominion to the realization that he had ushered in a new era.

At first Bonaparte was scarcely mentioned. Men wrote of the Italian campaign in 1796 and 1797 as of other operations of the French armies. Sometimes the commander of the Army of Italy was named; at other times he was not. Gradually, however, Napoleon Bonaparte emerged as a distinctive personality.

For Federalists General Bonaparte was usually another of the horrible generals, perhaps worse than the others, spewed forth by revolutionary France. English Tory newspapers supplied such Americans with the necessary political fare. On September 14, 1797, the mercantile *Norfolk Herald, & Public Advertiser*, published by Charles Willett and James O'Connor, reprinted a sketch of European politics from an English newspaper, in which the conduct of the French in Italy since the preliminary peace treaty with Austria earlier in the year was characterized as more atrocious, if that were possible, than before. " Buonaparte,[62] acting in the capacity of Universal

61 *Jefferson Papers*, LC, vol. CVI, p. 18137. The bill further to suspend commercial intercourse with France became law on February 27, 1800.

62 This spelling of Napoleon's cognomen was usual in Virginia prior to 1800. Only after Napoleon came to power did the spelling " Bo " gradually replace " Buo " and sooner among Republicans than Federalists.

Dictator, exercising powers subversive of the whole Constitutional Code of France, making Peace or War, overturning governments that have subsisted for centuries, and fabricating constitutions at the suggestions of interest, or the instigations of caprice, seems disposed to establish on the ruins of all existing institutions a supreme and despotic power for himself." France's ally Venice, the writer maintained, was annihilated under false pretences by that " Prince of Marauders."

The intimation that Napoleon was acting as a proconsul in Italy was elaborated in an editorial in the same newspaper on January 25, 1798. According to the article, Austria and France had fought until both were convinced that nothing could be gained by continuing the war. They, therefore, decided to shake hands and divide the small neutral states between themselves. Though this was usual, the hypocritical conduct of France was most glaring. Bonaparte encouraged the Venetians to subvert their government and place the republic in his hands so as to liberate it. He then gave it to the Austrian ruler [63] as the price of other territories for France and for himself. The Cisalpine Republic was really for Bonaparte. That state would undoubtedly soon comprise Sardinia, Tuscany, and the Papal States. An alliance between the general and the Emperor, the article concluded, would result from their joint fears of France.

The *Norfolk Herald* could, nevertheless, publish prior to the above articles a paean to Bonaparte. At that date—August 3, 1797—the paper had not yet become consistently Federalist. That was to occur soon afterwards. Furthermore, the occasion for the exultation was the release of Lafayette, the American hero, from his imprisonment at Olmütz. The editors, Willett and O'Connor, believed Napoleon to be the sole agent in its accomplishment. Thank you and bless you, great conqueror and benefactor Buonaparte, they exclaimed. " This only trait was wanting to complete thy character; and to present, to latest ages, in the name of BUONAPARTE, all that constitutes the perfect *hero*, and the perfect *man*. . . . O! may the nation which

63 Actually Venetia was partitioned between Austria and France.

thou servest, prove herself worthy of thy example; and finish with the same liberality, with which thou hast commenced the entire emancipation of the *Patron of Mankind*; that *Columbia* may once more wear her *Warrior* in her heart." A month later the *Norfolk Herald* was writing about the " Prince of Marauders."

It was the unfavorable view of Napoleon that prevailed in Federalist circles. In the midst of American preparations for war against France the *Virginia Herald* of Fredericksburg on August 12, 1798, compared the two chief protagonists in the European war, Great Britain and France. The editorial, taken from a non-Virginia newspaper, described England as confiding in her gigantic navy and bolstered up by national pride, while France relied upon its triumphant veterans and " the renowned Bonaparte, who unsatisfied with empire already obtained through seas of blood, pants for universal dominion; who, possessing a principle of ambition that would grasp the world, is determined to abridge the power of his rival or sacrifice his life in the attempt. . . . " Such a concept of Napoleon's personality was to become current among Federalists in the period of the Empire. Henry Gird, Jr., publisher of the Alexandria *Columbian Mirror and Alexandria Gazette*, brought the Napoleonic danger closer to home. On August 25, 1798, this newspaper agreed with a Boston prediction that the expedition of Bonaparte was destined for the southern part of the United States, whence the French would proceed to revolutionize and subjugate the whole country. Were the Federalists attempting to frighten the Republican slave-owners?

But the expedition landed in Egypt. Augustine Davis's *Virginia Gazette and General Advertiser* of May 24, 1799, speculated as to the objectives of France.[64] With Egypt under control, the French could develop commerce with India and Persia by way of the Arabian Gulf. French ambition, furthermore, looked greedily at the weak Ottoman Empire. French methods were to stir up discontent everywhere. Their armies

64 This editorial was discussed in part, *supra*, pp. 51-2.

were guided by a band of desperadoes in pursuit of spoils and power. The article concluded with the warning: America, be prepared!

Federalists hoped for and prophesied the defeat of Bonaparte in the land of the Pharaohs. The distance from the battlefront encouraged more than the normal crop of rumors and propaganda from the English conservative press. Napoleon and the French army were being or about to be annihilated weekly by plagues, Mamelukes, or what not. The Federalists generally believed it and rejoiced. Did not the safety of the world—which, of course, included the United States—depend on French defeats?

Quite different was the General Bonaparte of the Republicans. The latter doubted British stories of Napoleon's defeats in the Italian campaign and rejoiced at his victories. For emotional Republicans this general of the French Revolution became the exemplar of the republican hero.[65] He was another Mercer, exclaimed the Fredericksburg *Republican Citizen.*[66] Pleasants' *Richmond and Manchester Advertiser* of September 3, 1796, reprinted entirely in italics the following panegyric from a Philadelphia newspaper:[67]

> If any thing short of omnipotent power, can restore to the effeminate sons of modern Italy, the virtues of their illustrious predecessors, it must be the humane, dignified, and endearing treatment of Buonaparte. Did he speak the language of proud and unfeeling victory, he might say, 'creatures of superstition and folly, victims of indolence and error, submit to the sway of a conqueror, determined to hold you up to the universe as an awful example of merited punishment! The chains you

65 *Cf.* the attitude of the Corresponding Societies in England; F. J. Maccunn, *The Contemporary English View of Napoleon* (London, 1914), pp. 11-12.

66 Its full title was *The Republican Citizen, and Farmer and Planter's Chronicle*; issue of October 12, 1796. The Mercer referred to was probably General Hugh Mercer of Trenton and Princeton fame during the Revolutionary War.

67 The *New World.*

> have forged for others, shall now be rivetted on you!'—But with the heroic magnanimity, inspired by the spirit of rational and enlightened freedom, he announces, 'that all shall exercise their rights under the shield of virtue, that every one who acknowledges a God shall worship him in the manner his conscience dictates!'—Frenchmen! if these are your arms, victory is yours forever! there is magic in them.

Fulwar Skipwith, a Virginian by birth, recently dismissed by the federal administration from the position of consul-general in France, likewise admired the general. In a letter to Monroe on May 15, 1797, he contrasted Napoleon, nobly asking the Directory, after the preliminary peace treaty with Austria, to relieve him of his military duties, with the anti-republican Washington wallowing in pomp and adulation.[68]

Napoleon's victories, in particular from 1797 onwards, came at a very auspicious time for Republicans. Such events increased the possibilities of success of the party's anti-war policy by dampening the belligerence of the Federalists. That was the reasoning used by Republican leaders in their letters to each other.[69] Bonaparte, like other French generals, was fighting for republican America as well as for republican France.

The aims and significance of the Egyptian expedition as interpreted by Republicans were similar to those of the Federalists, but the former perceived advantages in it for the world. The *Times and Alexandria Advertiser* of September 18, 1798, reprinting an editorial from a New York newspaper, described a major objective as the trade of India and, hence, of the world. An expedition from Egypt against British India was to follow naturally. Moreover, the long-expected destruction of the Ottoman Empire in Europe now seemed imminent. That, the writer stated, would most probably be beneficial for mankind.

Republicans continued to admire Napoleon's military ability and personality in 1799. Bonaparte was referred to as a military

68 *Monroe Papers,* LC, vol. V, p. 800.

69 *E. g.,* Jefferson to Madison, June 8, 1797; *Madison Papers,* LC, vol. XX, no. 49. John Dawson to Madison, June 4, 1797; *ib.,* no. 48.

authority. The victories of Masséna recalled to Meriwether Jones of the Richmond *Examiner* that Napoleon had often spoken of Masséna very favorably. The pupil had justified the praise of his preceptor.[70] Republicans placed little reliance on the continuous stream of news from allied sources concerning Napoleon's disasters in the Near East. "The English & German papers are killing and eating Buonaparte every day," wrote Jefferson tersely on January 30, 1799.[71] The alleged atrocities of the French were especially untrue with regard to Bonaparte, declared the Richmond *Virginia Argus* of July 12. "Buonaparte . . . has displayed the virtues of humanity, and has rendered himself equally as highly esteemed for the mildness of his disposition, as he is dreaded for the energy of his victories. So far from slaughter, he has been the guardian of female virtue; 'he who violates a woman, said Buonaparte, is a MONSTER.' "[72]

Napoleon's return to France in October, 1799, instead of disturbing the Republicans, pleased them no end. Though the reasons for his return were not too clear to them, the occurrence could only have a propitious outcome. The Martinsburg *Potomak Guardian*[73] devoted a large portion of its issue of January 8, 1800, to the event. It described how Bonaparte and his companions upon landing at Fréjus passionately kissed the soil of liberty. The people's joy was unbounded. That hero, so generally beloved by his countrymen, would again resume the glorious task of chastising despotism, and in conjunction with Masséna break the newly-forged chains of the coalition. The grand cause of governments founded upon the sovereignty of the people was prospering.

This was written two months after the Man on Horseback had subverted the French Republic, though before the news

70 Issue of June 4, 1799.

71 To N. Lewis; *Jefferson Papers,* LC, vol. CV, p. 17948.

72 Reprinted from the Boston *Independent Chronicle.*

73 Previously the *Potowmac Guardian, and Berkeley Advertiser.*

had reached America. Virginians, whether Republican or Federalists, did not seem to foresee the events of November, 1799.

It was not surprising if Republicans could not have prescience of Brumaire. They were the devotees of the French Revolution, hoping and believing in its success. They were blind with faith. But the Federalists had generally feared or hated the later revolution. They had not, on the whole, considered the chances of moderate liberty as opposed to license in France as very great.

News from English sources concerning the instability of the Directory and the popular discontent in France became rife in the latter half of 1799. The Federalist press of Virginia harped on it. The *Norfolk Herald*[74] of September 26, 1799, related that an artist in Paris had been bold enough to publish a caricature representing the Abbé Sieyès administering extreme unction to the expiring Directory. The Richmond *Virginia Gazette and General Advertiser* of September 27 presented a lewd metaphorical summary of the French Revolution. France, satiated with the charms of Liberty, had sought illicit pleasures in the arms of the wanton Equality. After eight years of crimes, folly, and dissipation, impelled by unbridled passion, that emaciated nation was now being embraced by Death. "The climax of extravagance, the list of paramours very naturally stand,—Liberty!—Equality! Death!"

There was, moreover, a belief among conservatives that democracy or license must end in tyranny. Educated Virginia Federalists could not have been unacquainted with Plato's theory of the degeneration of governmental forms, with democracy and tyranny as the final stages. John Adams' well-known *Defence of the Constitutions of Government of the United States of America*... (1786) had developed the theory that democracy is succeeded by despotism. Edmund Burke's *Reflections on the Revolution in France*... (1790) had warned

74 Its title had been thus shortened in February, 1798.

of the emergence of a military despot from the anarchy that the National Assembly was allegedly engendering. Finally, there was the history of the Roman Republic and its Caesars.

There seems, however, to be no reliable evidence that Federalists of the Old Dominion applied this theory specifically and prognosticated Napoleon Bonaparte's coming to power.[75] Perhaps they had become confused by their own emotionalism and hatred of the French Revolution. Had they not characterized every French régime from 1793, at one time or another, as despotic, tyrannical, as well as anarchical? When English news of the instability of the Directorial régime began to flow to the United States in increasing volume in 1799, it was accompanied by reports of the imminent restoration of the Bourbons. The whole situation was beclouded. It was even difficult for an impartial observer to distinguish between all the information and misinformation that travelled three thousand miles or more.

For Republicans it was difficult to conceive of the army as a threat to the French Republic. For example, James Monroe, newly-arrived in Paris in 1794, disposed of talk of danger from the military in a letter to Secretary of State Edmund Randolph. It was incorrect, he maintained, to compare the French Republic with the Roman Empire. The French army was composed of French yeomen living in an age imbued with the spirit of rational libertarianism, while the Roman army had been one

75 Beveridge in his biography of John Marshall, II, 288, describes the latter's alleged thoughts during the celebration in Napoleon's honor at the Luxembourg on December 10, 1797. Marshall, according to his biographer, already saw in Bonaparte the Man on Horseback advancing out of the future. But Beveridge offers no proof whatsoever for his statement. Patrick Henry, turned Federalist in his last years, is likewise reported as having predicted that anarchy would be succeeded by despotism and that Napoleon would "Caesar-like, subvert the liberties of his country." (William Wirt Henry, *Patrick Henry, Life, Correspondence And Speeches*, New York, 1891, II, 576.) This is in a letter from an anonymous contemporary, presumably to William Wirt, in which the writer of the epistle relates what he overheard Henry say some time before in a public company. Such evidence can hardly be accepted as valid.

of foreigners living in a period of a corrupt and decaying monarchy.[76]

Rumors of the instability of the Directory in 1799 were re-evaluated by Republicans. Any change, wrote the *Virginia Argus* of September 6, " would most likely be injurious to the cause of monarchy and slavery " and beneficial to the Republic.[77]

By January 3, 1800, the same newspaper was describing the possible project of an offensive campaign by the Directory, which—according to the editorial—had now been convinced by allied actions that the war was one of extermination between monarchy and republicanism. The article listed the probable commands of the French generals, with Bonaparte at the head of the Army of Italy. It concluded in this remarkable vein:

> In the condition of a junction of the armies [at Vienna], Buonaparte will command in chief; but it is neither the wish nor the policy of the Republic to concentrate in any one man, the dangerous and aristocratic powers and influence of a Generalisimo [*sic*]. The immensity of their operations will enable them to accommodate their Generals with separate commands. The rivalry inspired by the efforts of an honest ambition will, in its progress, develope a luminous series of shining actions, and the nation instead of resting for her defence and reputation on a single chief, who may be a Caesar, will *repose amidst the spears of a thousand chieftains.*[78]

The vision of a Caesar thus appeared to a Quaker Republican editor or his writer, but there was no correlation with the practical issues facing the French Republic and no prophecy that Napoleon would become a dictator. The question somewhat naïvely revolved around a mere grant of an office, that of generalissimo. Virginia Republicans were still in a dream world. It was to be rudely shattered within several weeks.

76 August 15, 1794; *Monroe Writings*, Hamilton ed., II, 16 ff.

77 *V. s.*, p. 58.

78 This editorial was reprinted in the newly-founded, short-lived Republican newspaper the Richmond *Press* of January 31, 1800.

CHAPTER III

VIRGINIA AT THE THRESHOLD: BRUMAIRE AND PACIFICATION

LATE in January, 1800, Virginians were startled by news of another *bouleversement* in Paris. The *Norfolk Herald* of February 4, presenting the latest reports of the momentous event to its readers, described it as "that extraordinary explosion, which has burst forth at once, without warning us of its approach by any of those indications which usually precede a political storm."

While some Federalists in other states rejoiced at the coup d'état because it might terminate in the destruction of the hated republic and the restoration of the Bourbons,[1] the first reaction of the administration newspapers in the Old Dominion was quite different. They had shown some moderation toward France in the latter part of 1799, after President Adams' decision to send a special mission to end the quasi-war.[2] The Richmond *Virginia Federalist* could at first consider only the possible effects of Brumaire on the negotiations.[3] A return of the Bourbon dynasty was repugnant to it. Surprisingly accepting a fundamental Republican view, the editorial asserted that such an event would be followed by a combination to annihilate the republican system in every quarter of the globe. "That it [Brumaire] may terminate in a more desirable *restoration*—a restoration of the blessings of peace to all nations, we most sincerely wish; and if the representation of the temper and disposition of the reputed agents in these important occurrences, is not inaccurate, we perhaps have good reason to

1 *Cf.*, *e. g.*, the Philadelphia *Gazette of the United States*, quoted in the Richmond *Press* of February 7, 1800. *V.* also Jefferson to Dr. Wardlaw, January 28, 1800; *Jefferson Papers, Coolidge Collection*, MHS. *Cf.* the view of the Tory George Canning; Maccunn, *op. cit.*, p. 19.

2 *Supra*, pp. 50-51, 56, and n. 29, ch. II.

3 Editorial reprinted in the *Press* of February 7, 1800.

expect it." But on February 5, 1800, the same newspaper decided, on the basis of additional information, that, whatever benefits France might derive from the coup, it apparently would not usher in peace.

Interest in the character and domestic significance of the new development in France, nevertheless, was intense. Augustine Davis's *Virginia Gazette and General Advertiser* of February 7 reprinted an editorial from a South Carolina newspaper [4] in which the writer decided that the coup d'état could not have been conceived and matured since the return of Bonapartc. Sieyès, its probable author, required the genius and the popularity of a man such as Napoleon to execute it. Federalists did recognize the ability of Napoleon Bonaparte. The general, the article continued, was, therefore, recalled from Egypt. The result was the most glaring violation of the independence of a legislature since the beginning of the revolution.

Federalists, nevertheless, tended to feel some sympathy for Napoleon. Had he not defeated "the Jacobinic party" [5] and overthrown "an anarchical democratical despotism"? [6]

What was to be the outcome? The Federalist newspapers soon reached a decision. The *Virginia Federalist* of March 29, commenting on the constitution of the Consulate, the complete

4 The Charleston *Courier*.

5 Original editorial in the *Virginia Gazette*, February 7, 1800, preceding the above reprint.

6 Robert Goodloe Harper, influential Federalist of South Carolina, to his constituents, April 7, 1800; *Papers of James A. Bayard, 1796-1815*, ed. by Elizabeth Donnan (Annual Report of the American Historical Association For The Year 1913, vol. II; Washington, 1915), p. 99. Harper, therefore, pronounced the new régime as the best France had had in the preceding ten years. *Cf.* the Boston *Columbian Centinel & Massachusetts Federalist*, March 29, April 30, 1800; October 14, 1801.

Though the author has found no such explicit recognition of Napoleon's services to conservatism in the scanty expressions available for 1800 and 1801 of Virginia Federalist opinion of the French régime, there is every reason to believe that such attitudes did then exist in the Old Dominion. This is proved, for example, by opinion in Federalist circles outside of Virginia at that time and by Federalist opinion in Virginia in the first half of 1802; *vide infra*, pp. 107-09.

text of which had just been received, concluded that "the sole will of an individual, as during the [Bourbon] despotism, is therefore the law. . . ." The people were entirely excluded from an agency in their own affairs. The wars of the revolution had been fought in vain for the privilege of exchanging a Grand Monarch for a Consul.

The *Columbian Mirror and Alexandria Gazette*, now published by Ellis Price, stated on April 1, 1800, that such a constitution might conciliate the royalists to some extent. But what of the numerous Jacobins? The new régime was, therefore, considered unstable.[7] Timothy Green's Fredericksburg *Virginia Herald* of July 15 [8] sought for the fundamental cause of the instability. Human nature, it declared, is universally prone to envy, if not to abhor, the man who advances suddenly. For many years France has witnessed a scramble for power. "King Buonaparte like all his predecessors during the revolution, sits on a throne of sand."

Napoleon was thus considered as just another figure of the hated French Revolution. And Federalist newspapers still published editorials in 1800 denouncing it. The *Virginia Federalist* of February 26, for example, described the revolution as a continuous reign of terror with the perverted shibboleths of liberty, equality, and popular sovereignty. Bonaparte, the beloved general of the Jeffersonians, had also turned out to be a villain, wrote the same paper on March 29.[9] His alleged concern for liberty and equality was as reliable as that of the Republicans of the United States.

This was excellent political propaganda in a presidential election year. "The American Republican Ticket of Electors" in Virginia representing the Federalist minority of the last General Assembly—and including James Breckenridge of

7 Editorial reprinted from the *Baltimore Telegraphe.*

8 Copying a non-Virginia newspaper.

9 Quoting an editorial from the *Gazette of the United States.* This editorial item was distinct from the previously discussed editorial of the same date.

Botetourt County, a leader of the Federalist party and future congressman—presented a statement of its position on May 26, 1800.[10] The voters were asked whether they were willing to embark on the tempestuous sea of liberty *à la* Jefferson. That would mean enduring unceasing storms and bloodshed, only to find refuge in "the calm of a *real* despotism." Beware of the fate of the French Republic! was the terrifying warning.

While American conservative philosophy was unscathed, if not strengthened, by the coup d'état in France, American liberalism was shaken to its very foundations. At first, Republicans refused to believe it. The rumor that Bonaparte, Sieyès, and Ducos had usurped the French government was characterized as anti-French propaganda. ". . . After killing Buonaparte a thousand times," wrote Vice-President Jefferson from Philadelphia on January 23, 1800, "they [the British] still have a variety of parts to be acted by him."[11]

When the news of a new upheaval in France could no longer be denied, Republicans hopefully refused to consider it as monarchist. The stanch partisan Senator Stevens Thomson Mason wrote to Governor Monroe that the coup d'état was most probably a move to crush the royalist faction in the Councils.[12] Thomas Jefferson averred that if Bonaparte established a monarchy for himself or for Louis XVIII, he had but a few days to live. "In a nation of so much enthusiasm, there must be a million of Brutuses who will devote themselves to death to destroy him. But, without much faith in Buonaparte's heart, I have so much in his head, as to indulge another train of reflection. The republican world has been long looking with anxiety on the two experiments going on of a *single* elective Executive here, & a *plurality* there." Perhaps, after years of perpetual broils and factional strife in the Directory, the

10 *V.* the *Virginia Gazette and General Advertiser* of June 27, 1800.

11 To Harry Innes; *Jefferson Papers,* LC, vol. CVI, p. 18148.

12 January —, 1800; *Monroe Papers,* LC, vol. VI, p. 947. *Cf.* the Alexandria *Times; and District of Columbia Daily Advertiser* of January 30, 1800.

political philosopher continued, the French might have decided in favor of the American form. ". . . Buonaparte may be for a single executive, limited in time and power, and flatter himself with the election to that office. . . ." That Napoleon, after usurping power, would submit to a free election for a relatively weak presidential office did not seem at all incongruous to the Vice-President. In any case, Jefferson was prophetically fearful that France would still have to undergo a half century of disorders. The revolution had not yet ended.[13]

Those Republicans who had viewed General Bonaparte as an idol found it even more difficult to conceive of a monarchical revolution in France. The ephemeral Richmond *Press*, published by a triumvirate of Republican politicians—Meriwether Jones, Alexander McRae, and John H. Foushee [14]—for the defense of republicanism against "Anglo-monocrats," reprinted an article on February 7 from Philadelphia entitled "Highly Ridiculous." How could Bonaparte, the foremost hero of the greatest age and the greatest nation on earth, desire the empty title of king? Such a man could not be a conspirator against his country's freedom and his own fame. There were, moreover, other factors, according to the article, that would make the restoration of monarchy impossible: the strong love of freedom in the army and people, the transfer of property, and the characters of Sieyès and Ducos.[15]

13 To Innes, January 23, 1800; *Jefferson Papers,* LC, vol. CVI, p. 18148. This was the latter part of the letter mentioned above. It was written after confirmation of the coup had been received but while the details were still uncertain. A similar view that Napoleon was aiming to establish a government based on the American model was presented in the Norfolk *Epitome of the Times* of February 13, 1800, copying an article from the London *Morning Chronicle* of November 27, 1799. But, according to this report, the consuls would be ineligible for the presidency.

14 Jones was the fighting publisher-editor of the *Examiner* and printer to the commonwealth; McRae was a lawyer; and Foushee was a physician.

15 *Cf.* the *Times; and District of Columbia Daily Advertiser* of January 27, 1800.

Upon receipt of the details of the event the *Press* analyzed it and its causes.[16] Brumaire was placed in its proper background, namely, a struggle between the Jacobins and the moderates. The writer of the article believed that the former had been on the verge of a revolution when they were anticipated by the Council of Ancients and Bonaparte. ". . . Buonaparte . . . has indeed 'tarnished all his glory.'" But it was utterly improbable that he entertained the remotest hope or design of being king or of restoring the Bourbons. The article ended on this optimistic note: "We do not despair of the republic— . . . the people are immortal and the republic will be saved."

What was the significance of the coup d'état? What was to be the outcome? What would happen to the glorious French Revolution? And to the French Republic to which American republicanism was bound? These were heart-rending problems tormenting zealous Republicans.

Thomas Jefferson's letters from Philadelphia to his numerous friends and acquaintances for over a month after receipt of the news of Brumaire were replete with conjectures and hypotheses concerning the results. In a letter of January 29[17] he concluded that a "Dictatorial consulate" had been established, and that the Constitution of the Year III which had been acquiring "consistence & firmness from time"[18] had been demolished in an instant. How the nation would react was as yet unknown, he continued. Had the consuls been put to death immediately before France had had time to take sides, the Directory and Councils might have reëstablished themselves on the spot. "But that not being done, perhaps it is now to be wished that Buonaparte may be spared, as, according to his protestations, he is for liberty, equality, & representative government, and he is more able to keep the nation together, & to

16 In the same issue.

17 To John Brackenridge [*sic*]; *Jefferson Papers*, LC, vol. CVI, pp. 18156-7.

18 This was not exactly consistent with his views on the Directory as given in the letter to Innes on January 23.

ride out the storm, than any other. Perhaps it may end in their establishing a single executive, & that in his person. I hope it will not be for life."

Napoleon, Jefferson wrote on February 2, might become a Robespierre, a Caesar, or present "the new phaenomenon of an usurpation of the government for the purpose of making it free."[19] The liberal leader now recognized the weakness of the last conjecture. He wrote to his son-in-law Thomas Mann Randolph on the same day:

> . . . Whatever his talents may be for war, we have no proofs that he is skilled in forming governments friendly to the people. Wherever he has meddled we have seen nothing but fragments of the old Roman government stuck into materials with which they can form no cohesion: we see the bigotry of an Italian to the antient [*sic*] splendour of his country, but nothing which bespeaks a luminous view of the organisation of rational government. Perhaps however this may end better than we augur: and it certainly will if his head is equal to true & solid calculations of glory.[20]

In a letter to the revolutionary patriot Samuel Adams on February 26, the Virginian seemed to be giving up Bonaparte as lost to the republican cause. He now wrote that his confidence *had* been placed in the head, not in the heart, of Bonaparte and that he had hoped that Napoleon would realize the difference between the fame of a Washington and a Cromwell.[21] By March 4, 1800, Jefferson was writing, "Buonaparte seems to be given up by almost everyone."[22] Napoleon Bonaparte, the

19 To Dr. Bache; *Jefferson Papers,* LC, vol. CVI, p. 18168.

20 *Ibid.,* 18166.

21 *Ibid.,* 18194. The Washington edition of Jefferson's writings, IV, 321-2, makes the serious error of changing the tense and, therefore, the meaning of the vital sentence: "My confidence has [instead of "had"] been placed in the head, not in the heart of Bonaparte." In addition, Mr. Washington invariably begins Napoleon's cognomen with a "Bo" even when Jefferson spelled it "Buo."

22 To T. M. Randolph; *Jefferson Papers, Coolidge Collection,* MHS.

destroyer of the French Republic, became a pariah for Thomas Jefferson and other Republican leaders.

They had recognized from the outset that the events of November 9 and 10, 1799, were highly significant for France, the United States, and the world at large. The coup struck a deadly blow at republican principles, Representative John Dawson affirmed.[23] It transferred the destiny of the revolution from the civil to the military authority, wrote James Madison to his devoted friend and chieftain.[24] But, Thomas Jefferson fervently insisted, it did not prove the impracticability of republican government. Reaffirming his fundamental belief, he exclaimed, ". . . I will never believe that man is incapable of self-government; that he has no resources but in a master, who is but a man like himself, and generally a . . . [illegible] man, inasmuch as power tends to deprave him."[25]

The coup d'état was an additional lesson against a standing army, the Vice-President continued. Without it, Jefferson concluded, Bonaparte could not have succeeded, nor have maintained himself in power.[26] And it could happen here! Writing from Philadelphia, the Republican leader stated his belief that the enemies of the American constitution were hatching a conspiracy. ". . . The dissensions in this state[27] are too likely to bring things to the situation they [the enemies] wish; when

23 To ——, February 5, 1800. Monroe Papers (MSS., NYPL), 1796-1801 Box.

24 February 14, 1800; *Madison Papers*, LC, vol. XXI, no. 67. *V.* also Jefferson to Samuel Adams, February 26, 1800; *Jefferson Papers*, LC, vol. CVI, p. 18194.

25 To General E. Meade, April 8, 1800; *Jefferson Papers*, LC, vol. CVI, p. 18252.

26 *Id.*

27 Jefferson is probably referring to the close division between Federalists and Republicans in Pennsylvania, with the Senate being Federalist and the House Republican, both by small majorities. It was, consequently, difficult to reach an agreement as to the method of choosing the presidential electors.

our Buonaparte, surrounded by his comrades in arms may step in to give us political salvation in his way." [28]

But the American Republic had firmer roots than the French. According to Jefferson, the French people, not having developed the habit of self-government, had not yet acquired the habit of acknowledging the fundamental law of nature, the basis of popular government, namely the *lex majoris partis.* Reiterating his political relativism, he claimed that the character and situation of Americans were materially different from those of the French. Americans were so impressed from the cradle with the sacredness of the law of majority rule that it was almost innate in them. The United States might possibly be saved from the fate of France.[29]

But that was not predetermined. In the last analysis, it was the individual will that would decide the issue. "We are able to preserve our self-government if we will but think so," Thomas Jefferson maintained.[30] The moral of the coup d'état for Americans was clear to him:

> They [Americans] should see in it a necessity to rally firmly & in close bands round their constitution, never to suffer an iota of it to be infringed, to inculcate on minorities the duties of acquiescence in the will of the majority, and on majorities a respect for the rights of the minority; to beware of a military force even of citizens; and to beware of too much confidence in any man. The confidence of the French people in Buonaparte, has enabled him to kick down their constitution, & instead of that to leave them dependent on his will and his life.[31]

Whatever might be the fate of republicanism in France, therefore, Americans could preserve it inviolate in the United

28 To Thomas Mann Randolph, February 2, 1800; *Jefferson Papers,* LC, vol. CVI, p. 18166.

29 To John Brackenridge, January 29, 1800; *ibid.,* 18156-7.

30 To T. M. Randolph, February 2; *ibid.,* 18166.

31 To Dr. Bache, February 2; *ibid.,* 18168.

States.[32] Brumaire had compelled Thomas Jefferson to renounce—without contradicting himself[33]—the concept of the partial interdependence of the American and French Republics. The practical Republican philosopher had altered his political beliefs to harmonize with the new political realities. American republicanism could exist in a non-republican world!

Napoleon Bonaparte, however, was not abandoned so readily by other Virginia Republicans, particularly by the editors. The *Virginia Argus* asserted on February 14 that Bonaparte, fortuitously appearing on the scene, had saved France from ruin. The continued existence of the imperfect and much-abused constitution of the Year V would have subserved the interests of the enemies of civil liberty. True, the methods that had been used to effect the change were despotic. It was likewise dangerous to suffer any man, no matter how great his talents and virtue, to dictate a government to a whole people. But the consular administration was temporary.[34] Besides, the principles of the new system were the same as of the old. The world would most probably discover, the article concluded, that Bonaparte was a "hero whose high ambition is to be a citizen, and to see his country free" as the prelude to the establishment of the most durable European peace in a thousand years of monarchical rule.[35]

As Federalist mocking of the new French developments increased, the Republican editors found themselves at a loss. Meriwether Jones declared in the *Examiner* of February 14 that more important than the Napoleonic revolution was the imminent rise in taxes in the United States. On March 18,

32 To Brackenridge, January 29; *ibid.*, 18157. *Cf.*, Madison to Jefferson, April 4, 1800; *Madison Writings*, Hunt ed., VI, 408.

33 *V. s.*, pp. 58-9.

34 Only the existence of the provisional Consulate was then known.

35 Editorial reprinted from the Philadelphia *Aurora* edited by the fiery William Duane.

Pleasants clearly displayed his embarrassment in the *Virginia Argus*.[36]

> We are daily bored with enquiries concerning the present state of France. Is there no new arrival? What has become of Buonaparte? Don't you think he'll enslave the whole French nation? And, oh Sir! Is it not a terrible misfortune that all the glorious labors of the revolution should terminate in the tyranny of a second Cromwell?
>
> To the first query our answer is that we shall be very glad not to hear one syllable from France for six months to come. We have quite enough of business of our own to digest and publish, without the intervention of arretes [*sic*], republican battles, harangues, constitutions, and the Deuce knows what! How often must we remind our beloved fellow citizens that knowledge, like charity, should begin at home. If any good was to be expected from our ambassadors, we should indeed be glad to hear from France. But we cannot persuade ourselves that any negotiation will be serious, or that any treaty can be lasting, until Mr. Adams shall be dismissed from the presidency.
>
> 2d. As to what has become of Buonaparte, our guess is that he has reinforced the army of Italy and that the republicans have made considerable progress in the reconquest of that country.
>
> 3d. and 4th. As to these two queries, we are no more afraid that the little Corsican will reduce 30,000,000 people to slavery than that the King of Spain will put the rock of Gibraltar into his snuff box.

The Republican editors were on the defensive; but they were still clinging to a hope.

When, however, the official text of the constitution of the Consulate arrived, the few papers that commented on it found it necessary to criticize it. The *Virginia Argus* of April 1 [37]

36 The editorial column was dated March 17. The editorial, headed "From a Scots Correspondent," was reprinted in the *Examiner* of March 21.

37 Editorial taken from the New York *American Citizen*.

averred that it contained "some features of genuine liberty, united with very prominent organic arrangements, whose tendency lead directly to the establishment of the most odious and dreadful despotism." A still more vigorous denunciation came in an editorial of April 8, which maintained that the chief magistrate had kingly powers and the people none.[38] As the Petersburg paper the *Virginia Gazette and Petersburg Intelligencer* [39] had so picturesquely expressed it on April 1: "It [the constitution] is a monster in whose countenance the features of aristocracy alone can be discovered. France begins to have 'an awful squinting towards Monarchy'. . . . "

Though Republican editors were not generally satisfied with the new developments in France, they felt compelled to defend them, if possible. Had their faith in the revolution been so strong that they refused to abandon hope? Or were they embarrassed by the continued Federalist accusations that they had misunderstood the revolution? To have been wrong was a gross political blunder, especially in a presidential election year. The continued war between Great Britain and France and the uncertainty concerning the future of Franco-American relations reënforced their decision. They attempted to salvage what they could from the ruins. They presented a brave front. Perhaps everything would turn out all right in the end.

Accordingly, the Alexandria *Times; and District of Columbia Daily Advertiser* on April 14 and the *Virginia Argus* on April 18 presented the following line of reasoning.[40] In answer to the repeated question of the 'friends of order' "What think you now of Buonaparte?" the editorials declared that he was a man and nothing more. They affirmed that they were and continued to be attached to republican principles, not to the man. Throwing the challenge back in the faces of the Federalists, the editorials denounced them for ex-

38 Taken from the *Belfast News-Letter* of January 23.

39 The title was changed to the *Petersburg Intelligencer* within the next two months.

40 Both used the same editorial from a non-Virginia newspaper.

pecting Republicans to place implicit trust in those officials who have served republicanism in the past. No doubt, they stated, the same argument was used by Bonaparte's friends. Now he is in possession of almost unlimited power. But perhaps the present constitution is necessary to save French independence. ". . . That being secured we trust Republican Liberty may yet be established." Such optimistic conclusions undoubtedly expressed the hopes of many a partisan of the French Revolution.

Sometimes Republicans even glorified Napoleon's alleged republicanism, as if nothing had happened. An article in the editorial column of the *Virginia Argus* on September 19 signed "X.Y.Z." evinced the effect of Federalist goading. Perhaps Bonaparte might become a villain as the English faction so eagerly desired. "They dread nothing so much as his turning out to be, as good as he is great; as irreproachable in his political morality as he is wise in council and heroic in action. . . . But unhappily for them, he appears at present . . . as firmly determined to continue the Republican system upon its true principles in France, as he is almost miraculously successful in all his operations." [41] The *Annual Register and Virginian Repository For The Year 1800* presented a eulogistic biography of Bonaparte, as a republican hero, through the Italian campaign of 1797, and promised its readers a continuation of the amazing story of his life in the next issue.[42]

Meanwhile, Republicans continued to extol the French Revolution. It is truly remarkable, stated Pleasants' *Virginia Argus* on May 6, 1800,[43] that such a populous nation could emerge from a state of complete despotism and establish a political system based on republican principles. The editorial correctly distinguished between American and European conditions. If it is difficult, it continued, to establish republican-

41 Reprinted, without acknowledgment, from the Boston *Independent Chronicle* of September 8. Such action was not unusual.

42 Petersburg, [1801], LC, pp. 76 ff.

43 Editorial reprinted from the New York *American Citizen*.

ism on a firm basis in the United States, it certainly is much more difficult to renovate society in Europe, where there are powerful aristocracies, churches, and monarchies. The short-lived Richmond newspaper the *Friend of the People*, published by the most roving of early American printers James Lyon,[44] attempted to prove on May 16, 1800, that the French Revolution had not been in vain. Referring to a recent news item, the article acclaimed the unprecedented abundance of crops in France. That was attributed to the liberation of the peasants from the exorbitant taxes of church and state.

Yet, despite the Federalist-Republican controversy over the domestic developments in France, it had turned out, in reality, that there was an important degree of uniformity of opinion. Both Federalists and Republicans had censured the coup d'état proper; both had, in general, disapproved of the new French constitution.

With regard to French international relations, however, there was only a slight blending of partisan opinion. The first acts of the Consulate greatly facilitated whatever degree of uniformity of opinion existed. France manifested a desire to reëstablish harmonious relations with the leading neutral. The ordinance of January 18, 1798, providing for the confiscation of any ship carrying goods from England or its colonies, was repealed in December, 1799. The new attitude was also indicated by the liberation of American prisoners, the elimination of some of the worst abuses in the administration of prize court justice by the establishment of a Supreme Prize Court in Paris,[45] and the official honors accorded the departed George Washington.

44 Douglas C. McMurtrie, *The Beginnings of Printing in Virginia* (Lexington, Va., 1935), p. 34. Lyon was described by Jefferson on December 5, 1801, as "a young man of bold republicanism in the worst of times, of good character, son of the persecuted Matthew Lyon." Jefferson to G. Granger; *Jefferson Papers*, LC, vol. CXVIII, p. 20362.

45 Eli F. Heckscher, *The Continental System, An Economic Interpretation*; edited by H. Westergaard (Publications of the Carnegie Endowment for International Peace; Division of Economics and History; Oxford, 1922), p. 50.

The pro-Adams Federalists, supporting the administration policy of negotiation, were consequently hopeful at first that the new régime would promote a restoration of peace. Such an event would redound to the benefit of the administration in the election. The *Norfolk Herald* of May 13, 1800, noted—though somewhat distrustfully—the new pro-American attitude of the French press.[46]

The anxiety of the "French party" for peace between France and the United States continued unabated. As James Madison pointed out to his chief on April 20, continued embroilment with the Gallic power would prolong the ascendancy of the Federalists.[47] According to the Republican viewpoint, then, peace was absolutely essential for the victory of republicanism in the United States over Anglo-monarchism. It was also necessary for the economic welfare of the South. It would raise the price of tobacco, which had been falling since 1798.[48]

In Federalist and Republican circles alike expressions of hope for the pacification of Europe could be heard.[49] Peace abroad might facilitate a settlement of Franco-American differences. Throughout the year, both Federalists and Republicans continued to speculate on the possibility of peace.

Though the administration Federalists and the Republicans agreed partially on certain aspects of the international relations of France, the former had not developed a sudden affection for revolutionary France. France and Britain were still at war.

46 Editorial reprinted from the Boston *Columbian Centinel.*

47 *Madison Papers,* LC, vol. XXI, no. 80.

48 *Cf. supra,* p. 66; and Jefferson to J. W. Eppes, April 21, 1800 (Jefferson MSS., New York Historical Society).

49 *E. g.,* Leven Powell to Major Burr Powell, March 5, 1800; "The Leven Powell Correspondence," *Branch Historical Papers,* I, no. 3, p. 239. *Virginia Argus,* February 14, 1800; *v. s.,* p. 85. Yet Madison could discover an advantage in the continuation of the war. French entanglements would reenforce that country's disposition to come to terms with the United States. Madison to Jefferson, April 20, 1800; *Madison Papers,* LC, vol. XXI, no. 80. Meriwether Jones had written in a similar vein in the *Examiner* on March 21, 1800. But such were not typical Republican views.

Although Napoleon spelled partial reaction for France, he continued to disseminate basic principles of the revolution abroad. The old distrust of revolutionary France, therefore, persisted among Federalists. Representative Leven Powell expressed the belief on March 5 that it might suit the French government to grant our demands. France could then intrigue more easily in this divided country. Moreover, Powell asserted, France could repudiate the treaty whenever it pleased.[50]

News of continued French privateering in the West Indies and the delay in the conclusion of a treaty revived and strengthened old hatreds. The mercantile *Norfolk Herald* of Willett and O'Connor, on July 8, 1800, recommended that American merchant ships remain armed. If the French government seriously desired peace, it would not attempt to coerce the United States by acts of aggression against its commerce.

Secretary of State John Marshall wrote privately on September 13 of his fears that the recent French victories in Europe and "the hope which many of our papers are well calculated to inspire, that America is prepared once more to crouch at her feet, may render ineffectual our endeavors to obtain peace." But he was not certain. [51] He, therefore, commended patience and moderation to President Adams. Four days later, he informed the President of his belief that the new French government was inclined to correct, at least partly, the follies of the past.[52]

With regard to French-European relations, the previous Federalist antagonism toward France persisted despite the de-

50 To Major Burr Powell; "The Leven Powell Correspondence," *Branch Historical Papers*, I, no. 3, p. 239.

51 To Thomas Tinsly. *Washburn Papers* (MSS., MHS), vol. IV, *Statesmen and Orators.*

52 Quoted in Beveridge, *John Marshall*, II, 523. The Secretary of State maintained a neutral position between Great Britain and France. [*Cf.* his letter to Rufus King, the American minister to Great Britain, on September 20, 1800; in *American State Papers*, Class I, *Foreign Relations* (hereafter: *ASP, FR*), II, 486-9.] As Secretary of State, Marshall was thus more independent and less pro-British than when not in that office.

sire of some for peace in Europe. This was so even during the period when the news revealed Napoleon as a philo-American. Price's *Columbian Mirror and Alexandria Gazette* of February 18, 1800, described Switzerland as groaning under the heavy hand of French spoliation, with General Masséna demanding enormous contributions and requisitions.[53] Such were the miseries "attendant upon French fraternity," wrote this journal on May 1. On April 19, 1800, the Richmond *Virginia Federalist* had published in its editorial column a poem, glowing with patriotic zeal, which portrayed a tyrant ravaging Europe under the false and mocking pretense of freedom; in contrast, America's warriors were guarding the native soil, prepared to fight another Marathon, if need be, against the modern Persian conqueror. Reports of a famine in England caused the *Federalist* on May 14 to console its pro-British readers with the information that there were prospects of a plentiful harvest in the United States and that America would be able to provide relief.

In turn, no one reading the comments on European developments in the Republican publications of the day would have known that any change had occurred in France. The enthusiasm for the "republican arms" of France was as great as ever.[54] The crowned heads of Europe, it was maintained, had begun this crusade of tyranny against liberty. England, which hated republicanism so bitterly and had its faction in the United States, was the soul of the coalition.[55] And Great Britain planned world domination.[56] It was, consequently, the national interest of the United States that France give England a complete drubbing.[57] France was still our republican ally fighting

53 The same editorial appeared in the Boston *Columbian Centinel* of February 5.

54 *E. g.*, *v.* the *Examiner* of September 9, 1800.

55 *Virginia Argus,* April 22, 1800.

56 The *Times; and District of Columbia Daily Advertiser,* March 12, 1800.

57 *Examiner,* May 9, 1800.

a defensive war for freedom. The "deliverers and avengers of mankind" James Thomson Callender called them in his political tract *The Prospect Before Us*.[58]

The Napoleonic victory at Marengo was naturally acclaimed by Republicans. Copying the influential Philadelphia *Aurora*, Pleasants' *Virginia Argus* of August 19, 1800, declared that Austria would now be compelled to accept the peace offered "by the moderation of the French general." [59]

In the meantime, the Republicans, on the whole, were optimistic throughout the year 1800 that a treaty between the United States and France would be concluded. The only danger they feared was the opposition of the administration and of the American commissioners to peace. This idea was frequently reiterated. Jefferson, however, wrote to his son-in-law Thomas Mann Randolph on May 7 that he had the most authoritative information that the disposition of the Consulate was so favorable that a *carte blanche* would be given to the American envoys and that they would be unable to avoid a settlement.[60]

James Thomson Callender in his *Prospect Before Us* hammered away more dogmatically and virulently at the old arguments with regard to Franco-American relations. He maintained that the French attacks on American commerce began as a result of the treachery of the Federalists toward our ally. There was no danger of a French invasion of the United States. The author bemoaned the fact that President Adams had delayed the departure of the commissioners in 1799 until it was too late.

But in a footnote dated January 16, 1801, Callender informed his readers that a treaty with France had been concluded and was before the Senate. "The good sense and

58 (Richmond, 1800-1801); vol. II, pt. II, p. 92. This work earned him a jail sentence under the Sedition Act.

59 Napoleon was depicted by some Republicans as a master of the pen as well as of the sword. *Cf.* the *Virginia Argus*, March 21, 1800; Callender, *The Prospect Before Us*, vol. II, pt. II, p. 78, note.

60 *Jefferson Papers*, LC, vol. CVII, p. 18277.

moderation of the first consul have negatived the prediction of the text; but for that fortunate occurrence, we need not thank the president." [61] Callender, who was in jail because of the policies of the administration, could not have written in any other vein. He considered Napoleon a hero.[62] Moreover, the book was intended as political propaganda.

Peace between France and the United States, for which Republicans had yearned, had finally arrived. Without knowing the terms, the Norfolk *Epitome of the Times* on November 24, 1800, exulted: ". . . Two powerful nations engaged in the cause of freedom" have reëstablished harmonious relations. Had the dispute persisted, it added, the United States would have been throwing its balance into the scale of despotism and monarchy. A close union between the two republics, however, would strengthen the cause of liberty in both countries.[63]

Planter Thomas Jefferson informed the Philadelphia tobacconist Thomas Leiper on December 14, 1800, that he was still holding on to his tobacco crop. He was waiting for the rise in prices which the treaty would bring.[64] When Jefferson learned the provisions of the Convention of 1800 or the Treaty of Mortfontaine, as it is often called, he reported to Madison on December 19 that it had some undesirable features. "It has been a bungling negotiation," he concluded.[65] Two days later, however, the Vice-President indicated that he favored its ratification with a limitation of time as to its duration.[66] Thomas Newton, Jr., enterprising Norfolk merchant probably trading with the French West Indies and South America,[67] and a

61 Vol. II, pt. II, p. 91, footnote.

62 *E. g., v. s.*, n. 59.

63 Editorial reprinted from the New York *American Citizen.*

64 *Jefferson Papers*, LC, vol. CVIII, p. 18489.

65 *Jefferson Writings*, Washington ed., IV, 343.

66 To Caesar Rodney; *Jefferson Writings*, Ford ed., VII, 472-3.

67 *Cf.* Eugene P. Link, *Democratic-Republican Societies, 1790-1800* (New York, 1942), p. 75; and Newton to Madison, September 12, 1803, *Madison*

stanch Republican, found the treaty not so disagreeable as expected from reports. He hoped that it would be approved, for, above all things except independence, war must be avoided.[68] Likewise, James Madison advised Jefferson on January 10, 1801, that, if there was anything in the convention which could not be accepted, it would be better to ratify it with qualifications than to reject it *in toto*.[69] A rejection of the treaty, wrote Representative Samuel J. Cabell, would greatly depress southern agriculture.[70] The Republican senators from the Old Dominion, Stevens Thomson Mason and Wilson Cary Nicholas, consequently voted for the ratification of the Convention of 1800.

The Federalists received the treaty with especially mixed emotions. The tendency at first was in the direction of sharp criticism. Representative Leven Powell wrote on December 23, 1800, that the Senate did not know what to do with it. He pronounced certain provisions as unsatisfactory and concluded with the assertion that the French had outwitted the American envoys.[71] The prevalent opinion of the treaty, wrote the *Norfolk Herald* on December 29, seems to be that, considering the dignity and honor of the nation, it cannot be ratified. If the Senate should finally reject the treaty, it will be difficult to account for the present naval policy—for example, the frigate " Constellation " is ordered round to New York and laid up, and recruiting for the service is stopped. The *Alexandria Advertiser and Commercial Intelligencer,* newly

---

Papers, LC, vol. XXVI, no. 40. Newton's son of the same name was a congressional representative from the electoral district including Norfolk consecutively from March 4, 1801, throughout the remainder of the Napoleonic era.

68 To Jefferson, December 29, 1800; *Jefferson Papers,* LC, vol. CVIII, p. 18549.

69 *Madison Writings,* Hunt ed., VI, 413-4.

70 To Monroe, February 3, 1801; *Monroe Papers,* LC, vol. VI, p. 1023.

71 To Major Burr Powell; " The Leven Powell Correspondence," *Branch Historical Papers,* I, no. 3, p. 242.

founded for a clientele of merchants and shippers,[72] was critical of the Convention of 1800. The newspaper was worried about keeping faith with Great Britain under the terms of the Jay Treaty! [73]

Secretary of State Marshall wrote to Alexander Hamilton on the first day of the new century that he agreed with him in favoring ratification, though he was " far, very far from approving " the Treaty of Mortfontaine. There was one point especially that had be to be clarified. The American envoys undoubtedly—and correctly—were of the opinion that the prior treaty with Great Britain would retain its stipulated advantages. Were this treaty with any nation other than France, Marshall explained, he would feel no solicitude on the subject. " But France, the most encroaching nation on earth, will claim a literal interpretation, and our people will decide in her favor." Francophiles were seemingly preponderant in the United States, according to Marshall. Had not the Republicans won the presidential election? " In consequence of this temper in our country," the Secretary concluded, " I think the ratification of the treaty ought to be accompanied with a declaration of the sense in which it is agreed to." [74] The Jay Treaty, which had reëstablished commercial relations with Great Britain and made Great Britain the most favored nation, was the cornerstone of Federalist foreign policy.

On January 16, Edward Thornton, British chargé d'affaires, gloomily informed the foreign office in London that the American merchants impatiently awaited the ratification of the treaty with France in order to resume commercial intercourse.[75] The Senate, consequently, approved it on February

72 *V.* the prospectus in the issue of December 8, 1800.

73 Issues of December 31, 1800, and January 1, 1801. Since Alexandria became a part of the District of Columbia on February 27, 1801, no Alexandria newspapers after that date have been used.

74 Oster, *Political and Economic Doctrines of John Marshall*, pp. 91-2.

75 To Grenville; *Great Britain, F. O. 5*, LC, vol. XXXII, p. 8.

3, 1801, despite a prior rejection, with the reservation that Article II be expunged and the duration of the convention be fixed at eight years. It was Article II which provided for future negotiation on indemnities for French spoliations, the treaties of 1778 and the consular convention of 1788.

Attempts of extreme Federalists to continue the suspension of commercial intercourse with France until the final exchange of ratifications were doomed to failure. The Federalist representatives from Virginia split on the question, with Henry Lee of " Stratford " denouncing the proposal in a speech before the House on February 10, 1801. What would the world think, he asked, if the House passed a bill to continue non-intercourse with France, when the President and Senate had already ratified a convention of amity and commerce? It would certainly appear as a deed of the most degrading duplicity.[76] Lee was supported by Robert Page and Leven Powell. Only Thomas Evans and Josiah Parker of the Virginia Federalists voted for the bill.

The more moderate Federalists were vigorously assisted by the Virginia Republicans in the House of Representatives. Joseph Eggleston called attention to the extreme suffering of the tobacco growers and merchants of Virginia during the preceding two years because of the non-intercourse law. Tobacco, he averred, was " an article principally consumed in that country with which we had been prohibited to trade." He hoped the bill was lost.[77]

The non-intercourse law was not renewed. It expired on March 3, 1801. On the following day, Thomas Jefferson, the liberal leader, was inaugurated President of the United States. He had already decided that neutrality and isolation would be the bases of his foreign policy. According to Thornton, the new President informed him on the fifth that " for *republican* France he might have felt some interest, but that was long

76 *Annals of Congress*, 6th Cong., 2nd Sess., 1014-5.

77 *Ibid.*, 1013-4.

over, and there was assuredly nothing in the present Government of that country, which could naturally incline him to shew the smallest undue partiality to it at the expence of Great Britain or indeed of any other country." [78]

Although Jefferson minimized his sympathy for the French Revolution and exaggerated his impartiality toward England for reasons of state, his opinion of the Napoleonic government was portrayed correctly. He felt aloof from Europe. His long-held belief in a policy of neutrality for the young American Republic was strengthened thereby. Moreover, this lonely man, eager to execute the desires of the American people and receive their approbation, was convinced that they wanted to "haul off from European politics" [79] and be the sole arbiters of their destinies. "Peace, commerce, and honest friendship with all nations, entangling alliances with none," was, therefore, proclaimed in the first inaugural address as an essential principle of the American government.

Since the dispute with France seemed to be in train of accommodation, the administration would have to settle the issues outstanding with Great Britain. Throughout the year the American minister to London, the Federalist Rufus King of New York, under the constant pressure of Secretary of State James Madison, attempted to obtain satisfaction for British depredations on American commerce and for impressments. On July 25, 1801, Madison wrote to Governor Monroe that the English government was treating the United States with more respect and conciliation than theretofore.[80]

In the meantime, the new Republican administration was reëstablishing normal relations with France. The stanch Republican Representative John Dawson, anxious for a European trip, was dispatched as courier to France to exchange the rati-

78 Thornton to Grenville, March 7, 1801; *Great Britain, F. O. 5,* LC, vol. XXXII, p. 66.

79 To Stephen Sayre, February 14, 1801; *Jefferson Papers,* LC, vol. CIX, p. 18731.

80 *Madison Papers,* LC, vol. XXIII, no. 28.

fications of the convention. The Republican Robert R. Livingston of New York, who had served with Jefferson on the committee to draft the Declaration of Independence, was appointed minister. But he was not to leave for his post until the completion of ratification. In all other respects the administration acted as if pacification were complete. For example, Pichon, the new French chargé d'affaires, was informed of the recall of American warships.

"Beau" Dawson,[81] however, met lengthy, incomprehensible delays in Paris. He attributed them, ultimately, to the First Consul.[82] President Jefferson, tiring of the delay, decided that Livingston should depart, treaty or no treaty. Perhaps it would be best to have no treaties with any nation.[83] The real obstacle to ratification, he wrote to Madison, was probably the desire to obtain an express renunciation of the demand for indemnities.[84]

A copy of the Treaty of Mortfontaine as ratified by Napoleon was received in October. The First Consul consented to the changes made by the American government, with the understanding that the subjects which were comprehended in the expunged article, that is, treaties and indemnities, were reciprocally renounced. Jefferson considered this a superfluous reservation, because, according to him, it was an established principle that matter not provided for in a peace treaty was abandoned. Since the question of indemnities, however, was "a sore circumstance to the merchants," he would not proclaim the treaty, "but leave it on the shoulders of the senate to accept." [85]

81 John Dawson was so nicknamed because of his elegant manners, dress, and taste for society.

82 Dawson to Madison, August 5, 1801; *Madison Papers*, LC, vol. XXIII, no. 33.

83 To Secretary of Navy, September 5, 1801; *Jefferson Papers*, LC, vol. CXVI, p. 19983.

84 September 12, 1801; *Madison Papers*, LC, vol. XXIII, no. 52.

85 To Wilson Cary Nicholas, October 25, 1801; *Jefferson Papers*, LC, vol. CXVII, p. 20177.

The treaty was approved by the Senate on December 19, 1801. The mercantile *Norfolk Herald* of January 7 and February 6, 1802,[86] bewailed the fact that the treaty with Bonaparte did not provide for compensation for American merchants despoiled by France. The Jefferson administration had begun poorly so far as such merchants were concerned.

Though the foreign policy of the national administration was one of neutrality, the sentiments of Virginians concerning the European war continued to be far from neutral. The Federalist *Norfolk Herald* of November 21, 1801, criticized Napoleon's constant planning for aggrandizing his already overgrown empire.[87] Republicans, on the other hand, continued, in general, to sympathize with the French war effort. Did not Napoleon evince friendliness toward the United States? Did not Great Britain rule the seas tyrannically? Meriwether Jones of the *Examiner* expressed a popular Republican notion when he stated on March 20, 1801, that the destruction of the British navy would be one of the greatest boons to mankind. Governor James Monroe, an ardent Francophile during the 1790's, was still nursing the wounds of his recall from Paris by Washington's administration. He was bitterly anti-Federalist and anti-English. Every calamity, foreign and domestic, which the United States had experienced, he exclaimed on April 30, 1801, proceeded from Great Britain. Monroe maintained that only defeats made the British more amenable to American demands for justice.[88] But Pleasants' *Virginia Argus* of September 29, 1801, did not desire an invasion of England. The conquest of that country would be like "*thrusting out one of the eyes of Europe*." An Irish republic, however, would be satisfactory. (Sympathy for the Irish revolutionary movement was strong in Republican ranks.) Besides being generally hostile to Eng-

86 Editorials reprinted from non-Virginia newspapers.

87 The author has found few expressions of Federalist opinion in Virginia for the year 1801.

88 To Jefferson; letter marked: "not sent." *Monroe Papers*, LC, vol. VII, p. 1109.

land, Republicans could not forgive her hated allies. Partisans persisted in the view that the detested monarchs had begun the war with the intention of annihilating popular government in France.

Republicans still felt an affinity for France, though it was now largely based on French foreign relations rather than its domestic policy. Newspapers continued to refer to the "republican" armies of France. John Page of "Rosewell," Jefferson's close college friend, rejoiced on April 7, 1801, over "the late happy Triumphs of the republican Cause here, and at the Confusion and overthrow of the formidable Combination in Europe of its imperial Enemies." [89] Occasionally Republicans wrote eulogies on Napoleon's alleged ideological achievements in Europe. The editor of the Petersburg *Republican,* Thomas Field, recently acquitted for having killed a Federalist assailant in self-defense, compared Napoleon with Pitt the Younger. Both were characterized as conquerors, the former having gained victories over the enemies of his country, the latter over the liberties of his fellow-citizens. Bonaparte was pronounced the hope of mankind. He fought fanaticism in Europe, liberated oppressed nations, and founded republics.[90]

"A Correspondent" in a lengthy article in the editorial columns of the *Virginia Argus* of November 20, 1801, admitted that Bonaparte sometimes acted in defiance of the rights of his neighbors, like "the veriest King or Emperor." This was in reference to "that unheard of and astonishing measure," the territorial reorganization of the Germanies. Misinterpreting the character of the German "state," the writer affirmed that Napoleon was applying the maxim *divide et impera.* In the end this criticism was qualified by the remark that the petty principalities of the Holy Roman Empire were "a nest of ty-

89 Page to Madison; "Documents" in the *American Historical Review,* vol. I, no. 4 (July, 1896), pp. 699-700.

90 Issue of May 25, 1801; reprint from the New York *Republican Watch-Tower.*

rants, who richly deserve to be swept from the face of the earth."

It was the Anglo-French phase of the war that naturally attracted most attention. Speculation on the possibility of an invasion of England increased as the year progressed. John Dawson, observing the preparations from Paris, believed that there would be an attempt.[91] The *Virginia Argus* of September 29, 1801, thought it was feasible. The "talents and resources of the first Consul, [and] of that constellation of heroes and philosophers, which has burst upon the astonishment of mankind "[92] were beyond calculation. On the other hand, the "Correspondent" in the same paper on November 24, continuing his article of the 20th, affirmed that Napoleon did not need to invade England, now that its finances were on the verge of collapse. The conqueror of the Danube, the Alps, and the Nile, "the successor to the genius and the fortune of Frederick the Great," with his "comprehensive knowledge, . . . piercing sagacity, and . . . stern vigilance," was compelling Britain to ruin its industry by excessive taxation. He never intended invading Britain. "An angler might as well plunge into the stream to catch, with his bare hands, the salmon that is already writhing on his hook."[93]

The attitudes of Republicans toward the French régime, as toward the French war effort, generally experienced no marked changes during 1801. Brumaire, especially for the party's leaders, continued to serve as a frightful lesson for American politics.[94] The form of the French government did not generally

91 To Madison, June 25, 1801; *Madison Papers,* LC, vol. XXII, no. 115. To same, August 5, 1801; *ib.,* vol. XXIII, no. 33.

92 A reference to the French Revolution. Napoleon was thus considered a part of the revolution.

93 The Republicans sympathized with the French in their defeat in Egypt. Jefferson, for example, told Pichon on October 21, 1801, that the fall of Cairo would perpetuate the maritime tyranny of Great Britain. Pichon to Talleyrand, 3 *Brumaire, an* X; *Affaires Étrangères, États-Unis,* LC, vol. LIII, pt. 5, fol. 343[v].

94 *E. g.,* see Madison to Jefferson, February 28, 1801; *Madison Writings,* Hunt ed., VI, 418.

please Republicans. The Richmond *Examiner* of August 27, 1801, for example, condemned Bonaparte's government as a despotism. The editorial, however, proclaimed its willingness to trust in the dispositions of the talented Napoleon "until a peace shall test his choice between a glorious name and the freedom of his country, or the admiration mixed with the execration of mankind." [95] Many Republicans persisted in the opinion that General Bonaparte might have established an emergency régime in order to win the war. The Napoleonic régime was still a special phase of the French Revolution. Enthusiasm for the French war effort undoubtedly had its effect in encouraging such wishful thinking.

Some Republicans, indeed, continued to depict Napoleon as the republican head of France. If Jefferson is elected president, wrote James Monroe on February 12, 1801, "we are safe in part, and, unless Bounaparte [*sic*] turns royalist & villain, the commenc'ment [*sic*] of the 19th century will be more favorable to the cause of liberty, than any former epoch of time. America & France in republican hands can advance the cause with effect. France by arms, America by the form of example." [96]

In his memorandum book,[97] Monroe criticized Jefferson's inaugural address for having blatantly proclaimed that the United States desired no alliance with France. It could have been done privately, he wrote. One of the advantages of a conciliatory deportment toward France would be the preservation of the good esteem of France. Thereby the Republican administration at Washington could wield some influence over the future development of the French Revolution. It would be more difficult for France to leave the republican standard while in amity with the United States. Under such conditions the people of France would be doubly shocked, if their govern-

95 Editorial reprinted from the *Aurora.*

96 To ——; *Monroe Papers,* LC, vol. VI, p. 1042.

97 *Memoranda And Accounts—James Monroe; 1795-1801* (MSS., LC). It cannot be ascertained from the memorandum book when the various notes were actually written.

ment evinced monarchical tendencies. It would then be committing double perfidy, perfidy to the French and to their American friends.

Unlike Monroe, the "Correspondent" in the *Virginia Argus* of November 20, 1801, considered the "Little Corsican" as already a virtual monarch, though of a unique character. Notwithstanding the manner in which Bonaparte obtained power, the writer stated, it was very likely that during the "reign" of this great man France would be happier than under any sovereign since the time of Clovis. France's domestic happiness would probably be in direct proportion to its external grandeur. In the first place, the nation had eliminated an oppressive priesthood and aristocracy.

> Second. Buonaparte himself stands upon his good behaviour; for the moment that he shall forfeit his popularity, he must expect to quit his office; and most probably his life. Nothing but an eminent degree of justice and benevolence, as well as of vigour and sagacity, can make his situation tolerably secure. All these features have hitherto marked, and we may presume that they will continue to make [*sic*] the political deportment of the first consul. Alike intrepid & cool, enterprizing & provident, silent in his resentment, impenetrable in his designs, superior to every passion but that for the perpetuity of his power, . . . Buonaparte will not sacrifice the resources of his situation to the profligacy of a mistress, or the abyss of a gaming table. . . .
>
> Instead of a pampered phantom, fit for nothing but to act the farce of royal pageantry, the nation is now governed by a man whom nature had endowed with the most splendid talents, and who, in ascending the ladder of fortune, has acquired a complete knowledge of adversity, of mankind, and of military discipline.

In answer to the charge of some "Richmond critics" that Napoleon was a hypocrite as well as a renegade from the cause of religious freedom, the writer defended Bonaparte's religious policy as a means of closing the wounds of civil discord.[98] The papal letter inviting the emigrant bishops to resign proved to the " Correspondent's " satisfaction that the new pope [99] was a creature of the First Consul. Napoleon, with the sanction of *his* pope, would then fill the episcopal vacancies with men of his own choosing. The reëstablishment of a type of national church was necessary to gain the support of the clergy and, thereby, of many thousands or, perhaps, millions of Frenchmen. But Napoleon would never permit the restoration of the ancient church with its intolerance and its tithes. " The torch of reason, and the universal right of conscience," the writer concluded, " will forever prevent the midnight return of superstition and despotism. . . ."

Meanwhile, Federalist opinion of the Napoleonic régime, in general, apparently remained unchanged. Bolstering partisan propaganda, Federalists called the attention of Americans to the lessons of French history. Some aspiring leader in the United States—obviously of the opposite party—might become a despot like Bonaparte, wrote " Civis " in the *Norfolk Herald* of January 1, 1801. At a Federalist July 4 celebration in Fincastle, Botetourt County, one of the toasts was: " May the late usurpation in France admonition [*sic*] Amcricans to beware of the danger of Jacobinism." [100] Democracy leads to despotism. The *Norfolk Herald* of February 5, moreover, presented an inimical account of Napoleon's personal habits. He was upbraided, for example, for allegedly lacking in etiquette and for being a glutton. On November 21, however, the same newspaper applauded the reduction of the list of French émigrés.

Then came the news of the preliminaries of peace between France and Great Britain. Republicans generally welcomed it. President Jefferson breathed a sigh of relief. The only source

98 The article approved of the recall of lay émigrés on the same grounds. The Concordat of 1801 was not promulgated until April, 1802.

99 Pius VII, elected in 1800.

100 Reported in the *Fincastle Weekly Advertiser* of July 10, 1801.

of danger to the United States had been removed, he wrote with exaggeration on December 5, 1801. We could now proceed without risk to demolish all useless structures of expense, lightening the citizen's tax burdens, and, thereby, fortifying the principles of free government.[101] Frugality was a fundamental trait of Jefferson's republicanism.

Not all Virginians, however, were pleased with the pacification of Europe. Federalist Augustine Davis's Richmond paper, the *Virginia Gazette and General Advertiser* of March 16, 1802, echoing the displeasure of many merchants, described the harmful effects of peace on American commerce.

The return of peace to the western world removed, however temporarily, a catalyzer in the formation of Virginian opinion concerning France. Republicans need no longer worry about a possible victory of crowned heads. Federalists need no longer concern themselves with the fate of England. Napoleon Bonaparte stood more on his own merits than ever before. That was to be so until the retrocession of Louisiana to France seemed to endanger the national interests of the United States. The perception of such a danger—if reached at all—was to come at different times for different individuals.

Meanwhile, the time had come to test the Republican theory of the emergency character of the Consulate. Meriwether Jones wrote anxiously in the *Examiner* of December 1, 1801:

> Every friend to liberty, at this moment directs his attention to Buonaparte; and while they admire his wisdom and bravery, hope for much, but tremble at the fascinating allurements of grandeur and of power.—If he be really wise, he will pursue the generous & magnanimous route to Fame: he will restore to the people of France, the power which he so unwarrantably assumed. But if the reverse be the case, if uncontroled [*sic*] SWAY, has weakened his head & hardened his heart, the verdant fields of France may again be crimsoned o'er, and Liberty bemoan her blighted hopes.

101 To Governor Joseph Bloomfield; *Jefferson Papers,* LC, vol. CXVIII, p. 20360. *Cf.* Pichon to Talleyrand, 3 *Thermidor, an* IX; *Affaires Étrangères, États-Unis,* LC, vol. LIII, pt. 3, fol. 182^{v}.

The choice was of great importance to Europe, Jones asserted. If France became a representative democracy, its foreign policy would be pacific. But if it became monarchical, the same dominating spirit which directed Napoleon's internal policy would "lead him to pursue the illusory phantom of grandeur, through the murderous paths of war and conquest." The British navy would not always be able to obstruct Napoleon. Under such a capable ruler France could build a larger navy than England's. Great Britain and the continental powers, the editor concluded, should hope for the victory of republicanism in France.

A week later the *Virginia Argus* doubted whether Bonaparte would surrender his power. If he retained his position, disregarding the wishes and interests of the French people, this modern Caesar would find another Brutus.[102] On the other hand, on March 13, 1802, the Richmond *Recorder*,[103] published by James T. Callender and Henry Pace, characterized rumors that France was about to choose a king as absurd.

Federalists of the Old Dominion speculated differently. For them the French government continued to be a despotism. It had, nevertheless, certain admirable features. An extract of an address by youthful George W. P. Custis, grandson of Martha Washington, to the freeholders of Fairfax County,—published in the editorial columns of the *Virginia Gazette and General Advertiser* on April 10, 1802,—is an example of the latter viewpoint. Custis applauded the Napoleonic régime for having crushed Jacobinism, that poisonous philosophy concocted from a mixture of impiety, egalitarianism, and anarchism. The Jacobins had pulled down the church to erect the temple of anarchy. They had trampled the cross to raise the idol of democracy. They had destroyed the government to plant the tree of liberty. But now the name of a philosopher was

102 Editorial reprinted from the *Aurora*. *Cf. supra*, p. 79, Jefferson's reaction on January 23, 1800, to the coup d'état of Brumaire.

103 The complete title until November 3, 1802, was *The Recorder; or, Lady's and Gentleman's Miscellany.*

despised in France. The nation, having seen the error of its ways, subsided under an effective, energetic government. Instead of being a prey to faction, France had become an envied nation. Philosophy had been replaced by national utility.

A more detailed and somewhat different analysis of the relation between the revolution and Napoleon was contributed in *A Series of Letters Addressed To Thomas Jefferson, Esq., President of the United States, Concerning His Official Conduct And Principles* . . . by "Tacitus."[104] This was the pseudonym of a Thomas Evans of Virginia,[105] possibly the extreme Federalist ex-congressman from Accomac County. The author employed French history to prove his theory of the dangers inherent in Jefferson's alleged opposition to the separation of powers and belief in the supremacy of the legislative branch of the government. Steeped in the philosophy of Edmund Burke, "Tacitus" traced the ills of France to the alleged abolition of all existing institutions by the powerful revolutionary legislatures. Not only atrocities resulted, "but an avoidable general depravation of manners and perversion of ideas, springing from the worst passions of our nature, stimulated to a degree of madness, and turned loose by the licentiousness of anarchy."[106] An attempt was made under the Directory to return to the correct principle of the separation of powers. The French, however, experimented unwisely with a plural executive.

"Tacitus" averred that the successful coup d'état of Brumaire was prepared by the tyranny of the Directory, its discord, and the general state of manners inimical to all government. The Napoleonic régime was an inevitable consequence of the revolution. ". . . [The] depravation of manners and [the] perversion of ideas render hopeless a return to anything like 'the benign influence of good laws under a free govern-

104 (Philadelphia, 1802), NYPL. The work was dated March 27, 1802, by "Tacitus."

105 According to the LC catalogue.

106 *Op. cit.*, p. 90.

ment.' —Not peace, but barely a cessation from convulsions, is all that can be hoped for, and that too from the sternest military despotism." [107] Such a government was necessary to lay the foundations of enduring order. Whether the present government, therefore, was preparatory to the restoration of the Bourbons or the establishment of a new dynasty, it was fundamentally a transitional stage to a more permanent order. Only when the revolutionary state of France had been replaced by the Napoleonic régime, " Tacitus " noted, could the civilized nations of the world resume peaceful relations with that country.

The restoration of peace thus reënforced Federalist appreciation of Napoleon's services to conservatism. General Bonaparte had crushed the radicals of the revolution, the Jacobins. He had ended the French Revolution. He had established some " order " and " energy " in government. Napoleonic France, bad as it was, was better than revolutionary France. France was on the road to sanity!

Many Virginia Republicans, on the other hand, were on tenterhooks. What would be Napoleon Bonaparte's next political act? In the eyes of a man like Thomas Jefferson, however, the First Consul was already among the damned.

In the meantime, another element began to enter into the formation of opinion: Franco-American relations again became strained. But this time it was under a Republican federal administration.

107 *Id.*

CHAPTER IV
OPINION OF A NEIGHBOR

THE Republican administration in Washington was not unduly alarmed when it received a report in May, 1801, from Rufus King in London, that Spain had retroceded Louisiana to France. Rumors of such an event had been rife since 1796. Jefferson and his Secretary of State, Madison, endeavored to fathom the motives of the Consulate in the light of Franco-American relations in the heyday of the Federalists. They reasoned that if the retrocession had really occurred, it was, in all probability, the consequence of the anti-French policy of the American government in the preceding years. It was a means of counteracting the Anglomania of which New England was suspected as well as the danger of a British conquest of Louisiana.[1]

Yet the President was disturbed. It was "very ominous to us," he wrote to Governor Monroe on May 26.[2] It had long been a basic conviction of Jefferson that the Spanish borderlands must remain in the hands of weak Spain until the United States was prepared to acquire them.[3] The anxiety, therefore, was created not by hostility to Napoleon, but by fear of a strong neighbor. British control of Louisiana and the Floridas was dreaded by the administration even more than French control. Great Britain, mistress of the seas and of Canada, would under the circumstances encircle the United States.[4]

The immediate issue, however, was a probable French neighbor. In the ensuing months, the administration elaborated

1 Madison to Monroe, June 1, 1801; *Madison Writings*, Hunt ed., VI, 422. Secretary of State to Charles Pinckney, June 9, 1801; *ASP, FR*, II, 510.

2 *Monroe Papers*, LC, vol. VII, p. 1115.

3 *E. g., cf.* Jefferson to Archibald Stuart, January 25, 1786; *Jefferson Writings*, Ford ed., IV, 188-9.

4 Secretary of State to Rufus King, July 24, 1801; *Madison Writings*, Hunt ed., VI, 435.

upon its reasons for opposing a retrocession.[5] With the French in Louisiana, there would be danger of friction over the question of the navigation of the Mississippi and the right of deposit at New Orleans, both so essential to western trade. The frequent wars between France and Great Britain might embroil the West in the military expeditions between Canada and Louisiana.[6] The French, furthermore, were noted for their impetuosity of temper, and the energy and restlessness of their character.[7] Reports of a plan to use Louisiana as a safety-valve for the turbulent spirits of the French army were accepted as true.[8] A French neighbor would excite "inquietudes . . . in the Southern States, where numerous slaves have been taught to regard the French as the patrons of their cause. . . ."[9] Finally, Jefferson believed that the Napoleonic régime was "unequivocally hostile to a republican administration of this [government]."[10]

The trump card in the diplomatic maneuvering was the threat of an Anglo-American alliance. The strength of the young American Republic lay in its ability to exploit the national rivalries in Europe. But such a threat was to be used, if at all, with extreme caution. Livingston, the new minister to Paris, was thus informed.[11]

The uncertainty that prevailed in Washington in 1801 concerning the retrocession began to evaporate in February, 1802.

5 Madison merely seemed to be following Jefferson's lead. The Secretary of State, indeed, had originally thought that the French would pursue a policy in Louisiana favorable to the West. *Vid.* Madison to Wilson C. Nicholas, July 10, 1801; *Madison Writings*, Hunt ed., VI, 427n.

6 Secretary of State to C. Pinckney, June 9, 1801; to R. R. Livingston, September 28, 1801; *ASP, FR*, II, 510.

7 Jefferson to R. R. Livingston, April 18, 1802; *Jefferson Writings*, Washington ed., IV, 432.

8 Jefferson to T. M. Randolph, March 12, 1802; *Jefferson Papers*, LC, vol. CXXI, p. 20904.

9 Secretary of State to Livingston, September 28, 1801; *ASP, FR*, II, 510.

10 See n. 8 *supra*.

11 See n. 9 *supra*.

In that month General Leclerc, Napoleon's brother-in-law, landed with an expeditionary force in the hate-filled Caribbean isle of San Domingo in order to reëstablish French rule. Was there a connection between San Domingo and Louisiana? Leclerc's violent conduct toward American shippers augured ill for Franco-American relations. In February, too, there arrived King's dispatch from London enclosing a copy of the definitive treaty of retrocession, the Treaty of Aranjuez (March 21, 1801). Jefferson received at the same time the evasive answers of Talleyrand, the French foreign minister, as to the truth of such an arrangement.

The President's alarm was no longer subdued. The period of watchful waiting was over. This was the moment to play the trump card. Perhaps it might prevent the change of neighbors. The result was the famous letter of April 18, 1802, to Livingston. From the day that France took possession of New Orleans, "we must marry ourselves to the British fleet & nation," he fulminated. As soon as war broke out again between France and England, the United States would make common cause with the latter and hold "the two continents of America in sequestration for the common purposes of the United British & American nations." [12] Jefferson retained this belligerent pose throughout the spring and summer of 1802.

But war was the last thing he desired. On October 10, 1802, the President wrote calmly to Livingston, "No matter at present existing between them [the French] & us is important enough to risk a breach of peace; peace being indeed the most important of all things for us, except the preserving an erect & independent attitude." [13]

That was his policy despite his melancholy conclusion in the same letter: ". . . We stand completely corrected of the error that either the government or the nation of France has any remains of friendship for us. The portion of that country which forms an exception, though respectable in weight, is weak in

12 *Jefferson Papers,* LC, vol. CXXII, pp. 21078-80.

13 *Ibid.,* CXXVI, 21812.

numbers. On the contrary it appears evident that an unfriendly spirit prevails in the most important individuals of the government towards us." [14] French diplomacy toward the United States in the preceding months had not pleased the administration. Not only was Napoleon Bonaparte a pariah for Jefferson the republican, but even France, as a whole, was becoming such.

Meantime, the American press had become aroused over the Louisiana problem. Early in July, 1802, Pichon reported to Talleyrand that both Federalist and Republican newspapers in the United States were opposed to the retrocession.[15] Some Republican newspapers, however, after having written for so many years about "our ally," the French Republic, found it difficult to conceive of Napoleon Bonaparte as a menace to the United States. Meriwether Jones, a loyal and active Republican, criticized, in his Richmond *Examiner* of May 5, 1802, a Federalist proposal to foil the French acquisition of Louisiana by means of an alliance with England, and, if necessary, by war.

In an editorial on May 12, Jones attempted to prove that the retrocession would not be harmful to the interests of the West or of the United States as a whole. The event was the product of the Jay Treaty and the anti-French policy of the Adams administration. Theoretically, it was better to have a weak neighbor. In practice, however, weak Spain must ally with a great power, which could protect her colonies. Spain chose France rather than Great Britain, the editor asserted, because the former was an agricultural country, comparatively little dependent on foreign commerce, and inferior at sea. France became the neighbor of the United States more at the solicitation of Spain than at her own desire. America should approve the choice. Repeating some of the arguments of the administration, the editor expounded the dangers involved in British con-

14 *Id.*

15 Pichon to Talleyrand, 18 *Messidor, an* X; *Affaires Étrangères, États-Unis,* LC, vol. LIV, pt. 6, fols. 410-11.

trol of the Spanish border provinces. The United States would be encircled thereby. France, on the other hand, could, if necessary, be easily defeated with British aid. France's commercial policy was more liberal than England's. A more friendly line of conduct with regard to the navigation of the Mississippi might be expected from France than from Great Britain. The free use of that river for the benefit of the West, Jones concluded, was a principal object in all considerations respecting Louisiana. The Trans-Alleghany region of Virginia was part of the West.

A different approach to the problem was to be found in the columns of the *Recorder*. The persecution complex of its chief editor, James T. Callender,—a political refugee from Great Britain,—was beginning to focus on his former benefactor, Thomas Jefferson, and on the Virginia Republicans. Among other reasons, the hack writer could not forgive the President for refusing him a federal position. Callender, moreover, was personally at odds with Meriwether Jones. The fact that Jones saw no danger in the retrocession of Louisiana was sufficient cause for Callender to allege that it would beget serious problems.

The independence of the United States would be somewhat crippled by the event, an editorial in the *Recorder* asserted.[16] It meant the end of the use of the Mississippi by Americans. If Jefferson complained, Bonaparte would send two seventy-four-gun ships to the river, effectually ending the western trade with the West Indies.[17] Napoleon was eager to prevent any American supplies from reaching the British West Indies in the next war. Furthermore, a French colony at the mouth of the Mississippi would result in the western states falling under French influence. Callender was chuckling at Jefferson's discomfiture.

16 April 24, 1802. This was an answer to an earlier *Examiner* editorial accepting the retrocession.

17 Was Callender unaware of the flourishing grain trade between New Orleans and the French and Spanish West Indies? *V. s.*, p. 116.

But Callender offered no solution. He was apparently interested not so much in the independence of the United States as in the overthrow of the Jefferson administration. Napoleon, moreover, was still his idol.[18] On October 27 and November 24, 1802,[19] editorials rebuked the President for pursuing an anti-French foreign policy. Such a policy, they asserted, had been the strongest reason for overthrowing Adams. In the latter issue the *Recorder* endeavored to strike terror into the hearts of Republicans with the warning that a French fleet and army destined for the Mississippi might mistake their passage and cast anchor in the Chesapeake. Jefferson, in that case, might find it more prudent to go to Manchester. This was raking up old coals, the probably unavoidable flight of young Governor Jefferson from Benedict Arnold's army during the Revolutionary War.

Though Virginians might differ as to the significance of a French colony in Louisiana, they were virtually unanimous in their detestation and fear of the Negro rebellion in San Domingo. The example of the slave rebellion was dangerous for the South. San Domingo, moreover, might become another Algiers.[20] General Leclerc's anti-American policy, however, created resentment. It also dawned upon Virginians that the French road to Louisiana ran through the sugar and coffee plantations of that Caribbean isle. Pichon accurately summarized the Southern attitude toward the French expedition in a report to Talleyrand in November, 1802. Although the slave-owners hoped for French success, he wrote, they would probably not be displeased if it took some time. That would prevent the execution of the plans concerning Louisiana.[21] Toussaint

18 *Vid. infra*, pp. 119-20.

19 The editorial column for the latter issue, however, is dated November 17.

20 This was Jefferson's reasoning in July, 1801, according to the French chargé. Pichon to Talleyrand, 3 *Thermidor, an* IX; *Affaires Étrangères, États-Unis*, LC, vol. LIII, pt. 3, fol. 178ʳ.

21 3 *Frimaire, an* XI; *ibid.*, LV, pt. 2, fols. 83ʳ-84.

l'Ouverture's arrest and imprisonment by the French did, nevertheless, evoke some sympathy.[22]

At the time that the retrocession of Louisiana was beginning to create discontent among Virginia Republicans, constitutional changes were being engineered in France that lost General Napoleon Bonaparte most of the remaining sympathy of the liberals in the Old Dominion.

For their sagacious leader, however, Napoleon had been a renegade since 1800. On July 6, 1802, Thomas Jefferson wrote sarcastically about a new constitutional development in France. ". . . Republican Buonaparte is [*sic*] made of himself Consul for life, as he did for 10 years by a sham vote of the people. The next step will be to make them vote the succession to his heirs lineal or collateral." [23] Jefferson seemed to have the measure of his man. France was again a kingdom, he affirmed on July 14, but the revolution was not yet finished.[24] On November 29, he was more pessimistic. He could not agree that all was not lost. France had retrogressed "from a limited to an unlimited despotism." "The press, the only tocsin of a nation, is completely silenced there, and all means of a general effort taken away." [25]

The President's analysis of the implications of the constitutional change followed the pattern of the reasoning he had employed immediately after Brumaire. Who could have thought the French nation incapable of self-government? he asked.[26] Americans seemed to be the only people able to live under republican principles. Jefferson was now more confident of America's future. "So thoroughly are their minds imbued with the principle of obedience to the will of the majority,"

22 See the Fredericksburg *Virginia Herald* of December 14, 1802.

23 To Peter Carr; *Jefferson Papers*, LC, vol. CXXIV, p. 21434.

24 To John Trumbull; *ibid.*, 21469.

25 To Thomas Cooper; *ibid.*, CXXVII, 22007.

26 To Joseph Priestley, November 29, 1802; *Jefferson Writings*, Ford ed., VIII, 179.

he wrote, "that a majority of one even in the choice of their chief magistrate produces as absolute an acquiescence as an unanimous vote. The unbridled license too of our newspapers serve [*sic*] as chimnies to carry off the smoke. Ill humors, instead of being pent up, find vent through them & leave the party at ease." [27] He knew whereof he spoke.

The Americans, according to Jefferson, were the sole trustees for mankind. On the outcome of the American experiment depended the great question: Could man govern himself? It became doubly one's duty to suppress all local and personal views, and to consider but the one great object of proving that a government might be so free as to leave every man in the unrestricted exercise of all his rights, while it had energy enough to protect him from every wrong.[28] President Jefferson obviously believed that he was displaying such energy when he assumed a belligerent attitude toward France on the Louisiana question.

Unlike Thomas Jefferson, other Republicans of the Old Dominion were taken aback by Napoleon's assumption of the Consulate for life. Napoleon Bonaparte had finally bared his soul to them. Meriwether Jones frankly admitted his surprise. He declared in the *Examiner* of July 21, 1802, that it was probably the last step in the political career of that extraordinary man. Jones expected and hoped that ere long a Brutus would appear to strike the merited blow at the insidious usurper. He endeavored to prove the justice of tyrannicide in the case. Were a second Pharsalus [29] to decide the duration of the French Republic, with Augereau, Bernadotte, and the other republican generals arrayed under the standard of liberty against Bonaparte, the military adventurer would be forced—notwithstanding his military fame—to yield to the spirit of

27 To John Trumbull, July 14, 1802; *Jefferson Papers*, LC, vol. CXXIV, p. 21469.

28 To Nathaniel Macon, July 17, 1802; *ibid.*, 21484.

29 The battle between Julius Caesar and Pompey in 48 B. C., which was won by the former.

liberty and to the wishes of a majority of the French people. Republicanism was steeped in the classical tradition.[30]

Should Bonaparte, however, remain consul for life, the editor continued, what have the French gained by the revolution?

> They have gained the extinction of orders in society; the abolition of the most hateful and tyrannical aristocracy, that ever trode [*sic*] upon poor degraded human nature; and the suppression of the odious and oppressive parts of the power and revenue of the Priesthood. One article in the creed of admission into Bonaparte's Legion of Honor, is a sacred engagement ever to resist the revival of the feudal system. The destruction of this system was of itself, well worth a ten years war. The French too have got the *idea* if not the *substance* of liberty. They understand what it is, if they do not enjoy it. They have once tasted its sweets, but it is impossible that they should ever become the *slaves they have been.*

The revolution was ended; but it had not been in vain.[31]

Jones defended the Republicans against the charge of inconsistency leveled by the Federalists. Napoleon, not the Republicans, had changed, he insisted. "Should an eccentric luminary, that has dazzled half the globe, with its brilliancy; should a Bonaparte become the slave of ambition, and desert his principles—*the Republicans desert him.*" [32]

"Sydney" took the offensive against the Federalists in the editorial columns of the *Virginia Argus* on September 1, 1802.

30 The *Republican, & Petersburg Advertiser* of September 30, 1802, formerly the Petersburg *Republican*, thought that a better parallel to Bonaparte than Cromwell or Çaesar was Dionysius, the tyrant of Syracuse from 405 to 367 B. C. The editorial, reprinted from a non-Virginia newspaper, then proceeded to compare the two, concluding with the implied hope that Napoleon would not remain in power that long.

31 *Cf.* the last part of James Ogilvie's July 4, 1803, oration; in the *Examiner* of July 20, 1803. Ogilvie was a Scottish teacher and philosopher, who came to Virginia during the 1790's.

32 Some admiration for Napoleon still lurked in Republican hearts. This was especially true of his military ability. *Vid., e.g.*, the *Virginia Argus*, December 1, 1802; and the *Examiner*, June 11, 1803.

Taking advantage of the pleasure which many Federalists had evinced with the developments in France,[33] he wrote: ". . . The nation that admires and extols despotism abroad, however effulgent the glory that surrounds it, is prepared for slavery at home; and the moment it shall appear that we have so far forgotten or abandoned our republican feelings, as to cease to abhor tyranny in every shape, that moment we expose the republic to the assaults of any ambitious leader, who in secret deliberates the subversion of liberty. . . . *There are* such men *here* as well as *elsewhere*." "Sydney" exclaimed indignantly that the Federalists, pointing to France, laughed at republicanism as chimerical, and urged Americans to overthrow their republic.

Republicans continued publicly to recommend tyrannicide. One of the toasts at a Republican festival at Westmoreland Court-House in the Northern Neck in March, 1803, to celebrate the inauguration of Thomas Jefferson was to "Buonaparte.—Let him remember the Ides of March and the fate of Caesar." [34] Similar were the toasts at other Republican meetings in the Old Dominion.

Prominent in maligning the Republicans for urging the assassination of Napoleon was Callender of the *Recorder*. This unhappy Scot penned the following laudatory remarks concerning his hero on November 24, 1802: [35]

> He [Napoleon] is doing everything in his power, and that is a great deal, to promote the happiness of France. We believe that he will be, by far, the greatest benefactor that the French ever saw, since they existed as a nation. If circumstances compell [*sic*] him to commit some acts of despotism, still he has too much good sense to forfeit the affections of the people at large. The late king of Prussia was an arbitrary and often an offensive monarch. But still he possessed, in an unlimited degree, the admiration, the confidence, and the affection of his

33 *Vide infra*, pp. 121 f.

34 Reported in the *Examiner*, April 9, 1803.

35 The editorial column was, however, dated November 17.

> subjects. In various respects, the great Corsican may be considered a second Frederick; and while Smith [36] and Cheetham [37] and the rest of the Jefferson tribe of newsprinters are bawling for a *second* Brutus, we could wish to become acquainted with the advantages that arose to mankind from the dagger of the first one.

He was still writing in the same vein on June 4, 1803. He declared that Bonaparte had gained the confidence of the French nation by the splendor of his literary and political talents, the importance of his services, and the heroism of his actions. Despite the fact that the constitutional changes made by Napoleon exhibited a tendency toward hereditary monarchy, Callender averred, France was satisfied.

Thomas Field vigorously parried an onslaught by Callender on a Republican meeting in Petersburg, which had drunk the usual toast to General Bonaparte's demise. In the *Petersburg Republican* of April 12, 1803,[38] Field affirmed that Callender was offended because "the democrats of this town dared to wish that an usurper, who had flagrantly betrayed his trust; who had trampled on the liberties of a great nation; who, by a mixture of violence and imposition, had made himself the sole lord of the lives and property of forty millions of people, might, since he had put himself beyond the reach of the laws, be made to answer to an extraordinary tribunal." The assassination of despots, he continued, was sanctioned by the best and most enlightened of the ancients. The leading tyrannicides —Harmodius and Aristogiton! Timoleon and Brutus!—were men distinguished by every virtue. In a telling blow, Fields pointed out Callender's probable fate, had he dared publish in France a single one of such invectives against the First Consul as he had against President Jefferson.

36 Samuel Harrison Smith, publisher of the semi-official *National Intelligencer* of Washington, D. C.

37 James Cheetham, English refugee, then co-editor of the *Republican Watch-Tower* of New York.

38 Formerly the *Republican* and the *Republican, & Petersburg Advertiser.*

At the same time that Republicans disapproved of the domestic developments in France, voices were heard in the party censuring Napoleon's treatment of the minor states on the European continent. How could Napoleon, whom they no longer considered as the torch-bearer of republicanism in France, bring liberty to other countries? The *Virginia Argus* of December 15, 1802,[39] noted that Bonaparte had recently acquired great facility in the use of the imperative mood. The editorial cited as proof his proclamation to the Helvetic Republic, which stated that he would mediate between the discordant factions and which ordered the Swiss to send deputies to Paris. On December 25, the paper presented its readers with a sketch of Aloys Reding, "the person who is the leader of those brave men, who are now endeavoring to recover their liberties, and to free Switzerland from abject dependence on a foreign power." The right of the self-determination of peoples was a fundamental concept of Republicans. But the *Virginia Argus* was probably unaware that Reding was a leader of the forces of conservatism!

While Republicans in the Old Dominion were turning their backs on Napoleon Bonaparte in the latter half of 1802, many Federalists in the state were expressing considerable admiration for him. The fact that England and France were at peace eliminated a major hindrance to such a development in Federalist ranks. News that a plebiscite was to be held in France on a Consulate for life removed another. Federalists had continued to denounce Jacobinism, the term which covered all sins. Especially did they proclaim their loyalty to traditional religion as they castigated the "impious" philosophers Tom Jefferson and Tom Paine. The champions of "religion," "order," and "energetic government" were pleased with the consolidation of the Napoleonic dictatorship. It served Federalist propagandists as a politically useful contrast to the "anarchy" in the United States under the Monticello philosopher.

39 Editorial reprinted from the Worcester *National Aegis.*

Augustine Davis, dismissed Richmond postmaster, adhered to the normal pattern of Federalist ideology in his paper, the *Virginia Gazette and General Advertiser.* He reprinted an article on the Life Consulate from a New York journal [40] in his editorial column on August 7, 1802. It showed clearly what the Federalists then admired in Napoleon.

The news from France, the writer began, is evidence that the citizens have just discovered that they have been mad for the past ten years. Intoxicated by the fumes of liberty and equality, they have been quarreling, cutting each other's throats, and spreading misery and confusion among their neighbors. Now that the democratic mania has subsided among the French, it is to be hoped that they will lend their aid to cure it in other countries, where they have labored to spread the infection. Formerly, they talked of spreading liberty and destroying thrones and altars. Now, Jacobins are to be watched, anarchists deported, the church restored, and slavery reëstablished. Thus, the editorial concluded, the French are forever rushing to extremes, as will every society that follows demagogues or is subjected to a military despotism.

An article in the same issue from the Philadelphia *Gazette of the United States* charged the Republicans with inconsistency.[41] When Bonaparte was deluging Europe with blood, the indictment began, the Republicans adored him. Now, when he had given peace to Europe and was exerting his talents for the prosperity and happiness of France, he was styled a 'tyrant' and a 'traitor,' with death by assassination or poison too mild a punishment. All Republicans, the writer concluded with zest, hated law and order and opposed the protection of property!

Witness the poisonous fruits of Jacobinism in Switzerland! That was the theme of an editorial in the *Virginia Gazette and General Advertiser* of December 15, 1802. With a fervid im-

40 The *Spectator.*

41 Though not in the editorial column of the *Virginia Gazette,* the article accords with Davis's general attitude toward the French developments. It can, therefore, be considered as the opinion of the Virginia newspaper as well.

agination, the author depicted the products of democracy as infidelity, persecution of the learned—who had fled for asylum to the First Consul!—and rampant prostitution. Americans, learn the lesson well! was the parting warning. Every assault on the alleged principles of the revolution in Europe was an added blot on the escutcheon of the detested lord of Monticello.

In contrast was the First Consul of France. The significance of Bonaparte was the subject of an editorial in the same Richmond paper on December 22.[42]

> There has been no period in the life of this extraordinary man in which he has appeared surrounded with more dangers than at present. The sentiments of the whole world seem conspiring against him. Whether his fall would contribute to the happiness, or misery of mankind is hazardous to affirm. He has doubtless restored Europe to a calm that it had not experienced for many years. He has extended his protection to the arts and sciences in a more eminent degree, than ever was done by the most powerful monarchs. Notwithstanding many of his actions are arbitrary in the extreme, yet they all seem calculated for the public good. Even his threatened invasion of Switzerland, although a stretch of power that would have been unpardonable in an hereditary prince, yet when coming from Buonaparte and compared with his conduct hitherto, appears designed, solely, to reduce that formerly happy people, into a state of peace and quiet.

The brilliant guards, the magnificent palace, and the splendid retinue, the editorial continued, are necessary for a ruler who has risen to the highest pinnacle of power by the sword and not by hereditary right.

> Buonaparte is the only instance in the bloody catalogue of usurpers, who has made learning, virtue, religion and peace his study. Whether he has done this from self vanity, or from

42 Though these December editorials were written after the news of the closing of the deposit at New Orleans, the editor apparently was not yet affected by it. The editorials, therefore, belong to the preceding phase of the history of opinion. See his later reaction, *infra,* 131 f.

> a love to mankind it is not our business to enquire; we can only judge by the actions of men and not by their thoughts.
>
> As long as Buonaparte will retain his power, it is probable that Europe and the course of the whole world will preserve [a] [43] state of prosperity, and will approach nearer that appearance, which was displayed under the emperor Tragan [*sic*], than any other state that mankind have exhibited since that period.

Bonaparte's conduct, nevertheless, will serve as a dangerous example to ambitious characters, who have not the same virtues. Of the two evils, however, compliance with the views of the First Consul seems to be the lesser. "For in the event of his overthrow, Europe may expect several years of hostilities and bloodshed, perhaps more terrible, than even those, which it has already experienced."

A remark about the Republican attitude was in order. Tom Paine's hatred of Bonaparte, the writer asserted, appears to arise solely from the regard which the First Consul has shown for the preservation of the divine worship. By demagogues of that description the fall or assassination of Bonaparte would probably be the most desirable event that could take place.

Thus for many conservatives in Virginia in the latter half of 1802, the good qualities of Napoleon Bonaparte outweighed the bad. Though he was an upstart—that was not cricket—and his services to the abhorrent French Revolution were in very bad taste, he had become, in their opinion, the parricide of the revolution. He had replaced popular government with absolute rule. He had reëstablished the church; deism was apparently extinct. The Federalists, in other words, applauded those domestic accomplishments of the Man on Horseback which marked a return to the ways of the *Ancien Régime*. Napoleon, furthermore, seemed to desire peace. He was also reëstablishing order in neighboring Switzerland. What else could one expect of a usurper?

43 Illegible.

And then the Mississippi question reached a crisis. News of the ending of the right of deposit at New Orleans by order of the Spanish intendant of Louisiana had arrived in the eastern part of the United States late in November, 1802. America was shocked. Eastern merchants, whose trade with the West and with New Orleans was growing, as well as western farmers expected to suffer economically from the action.[44] "Was this a consequence of Napoleonic pressure?" Americans asked themselves. "An omen of things to come under French rule?"

The great opportunity of the Federalists had arrived. By posing as the vigorous champions of the western farming interests, they might win the frontiersmen to the fold. By clamoring for war, they hoped to increase the embarrassments of the Republican administration [45] and prove its weakness to all concerned. The Federalists were the champions of energetic government. Some Federalists also thought this a suitable occasion for achieving a latent dream of an alliance with "mother England." [46]

Thomas Jefferson, however, desired to avoid war, if possible. He disseminated the idea that the occlusion of New Orleans was not the result of the orders of Madrid or St. Cloud, but of the decision of the intendant on his own authority.[47] So he wrote to the governor of the vital western state of Kentucky on December 16, 1802; [48] so the administration informed the House of Representatives later in the month, though less positively.[49] The House agreed with this interpre-

44 *Vid.* Arthur P. Whitaker, *The Mississippi Question, 1795-1803; A Study in Trade, Politics, and Diplomacy* (New York, 1934), pp. 150-154.

45 *V.* John Randolph to Monroe, January 3, 1803; *Monroe Papers*, LC, vol. VII, p. 1174.

46 *V.* "Falkland" in the *Virginia Gazette and General Advertiser*, March 30, 1803.

47 In reality, the order originated in Madrid. Whitaker, *op. cit.*, pp. 191-2, concludes that France had nothing to do with it.

48 *Jefferson Papers*, LC, vol. CXXVIII, p. 22074.

49 Secretary of State to Jefferson for transmission to the House, December 21, 1801 [*sic*; error for 1802]; *ASP, FR*, II, 469.

tation.[50] Of the Virginia delegation, the lone Federalist John Stratton, representing a Tidewater district, was the only one on January 7, 1803, to vote against the resolution expressing confidence in the President's handling of the Mississippi question.[51]

On December 31, 1802, Jefferson had received a letter from his special emissary and friend, Pierre-Samuel du Pont de Nemours, informing him that the French government might sell New Orleans and the Floridas. The problem could be solved peacefully. On January 11, 1803, the President nominated Governor James Monroe, a reputed friend of the West and almost a westerner himself, with a 20,000-acre tract in Kentucky, to be minister plenipotentiary and envoy extraordinary to France and Spain. The next day a committee of the House of Representatives, which included Philip Rootes Thompson of Virginia, recommended an appropriation of $2,000,000 to settle the affair. Both moves of the administration were approved by a pliant, Republican-controlled Congress.

The Federalists did not yield so easily. Their major assault came in the Senate in mid-February. Senator James Ross from western Pennsylvania brought up the vanguard. He demanded that the government seize the mouth of the Mississippi immediately, before powerful, ambitious France assumed control. He introduced resolutions authorizing the president to call out 50,000 militiamen from the extreme South and the West, and employ them, together with the army and navy, to take possession of a place or places on the island of New Orleans which could serve as a deposit. The resolution actually left the choice between peace and war to the already hard-pressed administration. But the speeches of the Federalist senators were warlike.

Both Virginia senators delivered lengthy addresses on the 25th of February against the resolution and in defense of Jef-

50 *Annals of Congress,* 7th Cong., 2nd Sess., 341.

51 *Ib.,* 342.

ferson's policy of negotiation. They endeavored to expose the inconsistencies and the partisan character of the Federalist harangues. Stevens T. Mason, who was in bad health and was to die in less than three months, ironically depicted the senators of the opposition as crusading knights. They yearn for war, he asserted. Some gentlemen tell us that Spain is the aggressor, others that France is, and another that Great Britain wants to purchase Louisiana from France. Thus they know not, or care not, what they do and with whom they fight. If it should happen to be England, some gentlemen would certainly deplore their present impetuosity. Mason was hinting at British influence in the Federalist party.

We are told, he continued, of the extraordinary power of the First Consul to create and destroy nations and in the next breath that we must go to war with him. The Senate presents an amazing spectacle of the eastern delegates filled with the utmost solicitude for the interests of the West, while the western people appear to see no danger and have complete confidence in their government. In reality the Federalists desire war. War, Mason pointed out, leads to expense; the latter to discontent with the government which creates it. Frugality in government was a virtue to rural Virginians with a scarcity of hard money.

Wilson Cary Nicholas, close personal and political friend of the President, and owner of lands in the Ohio valley, likewise insisted upon negotiation first. The United States should not become entangled with Great Britain or any other European power, if it could be avoided. Neither the Spanish court nor the First Consul was responsible for the closure. The First Consul was not the person, Nicholas alleged, to throw responsibility for his measures upon others. The United States, moreover, need fear no colony of any European nation on this continent. The colonies ought rather to be considered as a pledge of the good conduct of the mother country toward the United States; for such possessions could be held only at the pleasure of the United States. Nicholas called attention to the slowness of settlement even of the American West, the distance of the Spanish and French colonies from Europe, and the possible desire of Spain and France to prevent an Anglo-American alliance.[52]

The threat of an alliance with England remained the bludgeon of the administration. But a close examination of the letters of the President and his Secretary of State in the succeeding months reveals, despite the warlike posing and the bellicose verbiage, a constant desire to prevent war, if at all possible. Only if France meditated hostilities or denied the free navigation of the Mississippi, were Livingston and Monroe positively authorized to form an alliance with Great Britain. And even then, the date of the declaration of war was to be left to the free choice of the American government! Procrastination was to be the policy, if the deposit alone were refused. Avoid entangling alliances, if possible, the American ministers were warned.[53]

"Resort to war, only if the negotiations to secure the free navigation of the Mississippi failed," became the party line of the Virginia Republicans. The General Assembly had, with only one dissenting vote, passed a resolution on January 28, 1803, voicing confidence in the federal government, and promising to support firmer measures, if negotiation failed.[54] Thomas Field's *Petersburg Republican* of February 1 declared that France's sole object in acquiring Louisiana was to prevent Britain from obtaining it. Such an interpretation justified the policy of negotiation. Yet Republicans were toasting the demise of the despot Napoleon. That might solve all problems, ideological and practical!

52 *Ib.*, Mason's speech: 215-226; Nicholas's: 228-237.

53 *Cf.* Jefferson's notes of the cabinet meeting of April 8, 1803; *Jefferson Papers*, LC, vol. CXII, p. 19297. Instructions of Madison to Livingston and Monroe, April 18, 1803; *ASP, FR*, II, 555-6. Coded letter of Madison to Monroe (decoded), April 20, 1803; *Madison Papers*, LC, vol. XXV, no. 63.

54 Reported in the *National Intelligencer* of February 11, 1803.

The war clouds in Europe thickened at what seemed to Republicans a highly opportune moment. Jefferson and Madison became optimistic as to the favorable outcome of the special mission. They believed that Napoleon could not retain Louisiana during a war with Britain. That consideration, together with the alleged languishing state of the French finances, the difficulties in reconquering San Domingo, and the recognition of America's destiny, would encourage Bonaparte to grant the American demands.[55]

By May, 1803, Jefferson and Madison were writing that hostilities between England and France were inevitable. Great Britain, Jefferson averred, believed its existence endangered by the extensive aggrandizement of its rival after the peace of Amiens. It considered that treaty as virtually subverted by Bonaparte's aggressions. Britain, therefore, demanded a remodification of the European map. Though Napoleon deprecated a war, he could not permit even the most equitable and necessary concession, since his "power resting on the transcendent opinion entertained of him, would sink with that on any retrograde movement."[56] Since neither England nor France would budge, war had to result.

Republican newspapers in Virginia realized the great importance of the Orient in the friction. The Richmond *Examiner* of June 4, 1803,[57] is an example. In an analysis of the causes of the probable war, it called attention to the clash between British fears and commerce, on the one hand, and French intrigues and ambition, on the other. The editorial maintained that Britain trembled for her distant colonies. Malta was, there-

55 *Cf.* instructions of Madison to Livingston and Monroe, March 2, 1803; *Monroe Papers*, LC, vol. VII, p. 1200. Madison to Livingston, May 25, 1803; *ASP, FR*, II, 561. Jefferson to Thomas M. Randolph, June 22, 1803; *Jefferson Papers*, LC, vol. CXXXII, p. 22892.

56 To Governor Claiborne, May 24, 1803; *ibid.*, 22747. The same ideas are repeated in other letters during May and June.

57 The newspaper was now probably published by Skelton Jones, brother of Meriwether. According to an editorial statement in the August 3rd issue, Skelton Jones had already been sole proprietor for several months.

fore, the bone of contention. Great Britain would not evacuate that Mediterranean isle on the route to the British colonies in Asia. Undoubtedly, the editorial continued, Bonaparte had plans for the partition or conquest of the Ottoman Empire. The possession and colonization of Egypt had for a century been a favorable object of the French government, whether that government was in the hands of an hereditary king, a Directory, or a military despot. The *Examiner* thus discerned the permanence of a nation's foreign policy and its independence of domestic revolutions of any sort. The fall of British India was the aim of France, the journal stated, for with it British commerce would collapse and, consequently, its navy and its ascendancy.[58]

The editor of the *Examiner* did not hesitate to declare his sentiments on the subject. He condemned the alleged atrocities of the British East India Company as unparalleled in history. He averred, furthermore, that England was the aggressor; it had violated the Treaty of Amiens by refusing to evacuate Malta. It would be best for humanity, he asserted, if Great Britain were stripped of her colonies. But Britain herself must not be dependent on another power![59]

On the other hand, President Jefferson, in letters to British acquaintances in the field of "scientific" agriculture, expressed his sympathy with Great Britain. He was still speaking and writing at that period about an Anglo-American alliance against France in Louisiana. The President declared in a letter to William Strickland on June 30, 1803, that he realized the necessity of England's resorting to war.[60] He hoped, he wrote to Sir John Sinclair on the same day, that England would continue to serve as "a bulwark against the torrent which has for some time been bearing down all before it." Britain's naval

58 *Cf.* the *Petersburg Intelligencer*, May 13, 1803; Fredericksburg *Virginia Express*, June 20, 1803.

59 Editorials of June 4 and 11.

60 *Jefferson Papers*, LC, vol. CXXXIII, p. 22922.

power and prowess seemed to warrant optimism, he concluded.[61] In truth, Thomas Jefferson had never desired a French conquest of Albion, not even during the period of the French Revolution.[62] Nor did he desire the subjugation of France by Great Britain.[63]

The trend in Republican opinion was toward neutrality. The *Virginia Argus* of June 22, 1803, proclaimed its impartiality in the approaching war.[64] It merely lamented the deplorable sacrifices of human blood about to be offered up at the shrine of an ambition, equally inordinate in both powers and equally to be abhorred. Republicans obviously hoped that England and France would restrain each other's aggressions. War in Europe, moreover, would provide the necessary environment for a successful conclusion to Jefferson's policy of negotiation on the Mississippi question.

Virginia Federalists, in the meantime, had virtually executed a *volte-face*. Though many of them had but recently expressed considerable admiration for Napoleon Bonaparte, those who clamored for war with France over the Louisiana problem changed their emphasis. They now stressed what, in their opinion, were his bad qualities and deeds. How else could they justify their jingoism?

The warmongering Federalist editors in the Old Dominion, as elsewhere, were seething. They railed at Thomas Jefferson and upbraided Napoleon Bonaparte. Augustine Davis's *Virginia Gazette and General Advertiser* of March 2, 1803, satirized a proposed Republican festival celebrating the election of Jefferson. How disgusting! the writer exclaimed. Even Bonaparte, the most despotic ruler on earth, would blush with shame, were his subjects to humble themselves before him in

61 *Ibid.*, 22918.

62 *V. s.*, p. 62 and n. 48, ch. II.

63 *Vide infra*, p. 146.

64 Editorial reprinted from the *Aurora*. Great Britain actually declared war on May 16.

that manner. Could this be the same Bonaparte as the one who was lauded in the editorial of December 22?[65]

The newspaper described the festival as the ceremony of Jacobinism for the most holy philosopher of Monticello. The Republicans would rejoice at the rule of Jacobinism as against morality and religion, law and justice. They would exult in the dissolution of the navy. America thus unprotected would become the sport of the first French army Bonaparte might decide to land on its coasts.[66]

The *Gazette* reported a rumor on March 5 that the French Senate had proclaimed Napoleon "Emperor of the Gauls," with the Italian Republic forming an integral part of his dominions. If true, there would again be an empire equal in extent and power to the most splendid era of Rome or Constantinople. The fortune of the Corsican usurper had no precedent in the history of any of the ancient conquerors. By his talents—admiration continued to linger—he had accomplished greater deeds than Alexander, Caesar, or Mahomet. It would not be surprising to find Napoleon in a few years the sovereign of all the nations on the other side of the Atlantic. Great Britain was the only power that could block his ambitious path. If she permitted him to extend his sway over Spain, Portugal, Germany, and the northern kingdoms, it would be too late. Her navy and army would then be of no avail.

In a blustering editorial on March 16, 1803, the *Gazette* asserted that Bonaparte—unlike Great Britain—had terminated treaties without cause and had manifested a disposition to usurp the sovereignty of the whole world. He was more ambitious than any other figure in history. The enslavement[67]

65 *Supra*, pp. 123-4.

66 The editorials in the newspaper prove that Davis's leanings were now definitely toward war, notwithstanding the publication of anti-war as well as pro-war articles, and the statement on July 16, 1803, after the Louisiana Purchase was known, that he had uniformly abhorred the occupation of that province by force.

67 See also the editorial of March 5, 1803, in the same newspaper.

of the Swiss and Italian Republics should serve as a lesson to America to beware of the treacherous designs of that man. The First Consul was no longer portrayed as the restorer of order but as the enslaver! The Corsican usurper was a world menace! Consistency was not an outstanding trait of many newspapers.

Would Bonaparte, who regarded all nations with contempt, the writer asked, pay more attention to the reasoning of Monroe? Napoleon's insults ought to be resisted, not by cringing negotiation but by manly fortitude! To bolster his argument the editor averred on April 9 that Bonaparte had acquired Louisiana in order to conquer the United States.

Expressions of approbation did occasionally outweigh censure. An article in the editorial column of the *Virginia Gazette and General Advertiser* on May 18, 1803, written by a Mr. Wood,[68] extolled the new constitution which Bonaparte had imposed upon Switzerland by the Act of Mediation (February 19). Although Napoleon's intervention was arbitrary and tyrannical, Wood stated, he thereby ended the scourge of anarchy. The new constitution was infinitely superior to both the pre-revolutionary régime and the Jacobinical democracy of the revolutionary period. It resembled the federal constitution of the United States more than any other that Wood knew. Had the First Consul acted with equal justice and wisdom in framing a constitution for France, he could have immortalized his name, and escaped the censure which his seemingly ambitious disposition had incurred.

A sympathetic interpretation of Napoleonic policies could be expected from those members of the Federalist party who doubted the wisdom of the Ross resolutions. In a series of

68 This may have been the recent immigrant from Scotland, ex-writer for Aaron Burr, author of an anti-revolutionary history of Switzerland (*cf. An Antidote to John Wood's Poison* by Warren [pseudonym of James Cheetham] (New York, 1802), p. 63) and of the famous *Suppressed History of the Administration of John Adams* (1802). The Mr. Wood of Richmond supported the bellicose Federalist position on Louisiana and denounced Bonaparte's ambitions in the *Virginia Gazette* of May 21, 1803. See also the *Recorder* of May 25, 1803.

anti-war articles in the *Virginia Gazette* in March and April,[69] a writer under the pseudonym " Falkland " depicted Napoleon as a reactionary and a pacifist. The French, tired of revolution and war, he wrote, bowed to a virtual monarch. Napoleon gave them order and peace. Conditions in France, though not yet perfect, were better than before. Bonaparte knew that his popularity depended on the maintenance of tranquillity and justice. He desired only peace with the United States. It was reported, the writer stated, that the Spanish intendant had acted without the authority of his own government or that of France.

Assuming that Napoleon was an ambitious tyrant, " Falkland " continued, he would require 100,000 men, 400 transport ships, and an equal number of vessels for supplies in order to conquer the United States. It would be an enormous undertaking to provision such a host. Bonaparte could not obtain his supplies from France, and the United States would not provide them. England, supported by the other European powers, would, in any case, prevent the conquest.

If, on the other hand, the United States were the aggressor, Bonaparte's defensive war would be justifiable in the eyes of his people. But that great man desired neither additional glory nor territory, but peace. Despite the weakness of the American government, " Falkland " concluded, Napoleon would inform Monroe immediately that there was no need for negotiation and that the rights of America were safe.

As the war clouds in Europe began to cast their shadows across the Atlantic, Federalist editors began to analyze the causes and possible outcome of the imminent rupture between England and France. The *Virginia Gazette* of May 7, 1803, attributed it to the " unparalleled insolence " of Bonaparte's conduct. "Ambition & the love of power seem to be the only passions of his heart. To be the sovereign of the European world, is his sole object." However, the editor affirmed, he would not be as successful as in the last war. Then he was

69 *Vide* especially the issues of March 30, April 6, and April 9.

supposed to have been fighting for the liberty of France. (That was the old Republican line.) Now his aim was to conquer and enslave. France was united in the previous war, Britain divided. The situation would now be reversed, the editorial concluded.

Bonaparte would, undoubtedly, prefer peace for the present in order to consolidate his control over France, the same newspaper declared on June 11.[70] But war was inevitable, since England refused to surrender Malta until its independence was guaranteed by the other European powers. This was impossible, because the neighboring Italian states were puppets of France. An editorial on June 22 described Malta as the gateway to Egypt and Egypt as the gateway to India.

Perhaps war would be averted this time, wrote the Valley newspaper the Lexington *Virginia Telegraphe, and Rockbridge Courier*, published by S. Walkup & Co., on May 17, 1803.[71] Bonaparte was not yet ready; England sincerely desired peace. True, so long as Napoleon lived, peace was temporary. His restless ambition would urge him on. Fortunately for other nations, however, one power watched him, anticipated his designs, and controlled his inclinations. Britain's firm and dignified stand against the ambitious strides of the First Consul, and the temperance and forbearance of her conduct since the Treaty of Amiens justly entitled her to the esteem and admiration of every friend of humanity. The British position in the Anglo-French dispute was thus, in general, accepted by Virginia Federalists as the righteous one. The anti-Napoleonic trend in Federalist opinion was reënforced.

What would be the effect of a renewal of the European war upon the United States? American commerce would benefit, an editorial in the *Virginia Gazette and General Advertiser* stated on April 27. But if the government was pusillanimous we would suffer depredations from the tyranny and caprice of both

70 Editorial reprinted from the *Boston Gazette.*

71 Editorial reprinted from the *Washington Federalist.*

France and England, with our commerce ultimately ruined. The solution was to have an army and navy.

So far as Louisiana was concerned, the editor of the *Gazette* wrote on May 11, it would be safe from the French army for the time being. Great Britain would now attempt to occupy the province, since the United States had exhibited no interest in it! England would in a few years deprive the Americans of the navigation of the Mississippi. Such would be the effect of weak government. And the United States could already have been in possession of New Orleans. It was the hope of Federalist partisans that, no matter what happened, Jefferson would be humiliated.

The chief editor of the *Recorder* had the same hope. James Thomson Callender was now being supported in the columns of the *Virginia Gazette* against Republican attacks. He, in turn, was praising the quality of that Federalist paper. Nevertheless, Callender pursued his individualistic course. Napoleon Bonaparte received the most consistent defense in his columns. As has already been indicated, he continued to rebuke the Republicans for urging the assassination of Bonaparte.

Since Napoleon was his hero, Callender opposed a war between the United States and France over the Mississippi question. On April 6, the *Recorder* expressed the opinion that war with France would ruin the United States. American commerce would be excluded from France. Much of the remainder would be destroyed by privateers. The American government would tax the public funds, since it feared levying internal taxes. The financial ruin of the United States would result. What was the *Recorder's* solution? The appropriation of money to purchase peace was rejected. Submission was the only way! Though it was a bitter pill, it was better, the editorial declared, than destruction.

Napoleon's foreign policy toward the rest of Europe was approved by Callender. Callender the exile had no love for Albion. In answer to English complaints about Bonaparte's oppression of Switzerland, the *Recorder* of March 19, 1803, had called attention to the British administration of Ireland and India. Where the British have the power, Callender thundered, they prove that they are the most ravenous, most insolent, and most barbarous people on earth.[72] The last editorials on Napoleon's foreign policy that appear to have been written by Callender, those of June 1 and 4, refused to believe the English accusations against the First Consul and their report of the humiliating treatment of the English ambassador. Napoleon desired peace, Callender insisted. Bonaparte had virtually no naval force and was fully occupied with San Domingo and the expedition to the Mississippi. Considering his good sense, the writer stated, it was ridiculous to assert that he courted a quarrel. He had everything to gain by delay. The belief that Napoleon was in favor of peace in 1803 was thus widespread in Virginia—from the President to his virulent enemy, the lowly Scot.

As for the old story about Bonaparte's ambition, Callender continued, there was not the slightest reason for suspecting that the British would have made a more moderate use of their good fortune than the French have done of theirs. British independence was based on the maintenance of its superiority at sea. France was now the dominant power on the continent of Europe. During peacetime France could build a navy in ten years. England had at present nothing to fear on the seas; while on land it had nothing to lose, except Hanover. Great Britain, therefore, desired war now.

Within six weeks James Thomson Callender was dead. An urbane commentator on Richmond life completes his story of that writer in the following words: "Poor Callender, a martyr

72 An editorial on May 14, 1803, which reprobated Napoleon's conduct toward the English ambassador and attributed Napoleon's desire for war to his need of diverting the French from his extraordinary elevation to power, could not have been written by Callender in his sober moments. It was so contrary to the tenor of the editorials in the *Recorder* during Callender's association with it. Perhaps it was written by his partner, Henry Pace. Callender left the paper by June 22, 1803, after quarreling with Pace.

to both democracy and federalism, and also to liquor, died a whiskey and watery death. He had one day imbibed too much whiskey before taking his daily bath in the river, and was drowned."[73] Thus died virtually unmourned an infamous writer of billingsgate in an age when invective was the norm.

Napoleon Bonaparte would have to wait a few years before another and more thoroughgoing eulogist appeared in the Old Dominion. In the meantime, significant praise could no longer be expected of the Federalists; Britain and France would be at war. Nor could too much be expected of the Republicans. Liberals were not given an opportunity to forget that republicanism had been betrayed.

73 Mordecai, *Virginia, Especially Richmond, In By-Gone Days*, p. 233.

CHAPTER V

NAPOLEON THE BETRAYER

(July, 1803-October, 1805)

VIRGINIANS—together with the rest of the American people —were astonished when news arrived in July, 1803, that Napoleon Bonaparte had sold the vast province of Louisiana to the United States. They learned at the same time that France and Great Britain had renewed hostilities. Why had the First Consul parted with Louisiana? Republicans of the Old Dominion attributed this action mainly to the wisdom of the administration's foreign policy. Bonaparte had "good sense enough," President Jefferson later explained, to appreciate the force of the American government's arguments. The immediate prospect of a rupture with England precipitated his decision.[1] By the Louisiana Purchase Treaty, Secretary Madison asserted on October 12, 1803, France had reverted to a basic policy adhered to since the American Revolution, namely, the prevention of an alliance between the United States and Great Britain.[2]

James Monroe, the special American minister to Paris, added a unique ideological interpretation of the sale of Louisiana to the United States.[3] The new French régime was unstable. The republican [4] opposition was strong enough to merit its

1 To Dr. Priestley, January 29, 1804; *Jefferson Writings*, Washington ed., IV, 525. *Cf.* Madison's letters before July for what the administration considered other contributory factors; *supra*, p. 129 and n. 55, ch. IV.

2 To Charles Pinckney; *ASP, FR*, II, 571.

3 In a private letter to Madison, dated May 6, 1804, but marked "not sent"; *Monroe Papers*, LC, vol. X, pp. 1721 f. It is included in the Hamilton edition of Monroe's writings, IV, 184 f., but the editor does not indicate that it was not sent.

4 Though Monroe does not name the party in this letter, that he meant such a group is apparent from the context. This conclusion is confirmed in a later, more elaborate, letter on the internal strains and stresses of the French dictatorship; to ——, June 21, 1804, *Monroe Papers*, LC, vol. XI, p. 1790. For a summary of the latter, *v. infra*, pp. 154-5.

attention. To have hazarded a controversy or, rather, a war with the only free nation on the earth for insufficient reasons, Monroe averred, would have strengthened the republican "party" in France.[5]

The Louisiana Purchase was particularly gratifying to James Monroe. He had redeemed himself; he had wiped out the blot of his recall from France in 1796. The Republican party of the United States had proved, Monroe wrote, that the charge of subservience to France was unfounded. He rejoiced that the Republican administration had gained more from France than any former administration.[6] He was grateful to the First Consul.

While Republicans in the Old Dominion acclaimed the purchase almost unanimously, the Federalist minority faced division in its ranks. It endeavored, nevertheless, to detract from the Jefferson administration. The *Virginia Gazette and General Advertiser* stated on July 13, 1803, that Livingston—whom it had called "Dullstone"—had undoubtedly apprehended the imminence of a war with Great Britain and the inability of France, because of British naval supremacy, to hold Louisiana during the war. He had proceeded far in the negotiations to purchase the province, before Monroe arrived. The special mission was thus unnecessary and costly.

On second thought, the same journal, in its issue of August 3, 1803, even withdrew its underhanded praise of the New Yorker. No one in the administration had the slightest influence on the decision of the French government, the writer insisted. France, foreseeing a rupture with England, was determined to prevent Louisiana from falling into its enemy's hands. It was prepared, if necessary, to donate it to the United States. But naturally it first attempted to obtain as much money as possible. This was the newspaper that only a few months earlier had clamored for the forcible occupation of New Orleans.

5 *Cf.* Monroe's analysis of the French régime in 1801; *supra*, pp. 103-4.

6 To ———, [*c.* September] 1803; *Monroe Papers*, LC, vol. VIII, p. 1411.

The sale, the editorial continued, was, consequently, not a result of the wisdom or of the popularity of the Republican leaders with the French government, as was alleged. How could any man surrounded by Tom Paine, Gallatin, Duane, and Cheetham be popular at the courts of France, Great Britain, or any other European power? Atheism and rebellion had sent at least three million Europeans to their untimely deaths. How could the patrons of such causes, the writer asked, be popular with Bonaparte? The "tyrant" Napoleon, the enemy of the French Revolution and of its principles, was thus better than Jefferson and his tribe.

Extreme Federalists opposed the purchase of Louisiana. The Lexington *Virginia Telegraphe; or Rockbridge Courier* [7] in the combined issue of November 1 and 3, 1803, presented its readers with an article from a New England newspaper.[8] Since it was not placed in the editorial column, it was probably not the opinion of the publishers, S. Walkup & Co., but it was of sufficient interest to them to be reprinted. The article depicted Napoleon as one who violated treaties and as a menace to the world. If France won the war, it maintained, the United States would have to purchase Louisiana over and over again. Should America pay a tribute of $15,000,000 to aid France in prosecuting a war of extermination against the only country willing and able to resist her by arms? Should the United States accelerate the period of its own trial by removing the sole barrier between itself and its foe? [9]

The Virginia Federalist representatives in the Eighth Congress acted in accordance with the views of such extremists. Joseph Lewis, Jr., of the Loudoun, Fairfax, Prince William district and Thomas Griffin of the Tidewater questioned the constitutionality of that article of the treaty which granted for twelve years to French and Spanish ships laden with their native wares the same customs treatment in Louisiana as to

7 In June, 1803, "or" had replaced "and" in the title.

8 The *New England Palladium* of Boston.

9 *Cf.* Henry Pace's *Recorder*, August 6, 1803.

American vessels coming from the French or Spanish empires.[10] After all, it would hurt the commercial interests of the Atlantic seaboard. In addition, as Littleton Waller Tazewell, prosperous young Republican lawyer of Norfolk, informed President Jefferson, merchants were opposed to the purchase of Louisiana because it might bring competitors into their commerce with the West Indies.[11] The mercantile interest, moreover, dreaded the strengthening of the agricultural elements and, hence, of the Republican party. Griffin, however, expressed a fear that the acquisition of Louisiana would result in a decrease of land values.[12] The economy of the Tidewater was in decay. Joseph Lewis and Thomas Griffin, supported by their Federalist colleagues from the Valley, Thomas Lewis and James Stephenson, voted on October 25, 1803, against the resolution that the necessary measures be taken to carry the Louisiana Purchase Treaty into effect.[13]

This, however, did not represent the sentiments of all Federalists in the Old Dominion. The *Virginia Telegraphe* of Lexington reprinted in the editorial column of the combined issue of November 8 and 10, 1803, an address delivered on October 25 in the House of Representatives by Samuel D. Purviance, a Federalist from North Carolina. S. Walkup & Co. seemed therein to have reached a decision on the Louisiana question.

Purviance urged the appropiation of the necessary amount as the only action possible under the present pusillanimous administration. Since it had not the courage to fight, it ought to be permitted to bribe France. France, with its spirit of universal domination, must be kept away from our doors. Events in Europe, Purviance warned, should serve as a lesson. The Corsican upstart had subjugated one-half of the Old World

10 October 25, 1803; *Annals of Congress,* 8th Cong., 1st Sess.; Lewis's speech: 440-1; Griffin's: 442-3.

11 March 8, 1804; *Jefferson Papers,* LC, vol. CXXXIX, p. 24000.

12 *Annals of Congress,* 8th Cong., 1st Sess., 443.

13 *Ib.,* 488.

and threatened the other half. Napoleon had perhaps acquired Louisiana in order to injure Britain, control Spain, and dismember the United States. The British king then declared war. Hence Bonaparte sold the province. Jefferson deserved no thanks for it; American diplomacy had no effect upon Bonaparte's decision. "The mind of that Great Man is not made of such soft materials as to receive an impress from the collision of every gentle hand; stern, collected and inflexible, he laughs to scorn the toying arts of persuasion. His soul is a stupendous rock which the rushing of mighty waters cannot shake from its place." What a wonderful contrast that presented to the pusillanimous philosopher of Monticello!

By the beginning of 1804, the two leading Federalist newspapers of that period in Virginia—the Fredericksburg *Virginia Herald* and the Richmond *Virginia Gazette and General Advertiser*—were enthusiastically approving the acquisition of Louisiana. What else could they do in an overwhelmingly agricultural state? [14]

The settlement of the Mississippi question had removed the major hurdle to friendly relations between the American and French governments. The intervention of France, furthermore, was necessary in order to influence Spain to acknowledge American claims to part of Florida and to cede the remainder.[15] Control of the rivers flowing from the South and Southwest into the Gulf of Mexico seemed indispensable to Jefferson and Madison.

President Jefferson's third annual message had exuded friendly sentiments toward Great Britain as well as toward France. He had not only referred to the liberal actions of "the

14 The *Herald* on January 20; the *Gazette* on February 8. In the latter case, there was an added reason for the journal's enthusiasm. Davis was eager to become the printer of the Republican commonwealth! (See his letter to the governor, March 17, 1804; *Calendar of Virginia State Papers*, IX, 390.)

15 Monroe reported on May 18, 1803, that France had promised its assistance in the negotiation for the Floridas. To Madison, *Monroe Writings*, Hamilton ed., IV, 24.

enlightened government" of the latter in the Louisiana affair, but also to the friendly disposition of France and England and "their wisdom and regard for justice."

True, Jefferson no longer discoursed on an Anglo-American alliance with the British diplomatic agents. The administration, moreover, increasingly complained in the latter half of 1803 and the first half of 1804 about impressments and the use of American ports by British warships as cruising stations for their observation of French and American vessels. Both the British minister, Anthony Merry, and the chargé d'affaires, Edward Thornton, were reporting home that the American government was unfriendly. The change could be dated from the first arrival of the news of the Louisiana Purchase, added Thornton.[16]

Such foreign conservatives, however, had only contempt for what they considered a barbarian republic and, inevitably, interpreted the slightest criticism of British actions as proof of hostility. Jefferson's private letters, contradicting the Britishers' biased testimony, displayed friendliness to England throughout the year from July, 1803, to July, 1804. He wrote on December 22, 1803, that, although both belligerents had proved their friendship to the United States, Britain had done so especially.[17] The President, learning of Thornton's charges, informed James Monroe on January 8, 1804, that they were totally without foundation.[18] Monroe had by then been in London a half year attempting to settle all matters outstanding between Britain and the United States. The roving minister was extremely anxious for an understanding; it would complete his redemption in the field of diplomacy. Wilson Cary Nich-

16 Merry to Hawkesbury, January 20, 1804; *Great Britain, F.O.5*, LC, vol. XLI, p. 61. Thornton to Hammond, January 29, 1804; *ib.*, 64-6. Henry Adams apparently takes the same position; *History Of The United States Of America During The Administration of Thomas Jefferson* (New York, 1930), Book II, pp. 355 f.

17 To John Langdon; *Jefferson Papers*, LC, vol. CXXXVII, p. 23650.

18 *Monroe Papers*, LC, vol. IX, p. 1589.

olas, acting in the name of the administration, asked the United States Senate on February 29 to postpone to the following session consideration of a bill to protect American seamen against impressment.[19] Merry and Thornton were proved wrong.

Virginia Republicans as a whole shared the friendly sentiments of the administration toward Great Britain. Judge Archibald Stuart, a stanch Jeffersonian from Staunton, Augusta County, informed Monroe on April 15, 1804, that the friendly disposition of the British government had produced a surprising effect in removing deep-rooted prejudices against that country for the injuries she had inflicted on America during the Revolutionary War and for her subsequent spoliations on American commerce. Her greatest enemies, he asserted, were beginning to relax.[20]

One of the important reasons for the Republicans' friendly attitude was the interest the party had—especially in a presidential election year—in "shunning not only the reality but the suspicion" of being anti-British. Those were the words of Secretary of State Madison.[21] John Tyler, Stuart's colleague in the General Court of Virginia and an ardent partisan,[22] wrote to the ex-Governor in London about the importance of maintaining amicable relations between the two countries so that even the infidels—*i.e.*, the Federalists—would be made to believe.[23]

Thomas Jefferson could, therefore, continue to manifest sympathy for Great Britain in its war with France.[24] But his policy was one of neutrality. In the letter of January 8, 1804, to James Monroe, in which he denied being unfriendly toward

19 *William Plumer's Memorandum Of Proceedings In the United States Senate, 1803-1807*, ed. by Everett S. Brown (New York, 1923), pp. 146-7.

20 Monroe Papers, 1802-5 Box, NYPL.

21 To Monroe, January 19, 1804; *Monroe Papers*, LC, vol. IX, p. 1601.

22 Tyler was the father of the future President.

23 January 1, 1804; Monroe Papers, 1802-5 Box, NYPL.

24 *Vide* his letter to the Earl of Buchan, July 10, 1803; *Jefferson Papers*, LC, vol. CXXXIII, p. 22983.

England with regard to Anglo-American relations, he expressed a hope that the island kingdom would maintain its standing, but that it would use its power on the ocean justly. Had Britain done that before, Jefferson continued, other nations would not have looked with unconcern on a war which endangered its existence. (England was then being threatened with an invasion.) "We are not indifferent to it's issue," he maintained, "nor should we be so on [*sic*] a conflict on which the existence of France should be in danger. We consider each as a necessary instrument to hold in check the disposition of the other to tyrannize over other nations." [25]

Jefferson's concern for the fate of Britain was shared, though in varying degrees, by most of his followers in the Old Dominion. Judge Stuart apprised Monroe in the aforementioned letter of April 15, 1804, that Republicans were becoming concerned lest a successful invasion of England be attended with dangerous consequences to the world. It was admitted, he wrote, that Great Britain had acted imperiously on the high seas. But the common interest of all maritime nations was to restrain her; and they would probably soon succeed. The United States had, therefore, less to fear from British control of the seas than from her complete overthrow, and the convulsion and anarchy which had to precede a new order of things.[26]

Even those Republicans who could not overcome their hatred for monarchical Britain generally did not wish to see it conquered. Skelton Jones, who had succeeded his brother as publisher of the Richmond *Examiner*,[27] declared on July 9, 1803, that Great Britain had entered its last war of ambition. Monarchy as an institution was on the decline, he claimed. The relative military strength of republicanism and monarchy on the continent of Europe had been precisely reversed in the

25 *V. s.*, n. 18. *Cf.* also his letter to Dr. Benjamin Rush, October 4, 1803; *Jefferson Writings*, Washington ed., IV, 508.

26 *V. s.*, n. 20.

27 *V. s.*, n. 57, ch. IV.

course of a decade. The continental powers now held aloof from the war. Great Britain, excluded from the balance of power, and facing national bankruptcy, had begun the war with many apologies and had expressly surrendered all pretensions to interference in the internal affairs of other states. It was most likely, the editor concluded, that the British would be stripped of all their colonies and of Ireland, with the latter becoming an independent republic. The island of Albion would be, and should be, their only remaining possession.

Though the *Examiner* reprinted an article on October 5, 1803, from the *National Intelligencer* which stressed the importance to Europe and the United States of an equipoise of Britain and France, Jones continued to criticize only the former's foreign policy. He claimed on November 9 that the general, though not universal, opinion of Republicans was that England was the aggressor in the present war. He stated that he had from the first believed that it had wantonly provoked and renewed hostilities. The English had galled and irritated Bonaparte to the most inveterate animosity, the editor wrote on November 26. Now the white cliffs of Albion were the destined scenes of bloodshed and death. "Three hundred thousand warriors are led by the greatest military character that has appeared . . . since Caesar's fortunes!" Jones exclaimed admiringly. The fate of unborn millions was at stake. It was desirable, he concluded, that the power of Britain should be diminished, but it was scarcely desirable that that diminution should increase France's strength. How such a development was possible, the editor did not indicate.

In contrast to these anti-British screeds, the editorial columns of the Fredericksburg *Apollo* consistently demonstrated the impartiality that should accompany complete neutrality. This newly-founded, short-lived Republican newspaper, published by James Walker, featured a series of editorials on the war in a number of issues. In a discussion of the problem of strategy on September 28, 1803, the writer declared that the First Consul's "genius or temerity" had led him to plan the invasion of the British isles. The ultimate fate of the perilous attempt depended on the successful landing of the troops and on the attitude of the English people. The attempt was to be made in flat-bottomed boats, which would have to trust their safety to a dark night and a favorable breeze. The issue, however, could not be foretold. On the one hand, was the hero of Lodi and Marengo, pointing out to his enthusiastic followers the white coast of Britain and displaying to their enraptured imaginations all the glories of conquest and all the treasures of London. On the other, was a formidable navy, manned by able sailors and officers. And on shore in England there was complete national unity.

But, the article continued, not in poor Ireland. The road to freedom for the Irish, however, was not through an alliance with France. How could they place their confidence in a man who had ended the long and arduous struggles of the French Revolution with a military usurpation? How could they hope that a man who labored to obliterate from the face of Europe every little state which aspired to the enjoyment of a moderate degree of freedom would establish a liberal government in a conquered country? How could the usurper of France be the deliverer of Ireland? [28]

The *Apollo* of October 8 analyzed the significance of the war to the United States. The previous war between France and the coalition, the writer stated, had been one of principle: a struggle between liberty and monarchy. The present war, on the contrary, would merely decide whether France or Great Britain would become more powerful. American interests were not now involved. What difference did it make to the United States whether England was drawn into the war by fear of French aggrandizement or by the desire to retain Malta? Or what mattered it to the United States whether France was impelled by the ambitious hope of extending its dominions or by its deep resentment at the retention of Malta?

28 The article was reprinted in the *Examiner* of October 8, 1803, and again in the newly-founded Richmond *Enquirer* of June 23, 1804.

America had nothing to fear, the article continued, even from the most improbable consequences of the war. Should the French invasion be repelled and France forced to accept the most dishonorable peace, would England receive such an accession of strength as to enable her to encounter a new enemy three thousand miles away—an enemy, whom she could not subdue twenty years before even though he lacked almost all the necessities of war? If France conquered Britain and added the British navy to its own, it would not dare to attack the United States while it had at its own doors a newly-acquired country that would revolt at any opportunity. Bonaparte would perhaps require all his resources at home to repress the free spirit of his own countrymen. Americans, therefore, had every possible motive for maintaining neutrality during the present war. The isolationist writer ended on an optimistic note: "When the nations of Europe shall cease from their conflict, who knows but that the peaceful honours of our country, and the splendid advantages of our government, may exhibit to them an example, which they shall be anxious to emulate." "A plague on both your houses" was the underlying opinion of the editor of the Fredericksburg *Apollo* as well as of other Republicans in the first year following the receipt of information concerning the renewal of the Anglo-French war.[29]

Federalists could sometimes display impartiality in criticism. The Lexington *Virginia Telegraphe* did state on one occasion that both belligerents might resort to acts of treachery and villainy in the conduct of hostilities.[30] More usually, however, Federalists expressed opinions that were one hundred per cent pro-British and equally anti-French. An editorial in Davis's *Virginia Gazette* on August 13, 1803, compared the two contestants. Its author described the vast power of France on the continent of Europe. But England would not be de-

29 *Cf.*, *e. g.*, the oration of Benjamin Watkins Leigh, fledgling Petersburg lawyer, delivered at the court-house of that town on February 18, 1804; printed in the *Virginia Argus* for February 29, 1804.

30 In the combined issue of June 9 and 12, 1804.

feated, he argued, because of her insular position and the predominance of her navy. In any event, Russia, Austria, and Prussia would not remain inactive, if France's great superiority in numbers should threaten to overwhelm the British. If Great Britain were conquered, the other European states would meet the same fate. The United States too would fall into the world pattern.

A writer with the pseudonym "Vindex" asserted in the *Gazette* of the 24th that Great Britain was fighting for her survival against a country that had been continually aggrandizing herself. Britain had theretofore been the only power to check Bonaparte's rapid advance toward world rule. With Great Britain in its control, France could conquer the world. And Napoleon denoted slavery! How could any American, under the circumstances, "Vindex" asked, hope for the subjugation of England?

The Republicans were traduced more explicitly in an editorial in the same journal on August 27.[31] A few months ago, the article stated, the Republicans were denouncing Bonaparte as the destroyer of liberty in France. Now poor England, the only barrier to restrain the mad ambition of the Corsican, is the object of democratic venom, and Napoleon is accorded ample justification for entering into war. Their caution in praising the "hero" is a temporary expedient to preserve a semblance of consistency with their former conduct. It will be finally demonstrated, the editorial concluded, that our most distinguished Jacobin newspapers are in the pay of a foreign master. The Federalists, continuing as the champions of the former mother country in its struggles, thus hurled the epithet "French influence" at their opponents.

There was some truth, however, in the Federalist charge that the Republicans had slightly modified their attitude toward Napoleon Bonaparte. Some anti-Federalists were partly sympathetic to Bonaparte's war effort. Extreme Anglophobes could not be too hostile to the ruler who was harassing the

31 Reprinted from the *Gazette of the United States.*

traditional foe of American liberty. How could any Republican, moreover, be very angry with the man who had sold Louisiana to the United States and thereby virtually assured President Jefferson's reëlection? Toasts and editorials proposing another Brutus seemed to vanish into thin air.

Fundamentally, though, there was no change in Republican opinion in Virginia from July, 1803, to July, 1804, concerning the character of the Napoleonic régime. Jeffersonians affirmed that the French Revolution had ended in a military despotism. The representative principle, the liberty of the press, and the freedom of the individual had been destroyed.[32]

Thomas Jefferson intimated, in a letter to Cabanis, a leader of the French school of ideology, what Napoleon could have done, had he been interested in liberty. Had he granted the French " as great a portion of liberty as the opinions, habits and character of the nation " were prepared for, progressive preparation might have fitted them for increasing portions of freedom, until rational government had been attained.[33]

32 *E. g., v.* the Fredericksburg *Apollo,* September 28, 1803, *supra,* p. 148; *Examiner,* October 5, 1803.

Despotism had come to France, many Republicans believed, because the French people were unprepared for free government. According to William Nelson, the moral state of the French people was perhaps not suited for a free country. The Bourbon régime had made some people too vicious and kept others in too great ignorance to enjoy rational freedom. Nelson to William Short, April 8, 1804; *William Short Papers* (MSS., LC), XXXII, 5776.

33 See Jefferson's political philosophy *supra,* n. 65, ch. I; pp. 34-5. The above letter to Cabanis, dated July 13, 1803 (*Jefferson Papers,* LC, vol. CXXXIII, pp. 23009-10; incorrectly: July 12, in the Washington ed. of *Jefferson Writings,* IV, 496), was, in reality, written in a different vein and seemed to imply that Napoleon might act in such a fashion. Actually, Jefferson had long considered Bonaparte as lost to the republican cause. The President always respected the opinions of his correspondents as well as their situation, so as not to compromise them, if the letter were intercepted. (Jefferson to Monroe, January 8, 1804; *Monroe Papers,* LC, vol. IX, p. 1589.) Cabanis was residing in France. The letter must, therefore, be interpreted as above.

The concept of progressive preparation for self-government was applied to Louisiana. But John G. Jackson of the Trans-Alleghany demanded in the

Republicans, however, noticed praiseworthy features in the Consulate when they compared it with other European governments and with the pre-revolutionary state. The French Revolution had not been in vain. The privileges of the aristocracy and clergy had been abolished and their property was now distributed among many individuals, affirmed the Lexington *Rockbridge Repository* of June 26, 1804.[34] Though the French had no more political liberty than under the Bourbons, the *Examiner* stated on October 5, 1803, they were infinitely happier. Much of this they undoubtedly owed to Napoleon's internal policy, the editorial continued; nor could too much praise be accorded him for it.[35] The *Virginia Argus* of May 2, 1804, adverted in amazement to the order and prosperity in France; to the small public debt, high annual revenue, and large surplus "for the maintenance of cumbrous and ostentatious establishments civil and military" ; and to its arts and manufactures prospering to an unprecedented degree.[36] In another editorial in the same issue, the writer noted that Bonaparte had established the security of property and ameliorated the laws.[37]

The Napoleonic régime, nevertheless, was unstable, according to some Republicans. ". . . It hangs on the thread of opinion which may break from one day to another," Jefferson stated on July 10, 1803.[38] James Monroe pointed to the weakness of the French government vis-à-vis the republican opposition.[39]

House of Representatives, on February 29, 1804, the immediate establishment of free government there. Man, he said, was the same everywhere in the world; a love of liberty was implanted in his nature. *Annals of Congress,* 8th Cong., 1st Sess., 1070-1.

34 Editorial taken from a New England paper, as given in the *Aurora.*

35 Editorial reprinted from the *National Intelligencer.*

36 Editorial reprinted from the *Aurora.*

37 *Do.*

38 To the Earl of Buchan; *Jefferson Papers,* LC, vol. CXXXIII, p. 22983. See, in contrast, his pessimistic opinion of November 29, 1802; *s.*, p. 116.

39 *V. s.*, pp. 139-40.

Reports of a plot against Napoleon arrived in the United States in the spring of 1804. Republicans became bitter against General Moreau when they learned of his alleged participation in the royalist conspiracy.[40] Tyranny should be struck down by a republican, not by a monarchist. It was not Napoleon as a person that they wished to destroy, but Napoleon as the author of reactionary policies. Now that Bonaparte, who was partly related to the revolution, was in danger from the royalists, many liberals came to his defense. Moreau was, consequently, denounced by the *Virginia Argus* on May 2, 1804, as another Arnold for engaging in a plot to make conditions worse for the French people.[41] There was no sympathy for the Duc d'Enghien, kidnaped and executed summarily by the French government. A princely assassin merited the same punishment as one who was only a chimney-sweep, declared the *Argus* on May 23.[42]

The Valley newspaper, the *Rockbridge Repository,* asserted on June 26, 1804, that, had the plot succeeded, civil war and bloodshed more horrible than that imputed to the revolution would have resulted. The aristocracy and clergy would have demanded from the Bourbon ruler the restoration of their privileges and property and would have received them. Was it just to strip thirty-nine million persons of property duly purchased in the national market in order to accommodate one million outlaws and refugees? " If the security of private property, be the great and legitimate end of good government, what would not be the misery of France, in this projected state of things? "[43]

While Republicans had shifted their position somewhat with regard to the Napoleonic régime, the renewal of the Anglo-French war reënforced the Federalist *volte-face* of early

40 They did not know then of his innocence nor of Napoleon's control of the plot.

41 Second editorial in that issue from the *Aurora.*

42 Editorial reprinted from the *Aurora.*

43 *V. s.*, n. 34.

1803. Federalists could agree with the opinion of their opponents that the revolution had ended in a military despotism.[44] But the agreement stopped there. The French Revolution and its principles was the basis of the differences. For Federalists Bonaparte was still somewhat better than the horrible atheistic revolution; he had brought order to France.[45] Nevertheless, it would have been best had there been no revolution at all.[46]

The *Virginia Gazette and General Advertiser* stated on December 10, 1803, that the royalist movement was growing rapidly in France. Only the use of terror and an army disciplined to obey the one who paid it prevented the monarchists from coming out into the open. Bonaparte, fearful that a British landing in the Vendée would immediately raise a royalist rebellion, threatened Great Britain with an invasion as a means of intimidating its government to keep British troops at home.[47]

Federalist sympathies tended to be with England's royalist allies in France. An article in the *Gazette* on October 15, 1803, depicted General Pichegru as a patriot struggling against a tyrant and usurper. By June 30, 1804, the same paper was writing that the reign of terror under the Consulate was as monstrous as that during the worst period of the "Republican Despotism" of Robespierre.[48]

Within a few weeks news arrived that the consolidation of the Napoleonic dictatorship had been perfected: Napoleon Bonaparte had become Emperor of the French. James Monroe, the special envoy, closest to the scene, had learned of this event

44 *Vide, e.g.*, Purviance's speech, in the Lexington *Virginia Telegraphe* of November 8 and 10, 1803.

45 See the *Virginia Gazette and General Advertiser*, August 3, 1803; *supra*, p. 141.

46 Representative Purviance, in the previously mentioned address, lamented the overthrow and execution of Louis XVI.

47 Editorial reprinted from the Charleston *Courier*.

48 Editorial taken from the *New York Herald*.

earlier and, on June 21, 1804, had analyzed impartially the character of the Napoleonic Empire and its relation to the French Revolution. The Napoleonic régime, he asserted, was founded in opposition both to the monarchists and the republicans. ". . . The present order of things, [*sic*] is supported by the armies, who constitute the actual gov^{t} [*sic*] of France." Many moderate royalists and republicans have rallied to Bonaparte's support. The purchasers of the national domain are in favor of any government which protects them against the restoration of the Old Régime and they will continue to support it while there is any danger of such an event. "I am strongly inclined to believe," the Virginian concluded this part of the letter, ". . . considering the age in which we live and other circumstances that the sentiment in favor of liberty gains ground and that every day which passes by without restoring the antient [*sic*] order, makes its restoration the more difficult & doubtful." [49] In the opinion of the ex-Governor, Napoleon thus stood as a barrier between the accomplishments of the revolution and complete reaction.

To some Republicans the establishment of the Empire was of no great significance. President Jefferson had prophesied such a change as early as July 6, 1802. He had, furthermore, characterized France under the Life Consulate as a kingdom.[50] He was, therefore, indifferent to Napoleon's change of title.[51]

The event, nevertheless, reopened fresh wounds. The liberal philosopher again indicated his profound disappointment in the outcome of the French Revolution. Instead of the absolute imperial government, he stated, he preferred the reëstablishment of the Constitution of 1789—despite its faults—in conjunction

49 To ——; *Monroe Papers*, LC, vol. XI, pp. 1790-1. This was an elaboration of the unsent letter of May 6; *v. s.*, pp. 139-40.

50 *Vide supra*, p. 116.

51 To Madison, August 18, 1804; *Jefferson Papers*, LC, vol. CXLII, p. 24752. Anthony Merry informed his superiors on December 26, 1804, that both Jefferson and Madison spoke of the change of government in France with an apparently unaffected indifference. To Hawkesbury; *Great Britain, F.O.5*, LC, vol. XLII, p. 133.

with the restoration of the Bourbons.[52] This was obviously to be the first step in the extension of popular government to the French people. Perhaps the Bourbons would accomplish what Napoleon had not.[53]

For many members of the Republican party in the Old Dominion the constitutional change was unexpectedly shocking and tragic news. They were taken completely off guard. Though they had apparently lost all faith in Napoleon with the establishment of the Life Consulate, they had more recently begun to consider him at least as a stepson of the revolution. Now he seemed to have struck the final blow. They wished to admire him, but he gave them no opportunity. They were so fanatically and emotionally *republican*, they abhorred and dreaded monarchical institutions so intensely, that to assume the title " Emperor " was in their minds to sink to the lowest depths of ignominy. They tended to exaggerate the significance of the transformation of the Life Consulate into the Empire. Mourning, combined with indignation, were, consequently, the general order of the day in the Republican press.[54]

The *Virginia Argus*, still relying on other newspapers for its editorials, selected for the issue of August 1, 1804, the comments of the *Alexandria Expositor* on the establishment of the Empire.[55] The article lamented the end of the revolution:

52 In a conversation with John Quincy Adams on October 23, 1804; Charles Francis Adams, ed., *Memoirs Of John Quincy Adams, Comprising Portions Of His Diary From 1795 To 1848*, vol. I (Philadelphia, 1874), p. 316. According to the President, the Constitution of 1789 was defective because it did not grant adequate powers to the government. It, furthermore, provided for a unicameral legislature.

53 *V. s.*, pp. 151, 35. *Cf.* Jefferson's opinions at the beginning of the French Revolution; *e. g.*, to St. Étienne, June 3, 1789, *Jefferson Writings*, Washington ed., III, 45 f.

54 *Cf.* the English Whig attitude; Maccunn, *English View of Napoleon*, 74.

55 The *Expositor* was published by James Lyon and a partner. For Lyon *v. s.*, p. 89 and n. 44, ch. III.

> Where was the honest heart which did not bound with joy, when a great nation declared it a practical fact 'that all men were born and continued equal in their rights'[56] yet who can see the presumptuous arrogance of the to be emperor of the Gauls, without cursing his ambition, and lamenting that such a man as Bonaparte, possessed so little a mind as to prefer, the tinsel robe, and the glittering crown, of an empty title, to the masculine pleasure of securing the rights of his fellow men, & the laudable ambition of rendering millions happy. We expect in Bonaparte an enlightened attention to the political interests of his empire, but we cannot we must not forget that to acquire this title of emperor, this nomen which may alike distinguish the fool, the madman, the infant and the superanuated [*sic*], he has destroyed the fairest hopes of humanity and forfeited a title which correct ambition, would have secured him, and by which he would have induced a world to have hailed him the Jefferson of Europe.

The lesson for Americans, the editorial asserted, was to place little confidence in their magistrates and to watch the conduct of military men sedulously.

On August 4, 1804, Thomas Ritchie wrote his first major editorial on the new constitutional development in France for the Richmond *Enquirer*. This paper, sponsored by the Republican party,[57] was the successor to the defunct *Examiner*.[58] In the editorial of August 4, young Ritchie could not conceal a lingering admiration for "the Little Corsican," aged thirty-four. Fortune's "favorite hero," he wrote, returned to France in 1799 to find the treasury exhausted, the Directory despised,

56 Inexact quotation from art. 1 of the Declaration of the Rights of Man and of the Citizen.

57 *V. s.*, p. 44.

58 The *Examiner* was discontinued with the issue of January 10, 1804. The *Enquirer's* first issue had been on May 9, 1804, with Ritchie and William W. Worsley, printer and former partner of Skelton Jones in the last days of the *Examiner*, as publishers. For Ritchie's early life, *v. s.*, p. 43. Beginning with the issue of July 30, 1805, Ritchie, the editor, was sole publisher.

the armies defeated, and the people ripe for a change. The Napoleonic legend was being established.

Yet any other hero could have usurped power, Ritchie asserted correctly. " The modest, the simple, the magnanimous Moreau " declined; Bonaparte established a dictatorship. Despite increasing difficulties, Napoleon, in the " wild career of his ambition," ultimately reached the summit of his hopes. Thus the early friend of liberty, the editorial continued, established a new empire upon the ruins of a throne, which the people of France had destroyed at the cost of a million brave men.

" What a ' glorious, golden opportunity ' was presented to Bonaparte, of giving a deathless glory to his name! " Ritchie exclaimed. Why could he not have conquered himself? " Why, after he was made First Consul of France, did he not silently and gradually attempt to habituate the people to the representative system? Why did he not organise the government upon such a model, as that he might be slowly and silently giving up his own power, and calling into action the power of the people? " [59] Was it because the French were unfit for free government? If so, " and our own ignorance of the condition of that nation prevents us from deciding, we can only pity the degradation of their character, and preserve our own from similar disgrace." Or, was it because Bonaparte was too ambitious to give them freedom? That was probably the case. If true, it was deplorable that Napoleon had reached the age of thirty-four. The great Moreau, who aspired to resume civilian life as an ordinary citizen, Ritchie concluded, was an example of what Bonaparte might have been.[60] Now that Republicans comprehended Moreau's true position, they eulogized him as the ideal, as opposed to the fallen, hero.[61]

59 *Cf.* Jefferson's idea; *supra*, p. 151.

60 The editorial was reprinted in the *Petersburg Republican*, August 7, 1804.

61 *Vide infra*, p. 167. That Napoleon's action was replete with dangers to the cause of liberty throughout the world was the theme of several

Federalists, meanwhile, seemed to minimize correctly the importance of the constitutional transformation. A writer, calling himself "Civis," averred in the Fredericksburg *Virginia Herald* of August 21, 1804, that, as First Consul, Napoleon had already been absolute.

But the Federalists again had the opportunity to gloat over the discomfiture of their Republican opponents. No longer sympathetic to Bonaparte, Federalists did not miss their chance. The *Virginia Telegraphe* of Lexington published [62] this mocking item from the *New York Gazette*:

To all genuine Republicans
Friends of Liberty and Equality!

IN the name of Freedom, we beseech you to assist at the Funeral Ceremony and Interment of the most high, most illustrious, and most powerful REPUBLIC OF FRANCE, our dearly beloved sister, one, indivisible, and imperishable; who, all 'enlightened' [63] as she was, departed this life the 28th Floreal (18th May, Old Style) in her Conservative Palace.[64] Her remains will be deposited in the family vault at Monticello, the 21st of September next, the day of her nativity, when she would fully have completed the twelfth year of her age.

REQUIESCANT IN PACE.

. . . .

---

editorials by Ritchie in 1805. For example, he wrote on June 28, "The late revolution of the French has exhibited a spectacle, which cannot fail to discourage all nations oppressed as they have been, from encountering the same perils." Napoleon's betrayal was a damper on progress.

62 In the combined issue of August 17 and 13 [*sic*], 1804.

63 Reference to Jefferson's characterization of the Napoleonic government in his annual message of October, 1803 (*v. s.*, pp. 143-4). Though the President had intended to praise Napoleon only for selling Louisiana and not to approve his régime, Federalists made much ado about this adjective.

64 The Conservative Senate adopted the new imperial constitution on that day.

But, Fellow-Republicans! console yourselves, you will lose nothing.
You! whom this sad accident touches sorely.
For, if the mother who was a *monster*, (although not 12 years of age) died in the Pains of Child-Birth,
The Son lives to perpetuate and immortalize
THE GLORIOUS RACE OF
LIBERTY AND EQUALITY.

DEMOCRATICUS.

The cliché that democracy leads to despotism was frequently reiterated in this presidential election year by the Federalist party.

The newly-founded *Norfolk Gazette and Publick Ledger*,[65] of July 28, 1804, for example, vilified the "monster" of a revolution, which had ended "where all men of foresight supposed . . . [it] would end. . . ." It was not surprising, therefore, when the journal indicated on August 14 that its sympathies were with the Bourbons. It stated its preference for their restoration rather than a continuation of the Corsican usurper's despotism. Now that France was again a monarchy, conservatives discovered in a Bourbon restoration the ideal solution for the French problem. Federalists could now freely express such opinions without fear of supplying additional proof for the Republican charge of royalism.

This high-caliber pro-commercial newspaper,[66] which referred to itself in brief as the *Publick Ledger*, was the first relatively long-lived Federalist journal in Virginia to rely constantly on original editorials as the basic method of expressing its opinions. It was published and edited by John Cowper,

65 Established on July 17, 1804.

66 *V. s.*, p. 45.

secretary of the Marine Insurance Company of Norfolk,[67] and George L. Gray.[68] With the issue of July 26, 1805, Gray was to retire and the paper was to be published by William Davis [69] for the proprietor and editor John Cowper. The *Publick Ledger* had entered the partisan struggle.

In response to the Federalist claim that despotism was the natural result of democracy, the *Virginia Argus* of September 8, 1804, asked whether a man should not attempt to live because he was certain of death at a future time. Americans might not have an emperor for ages, if they remained alert, the article concluded.[70] It was, however, in an editorial on the twelfth that the newspaper struck its most telling blow. Napoleon had become an emperor, the writer asserted, because he was a *federalist,* fond of war and standing armies. "The French nation was surrounded by a multitude of *energetic* governments; armies were judged necessary; the command was entrusted to Bonaparte; power and extensive patronage were lodged in his hands; and he made those *federal* blessings, *armies, war, taxes,* and *patronage,* the *sure* means of his elevation over the liberties of France." Such would have been the fate of America, had not the constant patriots—the Republicans—arrested the base designs of the advocates of aristocracy and despotism.[71]

67 See the newspaper for May 3, 1809, and September 18, 1810. There was a prominent merchant of Norfolk, an ex-mayor, with that name. *Cf., e. g.,* William Maxwell, ed., *The Virginia Historical Register and Literary Advertiser,* vol. II (Richmond, 1849), p. 146; H. W. Burton, *The History of Norfolk, Virginia* (Norfolk, 1877), p. 231. There was another John Cowper, probably the former's son. The author has been unable to determine which one was the editor.

68 Formerly editor of a Federalist paper at Baltimore; *v.* the prospectus in the *Publick Ledger,* July 17, 1804.

69 Previously a publisher of newspapers in Norfolk and Petersburg. Douglas C. McMurtrie, *A History Of Printing In The United States...,* vol. II, *Middle & South Atlantic States* (New York, 1936), p. 294.

70 Reprinted from the *Salem Register.*

71 Editorial reprinted from the *Columbian Gazette* of Utica, N. Y.

The most scholarly and elaborate reply to the Federalists was an essay entitled "French Revolution; And Emperorship Of Bonaparte" by "S—." This was the fourth number of a series of essays, originally published in the *Enquirer* by a group of Richmond intellectuals led by William Wirt. The series was also published separately as *The Rainbow*. Number IV, dated September 7, 1804, is accredited to Skelton Jones, the former editor.[72]

Jones began with a description of what he believed to be the reaction of others to the establishment of the Empire. The advocates of despotism—in which extreme Federalists were included by implication—were overjoyed at what, in their opinion, was the conclusive proof that man was incapable of governing himself and that he required a master to achieve happiness. Many well-meaning men—undoubtedly the moderate Federalists—were convinced by the outcome of the French Revolution that a limited monarchy, like Great Britain's, was the best safeguard against the miseries of despotism as well as the disorders of republicanism. On the other hand, the friends of liberty bewailed the outcome, cursed Napoleon as a renegade and tyrant, and feared a repetition of the events in the United States when age had ripened it for the repose of despotism. Jones pronounced all these views erroneous.

He admitted, however, that he had originally reacted in the same fashion as other Republicans. But maturer reflection diminished his grief and indignation and would similarly influence the others. Skelton Jones asserted, and then proceeded to demonstrate, that the usurpation of Napoleon was neither permanently inauspicious for liberty nor so disastrous for France.

72 This is the conclusion of Jay B. Hubbell, "William Wirt and the Familiar Essay in Virginia," *William and Mary College Quarterly*, ser. 2, vol. XXIII, no. 2 (April, 1943), p. 143. Number IV was printed in two installments in the *Enquirer*, on September 8 and 12, 1804, and reprinted in the Winchester (Frederick County) *Independent Register* on October 2 and 9. References in the text are to the essay (pp. 20-39) in *The Rainbow; First Series. Originally Published In The Richmond Enquirer* (Richmond, Published by Ritchie & Worsley, 1804), NYPL.

The fundamental reasons for Napoleon's success, he declared, were the apathy of the French people and the need for a strong military government to prevent civil war and foreign conquest. Napoleon was the savior of France. "The nation sleeps soundly after its Herculean efforts; Bonaparte alone watches at his post. He has connected the greatness of France with his own usurpation; but it must be confessed that under his auspices, the nation has arrived to an unexampled pitch of power and prosperity." [73] Some admiration still lingered.

The upstart took advantage of the emergency to establish an hereditary empire, Skelton Jones affirmed. But it would not endure; the French Revolution was not at an end. Its last stage would be the peaceful, definitive emancipation of the nation some time during the nineteenth century.

Even assuming that the revolution had ended with the despotism of Bonaparte, Jones continued, it had not been in vain. He found the following to be the gains of the revolution: [74] (1) The theoretical basis of the state had been recast. Instead of the divine-right theory, the new despot was chief magistrate of the people, Emperor of the French. Popular sovereignty, though abused, equality, including equality of taxation, religious toleration, and other principles were recognized as inherent rights. (2) The aristocracy and the clergy had been toppled from their lofty pedestals. The emigrant nobles had lost their lands. The common man had no respect for Napoleon's upstart nobles. He considered himself their equal. The land confiscations and the Concordat had similarly changed the cleric's position. "A French bishop of Bonaparte, compared with a French bishop of Louis XVI. is as powerless and insignificant as a Virginia parson. . . . In suppressing the ridiculous veneration for nobles, and the impious idolatry for priests, the French Revolution and Emperorship of Bonaparte, has been singularly happy, not only for France, but for the

73 *Op. cit.*, p. 28.

74 His description of the Old Régime exaggerated its abuses.

progress of liberal thinking." [75] (3) The Frenchman was now more certain of receiving justice than under the *Ancien Régime*. (4) Last, but not least of the gains of the revolution, was the abolition of the feudal system. The essay concluded with the observation that, "'notwithstanding some of the wanton and capricious freaks which ever follow in the train of absolute power, *personal safety* and *private property* are much more safe than before.'" [76]

While Skelton Jones was endeavoring to answer the Federalists and, at the same time, console himself and the other members of his party, the Federalist attack continued. The Norfolk *Publick Ledger* regaled its patrons on November 3, 1804, with a shrewd and blistering analysis of the attitude of many Republicans toward the establishment of the first French Empire. It began: "EMPEROUR NAPOLEON!—We feel an almost irresistible propensity to laugh, every time the idea of the wonderful metamorphosis of Napoleonè Buonapartè into a French Republican Emperour, presents itself to our mind's eye. And we should certainly be guilty of that most unpardonable act of indecorum, were we not admonished, restored to serenity, or forced into seriousness, by the miserable canting, or lugubrious whinings, of our democratick brethren."

Once the object of their idolatrous worship, the editorial continued, he has deceived them. "With some he is an object of compassion: they contemplate him, as Milton did Satan, in his faded glory." By others he is loaded with execration. "With the majority of Federalists," the *Ledger* stated incorrectly, "he is just what he ever was, and what they have ever represented him to be:—a grasping, ambitious, insatiable, and bloodthirsty tyrant." It enumerated some of the alleged atrocities of Napoleon prior to Brumaire and pointed out that he was then venerated by the Republicans. The assumption of the imperial title might render him ridiculous, but it added little

75 *Op. cit.*, 33.

76 *Ib.*, 39. The quotation is from a contemporary English work, Stephen's *Wars of the French Revolution.*

to the catalogue of his crimes. The editorial concluded with these effective arguments:

> And yet it would appear as if, not only the writer of this number of the RAINBOW [the fourth], but every other of his party, view this as the only reprehensible, the only disgraceful act of Buonaparte.—This was to be expected. The name, and not the thing, we have long since known to be the object of their attention. They had no objection to all power being possessed by Buonaparte, under the denomination of CONSUL FOR LIFE; [77] but the same powers become criminal the moment they are exercised under the title of KING or EMPEROUR. He who might lawfully, and in perfect consistency with the principles of liberty, do every arbitrary act under one title, attempting the same under another is guilty of treason against the liberties of his country. Consistent and profound Statesmen! Will ye pretend to say that the new constitution of France, confers on Buonaparte the exercise of any power, essentially connected with liberty, which he did not before possess?

Nevertheless, the basis of the differences between the Federalists and Republicans concerning the domestic developments in France continued to be their unchanged attitudes toward the French Revolution. It was Napoleon's relation to it that caused the differences. In most other respects, opinion in Virginia pertaining to the internal history of France was confluent in the year and a quarter after the news of the establishment of the Empire.

It is obvious by now that both Federalists and Republicans agreed that Napoleonic France was a despotism. The Norfolk *Publick Ledger* and the Richmond *Enquirer* alike ridiculed the coronation of Napoleon and were displeased with the pope's participation in it.[78] The Petersburg *Republican* [79] reprinted an

77 This was, of course, not true.

78 The *Ledger*, February 4, 1805; the *Enquirer*, July 16, 1805.

79 "Petersburg" was again dropped from the title on March 29, 1805.

editorial from a Baltimore newspaper on July 21, 1805, which satirized the overwhelming vote Napoleon allegedly received in the plebiscite on the imperial succession. Only about twenty-five hundred, " not satisfied with the glory his imperial majesty has united with the French name, dared withhold their mite from him, when nearly 4 millions of *liege* SUBJECTS, hailed him, with loud acclamations of joy, as their sovereign lord. . . . O tempora! O mores!"

Some Republicans not only agreed with the Federalists that France was an absolutism but even became worried that our republican system would in the near future undergo the same metamorphosis as that in France and be replaced by a despotism. Ex-Senator W. C. Nicholas, now collector of the port of Norfolk, wrote almost hysterically to President Jefferson on April 4, 1805. Frightened by the bitter disputes within the Republican party in Pennsylvania and New York, and seeing symptoms of it in Virginia and elsewhere, he asked whether the United States was destined to repeat the history of the French Revolution and finally be deprived of its liberty. Nicholas prayed that it would not happen here. Thousands and thousands of America's citizens would lose their lives before the end came.[80] This was written by a prominent, veteran Republican politician and planter of the Old Dominion!

William Wirt, who was becoming the literary representative of Virginia,[81] had similar apprehensions. This rising young Republican lawyer was bent upon making a fortune for himself and his family so that he could retire in fifteen or twenty years. However, he admitted to his friend Ninian Edwards on September 17, 1805, that his plans rested on an uncertain foundation, the political stability of the American Republic. " It surely would not be matter of more surprise if the twentieth year from

80 *Jefferson Papers*, LC, vol. CXLVIII, p. 25867.

81 Vernon L. Parrington, *Main Currents in American Thought . . .*, vol. II, *The Romantic Revolution in America, 1800-1860* (New York, 1927), p. 30.

this should find an Emperor enthroned in America, than that ten or twelve years should have conducted France through a complete revolution from despotism, through anarchy, democracy and aristocracy, back to despotism again!" When all our revolutionary leaders had died, state jealousies, faction, and ambition might result in anarchy, civil war, and ultimate subjugation to a Macedonian Philip, Corsican usurper, other foreign martial tyrant, or a Caesar or Cromwell at home. In conclusion, William Wirt placed his trust in the protection of Heaven.[82] The Federalist shafts had reached their mark.

Federalists and Republicans, furthermore, were in complete agreement in their opinion of General Moreau. For Virginians Moreau became the knight in shining armor, the paragon of virtue and patriotism. They reached the conclusion, and correctly so, that Moreau was innocent and that Napoleon's purpose had been to remove a leading opponent while he completed his usurpation. Republicans considered him now as the ideal republican military hero, that which Napoleon could have been. Federalists absolved him of all crimes of which French Revolutionary generals were allegedly guilty.[83] Both Federalists and Republicans welcomed the arrival of the victor of Hohenlinden to the United States.

In glaring contrast to the virtuous Moreau was the "Little Corsican." What Federalists thought of Bonaparte was expressed succinctly in the *Publick Ledger* of November 28, 1804: "Buonaparte! a man so universally stained with crimes that in all his soul it would be scarcely possible to find one pure spot." The Federalist newspapers averred his low and, probably, illegitimate birth. His unlimited criminal ambition,

82 *History Of Illinois, From 1778 To 1833; And Life And Times Of Ninian Edwards* By His Son, Ninian W. Edwards (Springfield, 1870), p. 414.

83 *E. g., v. Publick Ledger*, September 25, 1804; *Enquirer*, August 4, December 6, 1804. Carnot and the few other Frenchmen who publicly opposed the establishment of the hereditary empire were also lauded, but not so extravagantly. *E. g., v. Publick Ledger*, July 19, 1804; *Virginia Argus*, August 18, 1804.

his hypocrisy, and his other alleged vicious characteristics made him in Federalist eyes the incarnation of Beelzebub.

Though Federalists were more hysterical, outspoken, and facile in their vituperation of the French ruler, most Republicans agreed substantially with their characterization of the new Emperor. The *Virginia Argus* repeated on August 11, 1804, the recommendation of a London paper that Bonaparte employ the following form for promulgating laws: "NAPOLEON, by the instigation of the Devil, and by force & arms, Emperor of the French, &c." In the *Enquirer* of August 8, a writer with the pseudonym "Iramba" penned a characterization of Napoleon which ended:

> In short, Bonaparte seems to be a man impelled by the most inordinate ambition; destitute of domestic or social affections; connected with no party by any other tie than that of interest; attached to no principles except so far as they may promote his views; alternately a Republican and a Monarchist, a Christian and a Turk; cold, selfish, and arrogant; comprehensive in his plans, inscrutable in his designs; bold, rapid and hazardous in their execution; impatient of contradiction, and resolved to command, rather than to conciliate. Behold the Emperor of the Gauls!

Some Republicans went further than others in their agreement with their opponents. An occasional reference to the "unfortunate" Bourbons could be found.[84] President Jefferson expressed a desire for the restoration of the Bourbons, though as limited monarchs.[85] An editorial in the *Petersburg Intelligencer* on July 31, 1804, declared that the "upstart usurper" ruled with more despotic sway than any king that ever governed France. "If there must be a monarchy, perhaps it would be best to have a legitimate one, and restore at once Louis the Eighteenth to the throne of his ancestor—the French people could not be worsted; their condition might possibly be

84 *Cf.* the "Communication" to the *Enquirer*, September 19, 1804.

85 *V. s.*, pp. 155-6.

ameliorated." This equation of Napoleon with a legitimate monarch indicated a superficial reading of the revolutionary era. In any case, the journal's conclusions were similar to those of the Federalists.[86]

The transformation of the superstructure of the French state had no effect on the diplomatic relations of the Republican administration at Washington. Friendly relations with both Great Britain and France continued. ". . . It is our unquestionable interest and duty," President Jefferson wrote to his Secretary of State on August 15, 1804, "to conduct ourselves with such sincere friendship and impartiality towards both nations, as that each may see unequivocally, what is unquestionably true, that we may be very possibly driven into her scale by unjust conduct in the other." [87] Sanguine of French assistance in the American negotiations with Spain, which were opening, the administration was amicable toward France in the latter half of 1804. Though the administration did complain about the increasing activity of British warships off Sandy Hook in the summer of 1804 and the President's message of November 8, 1804, recommended counter-measures to Congress, it was done in a polite and gentlemanly manner.[88] This firm but friendly attitude toward Great Britain prevailed till late in 1805.

Meanwhile, James Monroe, the roving ambassador, left in doubt by Talleyrand's attitude in November, 1804, proceeded to Spain, still hoping for French support. Instead he and Charles Pinckney, who had been jointly deputed to take charge of the Florida negotiations at Madrid, found France aligned with the Spanish government in opposition. Monroe

86 Despite the hostility displayed by members of both parties toward Emperor Napoleon and his régime, they occasionally recognized and admired his political ability. *E. g.*, the Norfolk *Publick Ledger*, April 19, 1805, *infra*, pp. 178-9; Jones' attitude in *The Rainbow*, *supra*, p. 163.

87 *Jefferson Writings*, Washington ed., IV, 557.

88 *Cf.* Jefferson to Nicholson, November 20, 1804. *Joseph H. Nicholson Papers* (MSS., LC), II, 1185.

wrote indignantly on March 24, 1805, in his journal of the negotiations: "There are but two modes of appealing to the interest of the government of France, one by accommodating it with money, the other by exciting in it the apprehension of danger." He was opposed to the former.[89]

On April 9, Monroe noted the abject subservience of Spain to France. He asserted on the 24th that a French-Spanish victory over England would lead to the complete failure of the present American mission, though it would ultimately have no effect upon the negotiations.[90] On May 25, 1805, Monroe and Pinckney reported in a joint letter to the Secretary of State that there was a belief that Napoleon's policy in the Spanish question was not explicable wholly by pecuniary motives. According to that view, he had much more dangerous designs against the United States. If he was successful in Europe, the Spanish controversy could be used as a pretext to further them. The American ministers, however, believed that France's object theretofore had been purely financial. What it might be in the future depended on circumstances.[91]

Jefferson's attitude toward Napoleon with regard to Franco-American relations began to change markedly as the pessimistic reports began to arrive from France and Spain. He was chagrined.[92] But Madison continued hopeful. As soon as France despaired of any financial gains and apprehended the danger of Anglo-American cooperation, the Secretary wrote to Jefferson on March 27, 1805, it would transfer its support to the United States.[93]

89 Monroe's Journal of the negotiations at Aranjuez in Department of State MSS., *Spain*, vol. VIII (National Archives).

90 *Ibid.*

91 Dispatch from Madrid; Department of State, *Spain*, VII, 265 (National Archives).

92 *Cf.* Merry to Harrowby, March 4, 1805; *Great Britain, F.O.5*, LC, vol. XLV, pp. 41-2; and same to Mulgrave, June 2, 1805, *ib.*, 94.

93 *Jefferson Papers*, LC, vol. CXLVIII, p. 25830.

To add to the President's troubles, General Ferrand at San Domingo issued a drastic edict intended to halt all American trade with the Negroes. French privateers in Caribbean waters were becoming active. Jefferson expected General Turreau, the new ferocious-looking, wife-beating French minister, to act more readily than Bonaparte to cause a modification of Ferrand's edict.[94]

As soon as Washington received the information that the special mission to Spain had utterly failed, President Jefferson began to consider an Anglo-American alliance.[95] He was seriously alarmed. Were it merely a question of the boundaries of Louisiana or even the spoliation claims, delay might be advisable, he wrote to the Secretary of State on August 17. But "the cavalier conduct of Spain . . . [is] evidence that France is to settle with us for her: and the language of France confirms it. . . ." France was planning to wait till she was at peace and then force the United States by arms to submit to her will. Under such circumstances, America must not be friendless.[96] To Madison, however, the proposal for an alliance with England was impractical. Britain would require too much in return.[97]

In the midst of this came Turreau's attempt to dictate to the American government the treatment General Moreau should receive. The President's anger rose to fever pitch. "The style of that government [the French] in the Spanish business, was [also] calculated to excite indignation: but it was a case in which that might have done injury." It was not impolitic, how-

94 To Madison, April 11, 1805; *Madison Papers*, LC, vol. XXVIII, no. 107. For a description and characterization of Turreau, see Augustus J. Foster, *Notes on the United States*..., LC, vol. I, pp. 84-6.

95 *V.* Jefferson to Madison, August 7, 1805, in which the President refers to a letter of July 23 suggesting such a step; *Jefferson Papers, Coolidge Collection*, MHS.

96 *Jefferson Papers*, LC, vol. CLII, p. 26531.

97 *E. g.*, Madison to Jefferson, August 20, 1805; *ibid.*, 26552-3.

ever, to take a bold stand in the present case.[98] "Considering the character of Bonaparte, I think it material at once to let him see that we are not one of the powers who will receive his orders." [99]

In the meantime, the opinion of the Republican press of Virginia concerning American foreign relations in the year and a quarter after the news of the establishment of the French Empire had tended, in general, toward impartiality. Hostile acts of any country were criticized.

Thomas Ritchie, for example, expressed his resentment in the *Enquirer* of June 25, 1805, at the insulting presence of French vessels off Charleston and the "Leander" off New York.[100] Reports of the failure of the Spanish negotiations prompted him to ask on August 3, 1805, whether Napoleon had not received Florida from Spain as he had formerly obtained Louisiana. Yet on August 23, he adverted to Britain's "tyrannical deportment" on the sea. The French and Spanish naval reverse in July, Ritchie affirmed on September 24, would intensify the tyrannical conduct of Great Britain and its navy, though it might encourage Spain to settle the dispute with the United States.

On the other hand, Samuel Pleasants' *Virginia Argus* did not seem to follow the general trend. It chose for insertion those editorials from newspapers outside of the state which emphasized British impressments and depredations on American ships and exculpated the acts of French privateers as unauthorized. On August 3, 1805, it accused the Federalists of desiring to embroil the United States with France over such acts of French privateers while disregarding authorized British aggressions.

98 Jefferson to Madison, August 25, 1805; *Jefferson Papers, Coolidge Collection*, MHS.

99 Jefferson to Madison, August 27, 1805; *Jefferson Papers*, LC, vol. CLII, p. 26577.

100 *Cf. Petersburg Intelligencer*, July 5, 1805.

Though, in August, 1804, the small Federalist press of the commonwealth had criticized the action of British warships,[101] France was its exclusive target for the remainder of the period. The Norfolk *Publick Ledger* is a case in point. It published a series of articles in February, 1805, disapproving the Louisiana Purchase and warning that Napoleon might resume possession of that territory when he defeated Great Britain.[102] Editorials in the spring and summer found occasion only to denounce French and Spanish depredations in the West Indies.[103]

The obverse of Federalist concentration on the censure of France for its treatment of the United States was the generally constant apologia for the British position in the European war. Britain's entry into the war was justified by the *Norfolk Gazette and Publick Ledger* as an essential measure to preserve her independence, which was being assailed by France.[104] The journal expressed the hope that there were few "democrats" left who desired a French victory. "Our democrats have not now their standing reason for wishing success to France. It is no longer the war of *Liberty* against *Despotism*; it is no longer the war of a Republick against a Monarchy; but it is the war of a military tyrant against the only free government in Europe. . . ."[105]

The well-being and security of America, according to the *Publick Ledger*, were in a great degree dependent upon that of the nations of Europe. The latter could not be said to have either security or happiness, an editorial stated on November 19, 1804, while a French emperor had the power not merely to disturb but to destroy both the one and the other. By January, 1805, the situation was presented in a graver light. The editorial writer asserted on the 28th that "the friends of reg-

101 *E. g.*, Fredericksburg *Virginia Herald*, August 14, 1804.

102 *Vide, e. g.*, the issue of February 15, 1805.

103 *Cf.* Fredericksburg *Virginia Herald*, April 16, 1805.

104 August 16, 1804.

105 September 20, 1804.

ular government, the lovers of rational liberty" could not but hope for the success of any measure which was calculated to check that impetuous advance of tyranny and usurpation which threatened to overcome the world, and to destroy in its course everything that had theretofore been regarded as essential to the safety of nations and the happiness of man. Ever since the French had been in "a state of liberty," their unprincipled conduct had violated every common decency. England, the writer maintained, was the only rampart of defense against a universal and degrading domination.

Federalists occasionally intimated that there was an inherent national trait which impelled the Napoleonic régime to endeavor to rule the world. An article in the *Ledger* referred to Henry IV's "Grand Design" and described Bonaparte as the spiritual heir of that alleged scheme to subvert the independence of the civilized world. The writer affirmed that French ambition had caused nearly a century and a half of war with England.[106]

Talk of Bonaparte's unlimited ambition in foreign affairs could be heard in Republican as well as in Federalist circles.[107] Moreover, most Republicans were concerned over the fate of England.[108] The danger of an invasion was at its height. President Jefferson continued to demonstrate his solicitude.[109] Thomas Ritchie declared in the *Enquirer* on June 14, 1805, that no one regarded the naval power of England with more suspicion and indignation than he did. But rather than witness Bonaparte's triumph in Great Britain or even the disasters associated with an invasion, he would rather see the French navy swept from the ocean.[110]

106 February 13, 1805.

107 *E. g.*, *Enquirer*, April 16, 1805, *infra*, pp. 175-6.

108 In contrast, see below, p. 177 and n. 113, 118.

109 *V.* his letter to James Maury, July 20, 1804; *Jefferson Papers*, LC, vol. CXLII, p. 24638.

110 The editorial was reprinted in the non-partisan Staunton *Candid Review: and Staunton Weekly Register*, June 28, 1805. *Cf.* the *Petersburg Intelligencer*, July 16, 1805.

The differences between the political parties, nevertheless, were profound. The lodestar of the Republicans of the Old Dominion continued to be neutrality. The United States had disagreements with both France and England.

The establishment of the Empire had seemed to seal the neutrality of many Jeffersonians. The *Enquirer* deplored the fact that the political course of France no longer harmonized with that of the United States. France was not destined to be the deliverer of Europe, wrote Ritchie.[111] The *Virginia Argus* declared that the war was now between two despots. Americans had to be neutral, for both were hostile to American principles. If one crushed the other, it "would not unlikely become openly hostile to a system of government which although a silent is a severe critic on their conduct." [112]

Many Republicans oscillated between criticism of Napoleon's territorial aggrandizement and of the actions of his enemies. In the latter case the French Emperor necessarily received some approval. Thomas Ritchie is an example. He affirmed in the *Enquirer* of April 16, 1805, that peace between England and France was unlikely. The English government was probably still wedded to the concept of the balance of power. France was, therefore, required to withdraw from Holland, Italy, and other territories. "But will the new Emperor of France, with a growing navy, an army the best disciplined in Europe, with finances, not exacted from his own people, but from the neighboring states, and with a long lustre of military glory, submit to those conditions of pacification, which he . . . rejected, when he was a mere First Consul of France. . . .?" France had declared that it would not relinquish its control over its dependent allies. Who could, furthermore, prevent Bonaparte's extraordinary ambition from placing his brother Joseph on the throne of Lombardy and then of all Italy, or from appointing another brother, Louis, stadtholder of the

111 March 15, 1805.

112 August 1, 1804; reprinted from the *Alexandria Expositor*.

Netherlands? How simple it would be to stir up a disturbance among the Swiss and then assume complete control. "Who will even say," Ritchie asked prophetically, "that the Pyrenees are to furnish a more insurmountable obstacle to his ambition than the Alps? Or are we mistaken, when we already perceive in the meditated attack on Gibraltar, the means of subjugating Spain? . . . In fact, when such a man as Bonaparte wields the resources of such a nation as France, who shall pretend to set limits to his ambitious designs, or to calculate the catastrophe of Europe?" On July 23, 1805, however, the *Enquirer* not only censured Napoleon's ambition on the land, but equated it with British tyranny on the ocean.

Then came the editorial of August 23. This was after the coronation of the Corsican as King of Italy and after the annexation of Genoa. Ritchie now attempted to console his readers. The French, he stated, were extending their jurisdiction on the continent, while restricting the maritime power of Great Britain. The former object was most probably the means of accomplishing the latter. Every additional European country under French control signified more territory from which English trade was excluded, while France received special commercial privileges. In war, the French navy was reënforced by the ships of the allies or dependencies.

The editor did not believe that Napoleon was conquering territories in order to free the seas. Ritchie was, however, willing to concede that posterity would profit by his enterprising labors. "We believe that the increase of the maritime force of France, will serve to soften the tyrannical deportment of England. Without a formidable rival, she becomes the tyrant of the ocean; whereas competition makes her more regardful of the rights of others."

There would be a more important reason for future generations to be pleased with French foreign policy, the *Enquirer* continued. One effect of the French Revolution had been the extension of French authority over the small neighboring states. But that very aggrandizement was paving the way to a more intimate union among those states. Perhaps, as in the case of Alexander the Great, the Napoleonic Empire would dissolve after the death of its founder. Among the ensuing beneficial changes might be a united Italy under its own monarch. It could then demand respect from the Barbary corsairs and the British navy! The pendulum bob had reached the opposite side of the field of neutrality.

The view that French conquests would eventually benefit mankind was presented in a different and more original form by James Monroe on April 24, 1805:[113]

> I have been invariably of opinion of late that the only way to break the power of France, and to give free government to the world, was by extending the power of France, and overthrowing by means of it in the other nations the existing Dynasties. I have thought that by extending his conquests the power of Bonaparte would eventually be weakened, inasmuch as wherever he made a conquest, that of the people by being brought into action, would be increased, altho' the government substituted to the existing one might be of the same kind. To support the new dynasty a new army must be raised, officered by new officers, and composed in some measure of new men. These would be a species of revolutionary troops, who having more impulse and enterprise would not submit willingly to a domestick much less to a foreign yoke. Whenever he marched to the south to crush a revolt against a new subject-king, one might take place in the north. Besides where is the certainty that revolts might not take place among the French armies, as soon as the foreign danger disappeared, which is now one of the strong bonds of domestic union.

Monroe's interpretation of Napoleonic imperialism was in harmony with his conception of the French régime as a useful half-way house between royalism and republicanism.[114]

113 Entry for that date in his Journal of the negotiations at Aranjuez; Department of State MSS., *Spain*, vol. VIII (National Archives).

114 *V. s.*, pp. 154-5.

The continued threat to invade Great Britain, not continental developments, was the center of attraction in European international relations for Virginians during the year and a quarter after the news of the establishment of the Empire. Federalist ridicule of the possibility of a descent upon the British isles was frequent. Commenting on the establishment of the French Empire, the Fredericksburg *Virginia Herald* wrote satirically on August 7, 1804, "According to an old manoeuvre, *illuminations* will now shine throughout France, in order 'to keep the people in the dark,' and *tilts* and *tournaments* will be introduced among its armies, to dissipate their dreams of *invasion.*" When the Federalist press did not ridicule, it denied that an invasion could succeed.[115]

And then it was learned that the Rochefort squadron was in the West Indies raising havoc with the British possessions. The invasion became an imminent possibility. The Norfolk *Publick Ledger* asserted on April 19, 1805, that Britain was surprised and mortified to find her colonies assailed by a navy which she had so long been accustomed not only to conquer but to despise. Concentrating upon the protection of her homeland from invasion and believing it almost impossible that any part of the French navy would venture to sea, Great Britain had shamefully neglected the defense of her West Indian colonies.

The difference between the conduct of the two governments was striking, the editorial continued. The plans of the British government always transpired, thereby placing the enemy on his guard. The English press had frequently disclosed secret expeditions. In contrast was the action of the French government.

> The secrecy with which Buonaparte meditates his measures, and the promptitude with which he executes them, are the strongest proofs that can be adduced of his high qualifications for the eminent and hazardous duties of Minister of the re-

115 *V.*, *e. g.*, the *Publick Ledger*, January 16, 1805.

sources of a nation. Whatever of passion, whatever of entetement[116] [*sic*], whatever of rashness, and whatever of violence, he may have displayed in many parts of his diplomatick conduct, at different periods since his elevation to power, we are more inclined to ascribe to a haughty consciousness of the extent of that power, to a proud conviction of his complete knowledge, not only of the immense physical force of the machine placed in his hands, but also of his own thorough command over all its movements, than to any deficiency of political skill, or, indeed of political prudence. Where has he yet failed of success in any measure, the planning of which and the means of executing it were submitted entirely to himself, or were altogether under his own controul [*sic*]. To signalize the present war he has conceived one mighty project; a project which must either end in the disgrace of his arms, or in the absolute ruin of his enemy, and the consequent uncontroulable command over all Europe. Such a project once matured in the mind, of Buonaparte, we know enough of that mind to authorize us to discredit any idea that, while there is the slightest shadow of probability to justify hopes of success, it ever will be abandoned.

The writer declared that all other moves—the entry of Spain into the war, the attack on the West Indies, the threat of an assault on Gibraltar—were merely feints to draw off the English navy in preparation for the decisive blow. " Experience shows that Buonaparte has no regard for human blood: he cares not how large the current which may flow from the breast of his country, provided it be strong enough to float him to the accomplishment of some favourite wish." If, therefore, the present diversion succeeded, and no continental war intervened, an early, if not successful, invasion of the British isles would follow. The *Ledger* had now arrived at a correct appraisal of French strategy. In the process, it could not but help admiring Napoleon's statecraft.

Speculation about the movements of the French and Spanish warships was at its peak in the Virginia press from May

116 Obstinacy.

through July. Some conjectured that the ultimate aim was the conquest of India.[117] Many more, especially after the news of the escape of the Toulon fleet from port, surmised that the invasion of Great Britain was the object. The editor of the *Publick Ledger* continued to be one of those. But he was also greatly disturbed about the possible accomplishments of the combined French and Spanish squadrons in the Antilles. In an editorial in mid-June, which was reprinted in the Petersburg *Republican* for June 21, 1805, the writer asserted that, if the French succeeded in conquering the valuable colonies of Great Britain in that area, British commerce and finance would suffer a fatal blow. Without commerce, Britain could not exist.

Criticism of the ineptitude of the British admiralty was expressed in Republican, and even Federalist, ranks. "Every incident at sea during the present war is calculated to display the sagacity and energy of the French government, and to reflect a ridicule upon the boasted prowess of England," wrote Ritchie in the *Enquirer* on June 21, 1805. At the beginning of the war, Britain said that there was no danger of an invasion, since France did not have enough ships to transport troops. Shipbuilders soon appeared and a formidable fleet of gun-boats was launched in different ports. Then England said that there was no danger in such isolated detachments. In the very face of the British navy, these ships came together in the harbor of Boulogne. But there was no danger, the British cried; the French fleet was blockaded. Yet various French squadrons escaped to the West Indies and did as they pleased. This editorial was reprinted in the Federalist *Publick Ledger* on June 27.[118]

117 *E. g., Virginia Argus,* May 8, 1805; *Petersburg Intelligencer,* June 14, 1805.

118 More open snickering at John Bull's tribulations could occasionally be heard in Republican ranks. *V.* the *Aurora* editorial in the *Virginia Argus,* June 22, 1805, which gloated over a possible French conquest of Great Britain. This was not placed in the editorial columns of the *Argus,* however, and, hence, probably did not represent the opinion of S. Pleasants. *Vide*

On September 20, 1805, Ritchie analyzed the implications of the naval engagement off Cape Finesterre on July 22 between the combined French and Spanish squadrons, which had re-crossed the Atlantic, and the pursuing English fleet. Since the action had resulted in the entry of the combined fleet into a neighboring port, he stated, it had prevented a junction with the French squadron at Brest. The meditated invasion of England, the *Enquirer* editorial concluded, had probably been intercepted.

Though Thomas Ritchie's conclusion was exaggerated, for all practical purposes the invasion menace was at an end. On August 24, the French Emperor had ordered the Army of England to advance to the line of the upper Rhine.

The war was now to spread. International problems were henceforth to be uppermost in the minds of Virginians. No longer were domestic developments in France burning issues. The First French Republic had set with Napoleon Bonaparte's betrayal.

---

the reprint from the Boston *Independent Chronicle* in the Petersburg *Republican*, August 9, 1805. *Cf.* John Randolph to Nicholson, June 11, 1805; *Joseph H. Nicholson Papers*, LC, vol. II, p. 1234a.

CHAPTER VI

THE PACIFICATOR OR THE BEAST?

(*c.* October, 1805-December, 1807)

THE guns were booming again in Europe. The Twilight War had ended. No more were there indecisive thrusts by Gallic fleets and parries by British men-of-war. The Third Coalition against France—Britain, Austria, Russia, and Sweden—was in existence.

John Bull, meanwhile, had responded to the wails of his merchants and shipowners over the flourishing and competing carrier trade which his wayward American son had built up between the French and Spanish West Indies and their mother countries. James Stephen's *War in Disguise; or The Frauds of the Neutral Flags* (1805) was the most notorious expression of British mercantile opinion. They wanted all the trade for themselves. John Bull had no love for his froward child but responded as an affectionate parent to his loyal well-to-do bourgeois. A more rigorous enforcement by his admiralty courts of the so-called Rule of 1756 ensued. That rule forbade a neutral to prosecute in time of war a trade that was closed to it in peacetime—*viz.*, the above-mentioned commerce between the colonial and metropolitan territory of the enemies. The culminating decision—rendered by the High Court of Admiralty—was in the case of the *Essex* (July 23, 1805).

Federalists in the Old Dominion were compelled to criticize the new British policy. The Fredericksburg *Virginia Herald* of October 11, 1805, recommended counter-measures if the *Essex* decision were enforced.[1] John Cowper, now sole editor of the *Norfolk Gazette and Publick Ledger*, stated on the 25th that the recent British restrictions were the beginning of more rigid measures that would virtually terminate all commerce with the colonies of France, Spain, and Holland.

But France bore the brunt of Cowper's criticism in the closing months of the year. France would continue to disre-

1 Reprint from the *Enquirer* of October 8.

gard the rights of neutrals, particularly American, he wrote in the aforementioned editorial. Only fear, the editor declared meaningfully, could compel respect from that nation and its Spanish satellite. Respect from the coalition would follow naturally. On November 18, Cowper openly threatened the use of force by the United States, if the French and Spaniards continued their depredations. A week later he charged the Republicans with having disregarded French and Spanish aggressions in the preceding few weeks and having attempted to stir up public indignation against the British. At the same time the editor denied that he was a British apologist. There were reasons for complaint against all three powers, he stated. But Great Britain had been willing to discuss the points in dispute. On the other hand, the United States had negotiated with France and Spain under the most humiliating circumstances.

The Republican press of the Old Dominion, in reality, censured France and Spain as well as England for their actions toward the United States. Thomas Ritchie, editor of the Richmond *Enquirer*, suggested on October 8, in connection with an unfriendly act of the French consul at Alexandria, Egypt, toward the American adventurer William Eaton, that the French government might be planning to become the mediator between the United States and the bashaw of Tripoli in order to receive a handsome *douceur* for its services! As late as November 29, Ritchie was not certain of Napoleon's rôle in the apparent failure of the Spanish mission. He suggested that, if Spain had rejected America's just claims, a declaration of war be postponed while increasing our army on the southern frontier. Against the "haughty islanders," who would now become more arrogant and rapacious as a result of the new coalition, Ritchie proposed commercial restrictions in several editorials.[2] Other Republican journals denounced the Jay Treaty, the commercial sections of which were to expire in 1807.[3]

2 October 8; November 1, 29.

3 *E. g.*, *Virginia Argus*, November 2, 1805; Petersburg *Republican*, November 7, 1805.

Though Federalist and Republican editors in Virginia differed over the relative misdeeds of the European powers toward the United States, they agreed that the formation of another powerful coalition against France would "call forth a repetition of those wonderful energies, which the French nation has so often displayed, [*sic*] since the commencement of the revolution." [4] ". . . What cannot the genius and the good fortune of Bonaparte accomplish?" [5] In contrast to the unity of the French war effort would be the discord to which all coalitions were prone. Neither Federalists nor Republicans would gainsay General Bonaparte's ability.

The sympathies of Federalists, however, were with the coalition. If its aims, Cowper wrote in the *Publick Ledger* on December 2, 1805, are the independence of Holland, Spain, Portugal, and the Italian states as well as the reduction of France so that she may no longer endanger Europe and yet retain her ancient political importance, it will be entitled to the gratitude of mankind. Since France must have a king, the editor continued, the coalition should endeavor to restore the unfortunate Bourbons. "If their misfortunes do not excite the sympathy of every generous heart, the Bourbons have a claim on the gratitude of every American."

Republicans, on the other hand, were generally neutral. Those horrible beings, called monarchs—Napoleon was one of them—were again about to shed the blood of their unhappy subjects for personal aggrandizement. Disgust at the spread of the war and the carnage that was to follow diffused itself over the columns of the Republican press.[6] Disputes with both of the major belligerents maintained Republican neutrality at the opening of the War of the Third Coalition.

That war was President Jefferson's great opportunity. He would repeat the Louisiana stroke in the case of Florida. There

4 Norfolk *Ledger*, October 25, 1805.

5 *Petersburg Intelligencer*, November 1, 1805.

6 *Vide Enquirer*, November 1, 1805; *Petersburg Intelligencer*, November 26, 1805.

was no further need of considering an Anglo-American alliance. He wrote breathlessly to Madison on October 23 that France would be engaged in war for at least a year and in peace negotiations for another. That would provide ample time for attempting a pacific settlement with Spain for the purchase of the Floridas and the settlement of the other questions outstanding, with France acting as mediator. The President did not care who received the money![7] The continuation of peace, which Jefferson desired so intensely, was now possible. The cabinet acquiesced in the new policy on November 12. What Monroe and Madison had heretofore opposed was now the policy of the American government. The controversy with Spain had been turned into a "French job."[8]

Thoughts of an alliance with "perfidious Albion" were dropped at a most opportune time. Jefferson informed W. C. Nicholas on October 25 that it would have been disagreeable to have proposed closer connections with England at a moment when there was so much just clamor against that power for its new encroachments on neutral rights.[9] The Monticello planter had been alert enough to recognize the new trend in British admiralty policy as soon as it appeared. Through his Secretary of State, Monroe was instructed to make the necessary strong representations.[10] And Madison set about writing an essay against the Rule of 1756.

In a conversation with Senator William Plumer of New Hampshire on November 29, the President reviewed the international situation. He averred that Spain contemplated war. If the United States, however, took advantage of the present juncture of affairs in Europe, the problem might be solved peacefully. But quick action was necessary. If Bonaparte's rapid

7 *Jefferson Writings*, Ford ed., VIII, n. 1, pp. 380-1.

8 *Cf.* Madison to Jefferson, September 30, 1805; *Jefferson Papers*, LC, vol. CLIII, p. 26693.

9 *Jefferson Writings*, Ford ed., VIII, 383.

10 Madison to Monroe, April 12, 1805; *Madison Writings*, Hunt ed., VII, 176 ff. Same to same, September 24, 1805; *ib.*, 190-1.

movements placed him in Vienna, he might there compel Europe to sign a peace on his own terms. Jefferson, surprised at the speed of Napoleon's advance, changed his interpretation of the duration of the continental war. With the restoration of peace, the President continued, France and Spain would unite to fight against us. We had most to fear, however, from the court of London, for its policy was systematic and persevering.[11] Jefferson's message to Congress, December 3, 1805, vaguely threatened hostilities against one and sundry.

Publicly Jefferson seemed to be following the advice of his minister James Monroe, who was suggesting pressure against Spain and England. The European powers were our enemies, Monroe had implied.[12] His failure in Spain had affected his opinion of Napoleon.

Jefferson's confidential message on Spain (December 6), however, repeated the insinuations of his talk with Plumer. Congress was soon apprised of the President's desire for an appropriation for the Floridas. Furthermore, the President was eager to comply with Napoleon's demand that all trade with the blacks of San Domingo be ended. It suited the interests of the Southern slaveholders as well as fitting perfectly into the new foreign policy. The administration hinted at commercial restrictions as the weapon to be employed against England.

In accordance with this policy, Secretary of State Madison completed *An Examination Of The British Doctrine, Which Subjects To Capture A Neutral Trade, Not Open In Time Of Peace.*[13] It was published early in 1806. In it, Madison skillfully battered the Rule of 1756. The aim of the rule, he maintained, was to draw the West Indian colonial trade of Britain's

11 Plumer, *Proceedings In The United States Senate,* 335.

12 Monroe to Jefferson, September 26, 1805; *Monroe Writings,* Hamilton ed., IV, 335-7. As he stated later: "The moral sentiment is weak with them all.... All will insult us, encroach on our rights, & plunder us if they can do it with impunity." To same, November 1, 1805; *Jefferson Papers,* LC, vol. CLIII, p. 26805.

13 *Madison Writings,* Hunt ed., VII, 204-375.

enemies through her own warehouses and countinghouses. It was intended to end the American carrying trade. Yet England relaxed her own mercantilist regulations in time of war! A report by the Secretary, dated January 25, in response to a Senate resolution, stressed British—not French—violations of international law.[14]

The American public was at first cognizant only of the annual message. The United States seemed to be on the verge of war. Loyal Republican Virginia rallied to the support of Jefferson and country. The General Assembly passed a resolution censuring both Britain and Spain and expressing the readiness of the commonwealth, whenever Congress deemed it necessary, to go to war against any nation that had injured the United States.[15] A protest meeting in Petersburg on February 8 was presided over by Mayor William Prentis, former publisher of the *Petersburg Intelligencer*, with John Dickson, its present publisher, as secretary. Benjamin Watkins Leigh and John Daly Burk inveighed against both Great Britain and Spain and intimated that they were prepared to fight, if necessary. In passing, the Irishman censured Bonaparte for exchanging the wreaths and laurels of a republican hero for the bespangled crown of a despot. Both orators suggested a non-importation act against Britain.[16] The patriotic resolutions of the meeting were presented to the House of Representatives on February 13 by Representative Peterson Goodwyn.

Even Cowper's *Publick Ledger* of December 11, 1805, applauded the "manly attitude" of the executive's message. Jefferson seemed to be adopting the Federalist program of energetic government. And it might be directed against Spain, *i.e.*, France. The editor, however, opposed a proposal of the

14 *Annals of Congress*, 9th Cong., 1st Sess., 72-3.

15 January, 1806; *Journal Of The House Of Delegates Of The Commonwealth Of Virginia Begun And Held At The Capitol, In The City Of Richmond, On Monday The Second Day of December, One Thousand Eight Hundred And Five* (Richmond; Printed by Samuel Pleasants, Jr.) [NYPL]; pp. 38-9, 64.

16 *V. Petersburg Intelligencer*, February 14, 1806.

National Intelligencer for commercial restrictions against Great Britain. War—whether military or commercial—with that country would be at least as injurious to the United States as to England, he asserted. The cat was out of the bag. War with France was all right, but not war with Great Britain! Cowper's concluding statement threatening war against the latter, if she did not recede, was, therefore, mere window-dressing.

While Virginia Republicans criticized both Spain and Great Britain, the trend for the time being was toward emphasis on the latter. Ritchie averred on December 27, 1805, that England's object was to destroy the commerce of every nation rivaling her own. On January 23, 1806, he summarized Madison's pamphlet for the benefit of his readers. The Republican press favored non-importation against Great Britain.[17] The Rule of 1756 was the prime target of a meeting in Norfolk on February 12. A committee, which included the prominent Republican lawyers Littleton W. Tazewell and William Wirt, drafted resolutions to that effect. They were adopted by the assemblage and presented to Congress by Representative Thomas Newton, Jr.

Meanwhile, the devious foreign policy which the Jefferson administration proposed to the first session of the Ninth Congress was bearing fruit. It was the immediate cause of the secession of John Randolph of Roanoke from the party of Jefferson and Madison. The Tertium Quids came into being.[18] The anti-Napoleonic segment of Virginian opinion was reënforced.

Already dissatisfied over the Yazoo question and his failure to obtain a conviction in the impeachment proceedings against Associate Justice Chase, the majority leader of the Republicans in the House of Representatives severed his ties with the administration over the President's dual policy toward Spain.

17 *Vide* Petersburg *Republican*, February 6, 1806; *Enquirer*, February 21, 1806.

18 *V. s.*, pp. 37 f.

Randolph favored the public one, *i.e.*, aggressive measures against that country, or, at least, so he affirmed. As chairman of a House committee he introduced a resolution authorizing the president, whenever he deemed it necessary, to call troops [19] into service to protect the southern frontier against Spanish incursions.

In a House debate behind closed doors on January 7 and 8, 1806, the baron of Roanoke exclaimed,—according to Senator Plumer,—that he would never consent to the proposition that "the asses milk of the United States" should enrich "the consumptive coffers of France." It was mean and unjust to give American gold to avaricious France in order to compel Spain to cede the Floridas. Had not France ceded Louisiana to the United States, after having promised Spain not to alienate it? France had never performed its obligations to Spain under the Treaty of San Ildefonso.[20] France sold Louisiana with indeterminate boundaries, he asserted, so that French mediation would again be required. France would thereby obtain another *douceur* of millions. In any case, he continued, the purchase of the Floridas would not prevent war. We might be obliged to fight for this barren wasteland after we had bought it. Randolph thus ended by apparently opposing any attempt to acquire Florida. But this was in secret session.

In passing, he had commented on the suggestion that the United States reserve its military force for Great Britain. True, he declared, England had committed acts of aggression against us. He had, however, more confidence in British justice and honor than in French. Britain might be a highwayman, but not a swindler. In any case, how could America punish powerful England headed by the great Pitt? A non-importation act would injure us infinitely more than Great Britain.[21] Ran-

19 The number of troops was not specified.

20 Had Randolph conveniently forgotten that, back in October, 1803, he had disregarded such arguments against the Louisiana Purchase Treaty? *Annals of Congress*, 8th Cong., 1st Sess., 409.

21 Plumer, *op. cit.*, pp. 367-370. Contrast his attitude toward Pitt and England in the letter to Nicholson, June 11, 1805; *v. s.*, n. 118, ch. V.

dolph's position in the coming battle over commercial restrictions was established.

Of the twenty-two representatives from Virginia, twelve,[22] including Randolph, voted on January 14 against the resolution appropriating blank dollars for the purchase of the Floridas. The resolution was carried in the chamber by a vote of 77 to 54.[23] (Not one Virginian, however, voted against the bill to end commercial intercourse with San Domingo.) When news about the Florida appropriation finally transpired, the *Enquirer* reluctantly endorsed it, but the *Ledger* opposed it.[24]

In difficulties with both major belligerents, the administration and its partisan following continued to be neutral in the intensified European war. " The moral duties make no part of the political system of those governments of Europe which are habitually belligerent," wrote the President.[25] " What an awful spectacle does the world exhibit at this instant," he stated on another occasion. " One man bestriding the continent of Europe like a Colossus, and another roaming unbridled on the ocean [*sic*]. But even this is better than that one should rule both elements. Our wish ought to be that he who has armies may not have the dominion of the sea, and that he who has dominion of the sea may be one who has no armies. In this way we may be quiet, at home at least." [26] The sage of Monticello thus aptly summarized the main current in Republican opinion of Europe at the close of 1805 and in the early months of 1806.

Republican oscillation between opposing and favoring the French Emperor's war effort was, therefore, to be expected.

22 The lone Federalist, Joseph Lewis, Jr., was one of them.

23 *Annals of Congress*, 9th Cong., 1st Sess., 1126.

24 *Enquirer*, February 18, 1806; *Ledger*, February 21, 1806.

25 To Judge Cooper, February 18, 1806; *Jefferson Papers, Coolidge Collection*, MHS.

26 To Thos. Lomax, January 11, 1806; *Jefferson Papers*, LC, vol. CLV, p. 27225.

Fortunately for Bonaparte, Republicans generally rejected the Federalist contention that American opinion of French policies in Europe should be determined by one's attitude toward the government of France.[27] Hatred of the Napoleonic régime could thus be combined with approval of its foreign policies.

At the same time, Federalists were restrained from being hysterically hostile to Napoleon. He was occupied in central Europe; England appeared safe, especially after Trafalgar.

Much overlapping of opinion was, therefore, to be found among Virginians. Dislike of the vacillating Prussian King was universal. He was not honorable enough for Virginians. Admiration of Napoleon's military achievements was common. Both Federalists and anti-Federalists, nevertheless, considered the French war bulletins exaggerated. Yet some Republicans as well as the Federalists believed that Bonaparte was a possible menace to the United States.

When Republicans thought in terms of American difficulties with Spain, they were pleased with the formation of a new coalition [28] and the spectacular British naval victory off Cape Trafalgar.[29] Such developments might facilitate an adjustment of American differences with Spain. But Wilson Cary Nicholas was apprehensive on December 24, 1805, that Bonaparte would prevent the Austrian ruler from rendering the United States the services that were expected of him! [30]

On the contrary, when Jeffersonians thought in terms of American differences with England, or in terms of domestic politics and the pro-British Federalists, they tended to appreciate Napoleon. Edward Pescud, the new editor of the Petersburg *Republican*, was pleased that the news from the front

27 *E. g.*, *Virginia Argus*, January 14, 1806.

28 *Enquirer*, December 14, 17, 1805.

29 Monroe to Secretary of State, November 11, 1805; *James Monroe Papers—Letter Book* (MSS., LC), vol. I, p. 247. *Cf.* "Americus" in the *Enquirer*, December 31, 1805.

30 To Jefferson; *Jefferson Papers*, LC, vol. CLV, p. 27055.

saddened the Anglo-Federalists.[31] Thomas Ritchie declared on February 25 that French victories in the heart of Europe diminished British encroachments on the seas.[32]

A *Virginia Argus* editorial on February 21—reprinted from the *Aurora*—rejoiced at the discomfiture of the English with the rapid defeat of Austria. Bonaparte merely had to reëstablish Poland to balance whatever vicious acts he had committed. He now ruled virtually all of western and central Europe. The monarchical coalition formed for the purpose of destroying revolutionary France, the editorial concluded, had instead created a scourge for itself.[33]

But hatred of Napoleon as well as the members of the coalition was the norm. The European powers, the *Enquirer* declared in editorials on December 27, 1805, and January 2, 1806, were vultures struggling for their prey, the weak states. What an incongruous coalition! Russia, former member of an armed neutrality for the freedom of the seas was allied with England, which claimed the sovereignty of the seas. The ambitious French usurper was endeavoring to divert the eyes of Europe from his own immediate aggrandizement to the danger of Russia. It was ridiculous, Ritchie stated, to aver that the Tatars might again destroy European civilization. There was, however, some truth in Napoleon's allegation of a Russian menace. The Russians did intend to conquer Turkish territory in southern Europe. Despite one's wish that the Turks be expelled from that continent, it was to the interest of Europe to prevent such Russian expansion in Turkey. The semi-barbarous Russian bear was emerging from the wilds of Asia to worry Virginians. The maritime tyrant, Britain, Ritchie asserted was a counterpoise to the present power of France and the growing strength of Russia.

31 *Vide* issues of January 13 and February 17, 1806. Pescud, previously associated with the *Petersburg Intelligencer*, succeeded Thomas Field as publisher of the *Republican* with the issue of October 21, 1805.

32 *Cf.* Monroe to Madison, December 23, 1805; *ASP*, *FR*, III, 110.

33 *Cf.* the English Whig view; Maccunn, *op. cit.*, 92.

The *Enquirer* stated on January 16, 1806, that Bonaparte, who could have done more for the cause of freedom and humanity than any other man, had become its most dangerous and inexorable foe. He hated the United States perhaps because the happiness of the American Republic was "the severest satire . . . upon his own apostacy." A rumor that Napoleon had dictated an armistice at Vienna depressed Ritchie. But for the maritime ascendancy of England, an editorial declared on January 30, there would be a real danger of a universal monarchy. Federalist alarums were having their effect. Charles V and Louis XIV, Ritchie maintained, had been "miserable drivellers" in contrast to Bonaparte. In what an appalling state the world was: the French monster could only be checked by the British monster.

Meanwhile, the Federalist journals in the Old Dominion were expressing opinions which were not too far removed from those of the Republicans. John Cowper of the Norfolk *Publick Ledger* was deeply stirred at the news of Trafalgar. "The IMMORTAL NELSON . . . the hero of his country, and of the age is no more!" he exclaimed.[34] The destruction of such a mighty fleet at one blow was unprecedented. As a result of this memorable battle Spain would drop her haughty tone toward the United States.[35] Trafalgar, wrote Augustine Davis in the Richmond *Virginia Gazette and General Advertiser*, should delay, if not entirely prevent Bonaparte's long-threatened invasion of England.[36]

Both Cowper and Davis, however, were impressed by Napoleon's military exploits. On December 24, 1805, the latter depicted the Corsican exhibiting his accustomed activity and indefatigable zeal in the midst of his 'throng'd legions.' The military achievements of this phenomenon in war and prodigy in council had already filled the world with astonishment,

34 December 23, 1805.

35 December 30, 1805.

36 February 5, 1806.

Davis affirmed. No human could foretell his future. In the meantime, the United States need not fear Bonaparte. Every inch of his capacious mind would be occupied for at least a year, the *Gazette* editorial concluded. The Norfolk paper expressed its amazement on January 6, 1806, at the overthrow of the mighty Austrian empire in six weeks, and without one battle in which the ancient valour of that nation was displayed. It appeared, the editor continued, that the meeting of the enemy by the modern Caesar was the same as defeating it. But Bonaparte would not be able to conquer England.

On February 5, Davis seemed to recant his excessive praise of Napoleon. His victories were not to be ascribed solely to his talents, the ex-postmaster wrote, but also—and more so—to his subordinate commanders and to the fervor and heroism of their undaunted soldiers. Cowper's admiration lingered however. Commenting on the rumor that Prussia had joined the coalition, he declared on February 14 that Napoleon was in great danger. But, he concluded, Napoleon, with his military skill and courage, assisted by a victorious and loyal army and experienced generals, would not be vanquished so easily.

In the month of March, 1806, the general public became aware of the schism in the Republican party. The occasion was the debate in the House of Representatives over a proposed resolution by Andrew Gregg, Republican of Pennsylvania, to retaliate against British impressments and the Rule of 1756 by means of non-importation. On the fifth, John Randolph delivered to crowded galleries what Senator Plumer described as "the most bitter, severe & eloquent philippic" he had ever heard.[37] Randolph even included the President in his diatribe.

The planter of Roanoke, representing the Southside [38] congressional district composed of Charlotte, Prince Edward, Buckingham, and Cumberland counties, proclaimed himself the spokesman of agrarianism.

37 Plumer, *op. cit.*, p. 444.

38 The base or southern stretch of Virginia.

> What is the question in dispute? The carrying trade. What part of it? The fair, the honest, and the useful trade that is engaged in carrying our own productions to foreign markets, and bringing back their productions in exchange? No, sir. It is that carrying trade which covers enemy's property, and carries the coffee, the sugar, and other West India products, to the mother country. No, sir, if this agricultural nation is to be governed by Salem and Boston, New York and Philadelphia, and Baltimore and Norfolk and Charleston, let gentlemen come out and say so; and let a committee of public safety be appointed from those towns to carry on the Government. I, for one, will not mortgage my property and my liberty, to carry on this trade.[39]

This trade, moreover, will disappear with the return of peace.

After shrinking from the Spanish jackal, do you presume to bully the British lion? Randolph asked. But there are no longer any Pyrenees. Our differences are really with France. For Spain and France you are carriers, and from good customers every indignity is to be endured. Britain, however, is your competitor, " and governed as you are by counting-house politicians, you would sacrifice the paramount interests of the country, to wound that rival." [40]

Non-importation, Randolph continued, is an incipient war measure. Can we fight against a country that has destroyed the fleets of France, Spain, and Holland? There is no indignity in refusing to fight the Leviathan of the deep in his own element. " What! shall this great mammoth of the American forest leave his native element and plunge into the water in a mad contest with the shark?" [41]

Randolph had completely reversed his position of December 6, 1804, when he had threatened England with a war on the ocean until the destruction of the last American vessel. But then the " useful trade " seemed to be at stake.[42] Now he de-

39 *Annals of Congress*, 9th Cong., 1st Sess., 557.

40 *Ib.*, 564.

41 *Ib.*, 559.

42 *Op. cit.*, 8th Cong., 2nd Sess., 767-70.

clared that he was opposed to a naval war with any nation, just as he had opposed the naval war of the Adams administration. It would result in the transformation of the executive into a First Consul and eventually an Emperor, *viz.*, a despot.

After asserting that the United States was no match for Great Britain, he proceeded to the contradictory argument that it would be impolitic on our part to help France overthrow the British dominion of the seas. "Take away the British navy and France to-morrow is the tyrant of the ocean." [43] The deep and wide Atlantic would then prove as much a barrier against the conqueror's ambition as the Mediterranean to the power of the Caesars. Bonaparte's gigantic ambition, Randolph exclaimed, was to become ruler of the sea and the land. This was also the Federalist position.

This was not 1793, the speaker continued. France was then fighting the battles of the human race against the combined enemies of its liberty. Britain was now performing the same rôle; it was the sole bulwark against universal dominion. "No thanks to her for it." England, unlike France, could not become a military and naval power. Her maritime power might not even be formidable for long. It was poor comfort to Americans to be told by some that France looked to Egypt or the Barbary coast and, at the worst, that we would be the last devoured.

John Randolph stated that he admired neither nation. "But with all my abhorrence of the British Government, I should not hesitate between Westminster Hall and a Middlesex jury, on the one hand, and the wood of Vincennes and a file of grenadiers on the other. That jury trial, which walked with Horne Tooke and Hardy through the flames of ministerial persecution [44] is, I confess, more to my taste than the trial of the Duke d'Enghien." [45]

43 *Op. cit.*, 9th Cong., 1st Sess., 559.

44 Horne Tooke and Hardy were prosecuted for treason in 1794 for founding and belonging to the London Corresponding Society. They were acquitted by the jury.

45 *Annals of Congress*, 9th Cong., 1st Sess., 573.

The ex-majority leader's proposed solution was to negotiate with Great Britain. Why, he asked, were the administration's supporters hostile to that country but not to Spain, or rather France, despite the failure of the mission to Spain?

The intra-party debate that ensued raged for the remainder of the month. The hopeless Federalist minority contented itself with following Randolph's lead.[46] The debate seemed for a time to produce a sectional split between Northern Republicans, mainly in favor of Gregg's resolution, and Southern Republicans, led by Randolph, generally opposed to it. Actually, however, the schism was more profound.

That was demonstrated in the reactions of the Virginia delegation. Only three representatives from that state spoke in favor of drastic commercial restrictions against Great Britain. Of these, John George Jackson, Madison's brother-in-law, expressed the interests of many western farmers. He represented the northwestern part of the state, which included the panhandle of what is now West Virginia. Jackson vigorously defended the American trade with the French and Spanish West Indies as beneficial to farmers as well as merchants, for those islands were provisioned exclusively by the United States.[47] Let there be no sectional conflicts between North and South, he pleaded. The North supported the South when the New Orleans deposit was closed. The South should reciprocate now. Jackson spoke the language of the young nationalistic West.[48] Thomas Newton, Jr.,—son of the prominent merchant of the same name,[49]

46 *Vide* Edmund Quincy, *Life of Josiah Quincy*, pp. 93-4.

47 March 11; *Annals of Congress*, 9th Cong., 1st Sess., 726. *V. s.*, pp. 14-16. Jackson's position disproves Henry Adams' statement that farmers were indifferent to the dispute about impressment and the Rule of 1756 (*History ... During The Administration Of Thomas Jefferson*, Bk. III, p. 211). Jackson's description of the horrors of impressment was most eloquent. *Annals of Congress*, 9th Cong., 1st Sess., 733-4.

48 March 12; *ibid.*, 731. John Clopton was the second Virginian to favor Gregg's resolution; *ibid.*, 852-62.

49 *V. s.*, pp. 94-5 and n. 67, ch. III.

—representing the congressional district which included Norfolk, spoke for the native American merchants trading on their own capital with the French and Spanish West Indies.[50] Independent merchant capitalists and many western farmers were united against "perfidious Albion."

In contrast, John Randolph and Christopher Clark stressed the dependence of the tobacco and cotton planters on Great Britain for their market and for their manufactured goods.[51] Were these the spokesmen of the planters of prime tobacco? Wheat growers with a British market must have hearkened.[52] Furthermore, many Virginia planters were not directly affected by the Rule of 1756. In any case, John W. Eppes, Jefferson's former son-in-law,[53] a loyal administration supporter,—representing the James River counties of Amelia, Goochland, Powhatan, and Chesterfield,—hemmed and hawed about the Gregg resolution when he finally addressed the House on March 10. He referred to Britain as our best market, the importance of British credit, especially to Southern merchants, and finally proposed a weaker measure as the first step.[54]

When the Gregg resolution came up for a vote on March 13, of the twenty-four representatives who voted to discharge the Committee of the Whole from further consideration of the resolution, eleven were from Virginia. Thirteen of the twenty-six votes cast against a resolution to end all commercial intercourse with Great Britain were from Virginia.[55] The compromise Non-Importation Bill, which Randolph described as "a milk and water bill, a dose of chicken broth to be taken nine

50 *Vid. Annals of Congress*, 9th Cong., 1st Sess., 868.

51 *E. g.*, *v.* Clark's speech, *ib.*, 663-4.

52 Randolph himself raised wheat as well as tobacco in 1805; to Joseph H. Nicholson, April 12, 1805, *Nicholson Papers*, LC, vol. II, p. 1211c. His plantation also produced wheat in 1806; to Garnett, April 27, 1806, *Letters of John Randolph ... and James M. Garnett*, LC, p. 2. His wheat and flour were probably sold ultimately in a British area; *v. s.*, pp. 15-16.

53 Maria Jefferson, his first wife, had died in 1804.

54 *Annals*, *ib.*, 666-71.

55 *Ib.*, 767.

months hence " [56] passed the House on March 26 with the Virginia delegation split 17-5 in favor of it.[57] The five who voted against it were Randolph, his close friend, James Mercer Garnett (representing King and Queen, Essex, King William, and Caroline counties); Lewis, the Federalist representative of the important wheat district of the northern Piedmont (Loudoun, Fairfax, and Prince William counties);[58] Philip Rootes Thompson (representing Culpeper and Fauquier, the neighboring counties); and Abram Trigg of southwest Virginia. Each one of these congressmen had also voted against the Florida appropriation.[59]

Before the final vote was reached on the Non-Importation Bill, many speakers discoursed upon Napoleon Bonaparte, European developments, and American foreign policy. Randolph and Clark bitterly repelled charges that they were British apologists. They admitted that Britain was a tyrant of the seas. They, however, defended England's right to apply the Rule of 1756 as a war measure against France. They talked of Napoleon's ambition " bounded only by the habitable world," of his pointed hatred of the American government, and of Great Britain contending for her existence and her liberties.[60]

While Napoleon's military victories would facilitate our negotiations with England, Randolph asserted, they should reënforce the argument against weakening her.[61] In reply to an assertion that it would take years before Bonaparte had a navy large enough to defeat the British, and that Napoleon's empire was only as permanent as his life, Randolph maintained that the fate of the French military despotism did not hang on the life of a man. If Mahomet II had been killed under the walls

56 *Ib.*, 851.

57 *Ib.*, 877. Clark voted for the compromise.

58 *V. s.*, pp. 15-16.

59 *Annals, ib.*, 1131-2.

60 *Vide* particularly Clark's speech of March 10; *ib.*, 661-6.

61 March 14; *ib.*, 793.

of Constantinople, he asked, would the destiny of the Greek Empire have been changed? Would not the power have passed into the hands of another terror of the civilized world? Napoleon must have ranked very low in Randolph's opinion, if he could be compared with the Turks, who were still detested in Christendom.[62]

The proponents of commercial restrictions, on the other hand, insisted that Great Britain was perpetrating her aggressions against the United States now. Was the United States to be tolerant and wait, because it was alleged that Britain was fighting for her existence? [63] In answer to the statement that her encroachments would continue only during the war, Jackson indicated that the war had lasted fifteen years already and that there was still no end in sight.[64] John Clopton pointed out the inconsistency of Randolph's argument that our little navy would be easily destroyed in a contest with England, but would nevertheless be able to assist France to acquire control of the seas. The British navy would not lose its predominance so soon, Clopton consoled his opponents.[65] The supporters of commercial restrictions declared that they were in favor of a balance of power between England and France.[66]

After the disposal of the British problem, the House of Representatives turned, in an anti-climax, to the question of whether to make the proceedings on the Florida appropriation public. Randolph castigated the administration and, especially, Madison. The disgruntled politician reiterated his arguments of the secret session. He heaped ridicule on the pusillanimous policy toward Spain and France. He even accused the administration of having adopted a hostile attitude toward Great Britain in order to obtain the assistance of the Emperor of France

62 March 6; *ib.*, 601.

63 Jackson, March 11; *ib.*, 727-8.

64 March 12; *ib.*, 731.

65 March 26; *ib.*, 857-8.

66 *E. g.*, Newton, March 26; *ib.*, 872.

in the Florida question. The negotiation would fail nevertheless, Randolph averred; the battle of Austerlitz had settled that question. If peace came to Europe, a strong Spanish squadron, aided perhaps by a French force, would appear in the bay of Pensacola. The administration would be glad, in those circumstances, to get off with a loss of twenty millions.[67] In rebuttal, Eppes and Jackson endeavored to prove that the Florida appropriation was similar to the Louisiana appropriation, that it was not dishonorable, and that if France ultimately obtained the money, it would be attributable to Spain's transferring it to her more powerful ally.[68]

Meanwhile, outside of Congress, partisan opinion of Napoleon had, in general, undergone no change in March and April, 1806, except for the increase of Republican concern and the return of Federalist emotionalism over the fate of England.

As the truth about Austerlitz dawned upon Virginians, many Republicans became as worried as their Federalist opponents. Although Edward Pescud had exclaimed in the Petersburg *Republican* of March 13 that he hoped that Bonaparte's troops continued to advance till Poland was liberated, England was humbled through the defeat of her allies, and the oppressed nations of the earth enjoyed their natural rights on the ocean, he now sang a different tune. On March 20, the *Republican* stated in amazement that Napoleon had beaten Austria and annihilated a Russian force of 80,000 in two short months. Britain was left to contend alone with the genius of Bonaparte. "But perish his immense resources, ere England sink beneath his giant arm." [69] Truth to tell, Pescud, like most Republicans, really desired a balance between the two major belligerents. Ritchie's *Enquirer* of March 18 declared that it would be better if Napoleon were assassinated than if he were "'king of Great Britain, Ireland, and France,'" and thereby menaced the Ameri-

67 Speech of April 5, *ib.*, 947-8; speeches of April 7, 959-62, 981-5.

68 *E. g.*, Jackson, April 5, *ib.*, 949; Eppes, April 7, *ib.*, 978-81.

69 *Cf. Petersburg Intelligencer*, July 16, 1805, when Pescud and John Dickson were joint publishers of that newspaper.

can continent. The Federalist *Publick Ledger* of March 17 revived its theme that only one barrier remained to oppose the gigantic views of Bonaparte. Another effort of the continental powers to restrain the inordinate ambition of the French government was not to be expected, Cowper affirmed.[70]

No love for Britain or mourning for the decease of Pitt could, however, be discovered in Republican ranks. Republicans sometimes imputed French aggrandizement to England's renewal of the war. England, they said, now stood alone, an armed camp, menaced with economic ruin and invasion. She was the cause of her own and Europe's ills.[71]

Republicans, moreover, saw national advantages in the Napoleonic victory at Austerlitz. Ritchie, defending commercial restrictions against England on March 25, hedged on the Napoleonic danger to the United States. In reply to the argument that such action on our part would hurt England, the bulwark against world rule, he declared that Britain was trampling on us now. What might happen in the future was irrelevant. In any case, the death of Pitt and the battle at Austerlitz would produce a settlement of our differences before the Non-Importation Bill became operative.[72]

President Jefferson was also writing on the same day that our dispute with Great Britain would be settled in consequence of the defeat of her allies and the change in the British ministry. The Non-Importation Bill, which Congress would probably pass, would facilitate that result. Napoleon and, probably, Alexander were in favor of neutral rights, he continued. The United States could encourage them by excluding all intercourse with any nation which infringed upon the rights of neutrals.[73]

70 *Cf.* the Federalist Frederickburg *Virginia Herald*, March 18, 1806.

71 *E. g., Enquirer*, April 25; *Virginia Argus*, April 22; Winchester *Philanthropist*, April 29.

72 The editorial was reprinted in the Winchester *Philanthropist* of April 8, 1806, without acknowledgment.

73 To Thomas Paine; *Jefferson Papers, Coolidge Collection*, MHS. *Cf.* John Tyler to Jefferson, March 25, 1806; *Jefferson Papers*, LC, vol. CLVII, p. 27613.

When asked by Senator Plumer in a private conversation on April 2 whether he apprehended any danger from France, the President replied in the negative. Yet the Republican leader, referred to Napoleon's ambition and his vast power. Napoleon planned to establish a federation of kings in Europe with himself as their emperor and master. Prussia would have to bow to his will. Bonaparte would make peace with England and then build up his navy. But he would not disturb the United States.[74] Jefferson, however, wrote to John Tyler on April 26 that he was concerned lest Randolph's attacks on the French government stir up hostility there. It might be especially dangerous if peace were established in Europe. But if the war continued another year, sober sense on both sides might produce a solution of the Spanish question.[75]

. . . .

Henry Banks, however, apprehended no danger at all from Napoleon Bonaparte. On the contrary, this prolific, though diffuse, author was then eulogizing the French ruler. The high watermark of Banks' writings on Napoleon was reached in 1806. During that year he wrote chiefly under the pen names "Pacificator" and "An American" in various Republican newspapers, including the *Enquirer* and the *Virginia Argus*. In the month of February there was also published separately his *Sketches Of The History Of France, From The Earliest Historical Accounts, To The Present Time—1806: With Some Remarks Concerning The Life And Achievements Of The Celebrated Napoleon Bonaparte, Now Emperor Of France* under the pseudonym "An American." [76] Henry Banks' works

74 Plumer, *op. cit.*, 470-1.

75 *Jefferson Writings*, Ford ed., VIII, 441-2.

76 Richmond, Printed by Seaton Grantland, 103 pp.; available in LC. Excerpts from the book were reprinted in various Virginia papers, especially in the *Lynchburg Star* from May through August. For proof that the *Sketches* were written by "Pacificator" see an article under the latter name in the *Virginia Gazette and General Advertiser* of January 10, 1807. Conclusive proof that the "Pacificator" articles were written by Banks is to be found in an article signed "Henry Banks" in the Richmond *Spirit of*

gained national prominence.[77]

Henry Banks, born in 1761, had become a wealthy patriot merchant by the close of the Revolutionary War. Extensive land speculations followed in the next decade and a half. He overreached himself by the end of the century and "came a cropper." In the first decade of the new century he resided in Richmond, practising as a lawyer, meddling in newspaper and political controversies, and expressing his views in the press on everything about which he had an opinion. His wife died childless in 1804. Thereafter he led a lonely life, interrupted only by his violent polemics in the Virginia journals.[78] He did not pull his punches.

Though non-partisan in the 1790's and early 1800's, his leanings had been toward Federalism. Gradually, however, he was won over to the support of the Jefferson administration. Meanwhile, the adventurous spirit of his earlier days combined with his solitude to glorify in his mind the great adventurer on the stage of Europe. An enemy of hereditary aristocracy and of "the wild theories of an unrestrained and licentious democracy," and believing that reason should rule,[79] Henry Banks found in Napoleon the answer to Europe's needs.

The eighteenth century longing of the European bourgeoisie for the enlightened ruler, the philosopher-prince, was vibrantly expressed in Banks' writings on Napoleon Bonaparte. Banks

---

'Seventy-Six of October 17, 1809. Similarity of views and phrases, plus a variety of other clues, in other writings under different pseudonyms also led to their identification as the work of Banks.

77 *V.* "Pacificator" in the *Virginia Gazette,* January 10, 1807.

78 *Résumé* of the Henry Banks Papers in the Virginia Historical Society by Elizabeth H. Ryland (courtesy of the Virginia Historical Society); ms. in my possession. Also see the genealogical article on Adam Banks of Stafford County by Mrs. P. W. Hiden in *Tyler's Quarterly Historical and Genealogical Magazine,* XV (July, 1933-April, 1934), pp. 122-3, 237-8; *Calendar of Virginia State Papers,* vols. III-VIII, items on Henry Banks; anti-"Pacificator" article by "An Impartial Native of England" in the *Virginia Gazette,* February 18, 1807.

79 "Candidus" in the Richmond *Recorder,* July 14, 1802.

believed that the coup d'état of Brumaire was necessary to save France. Since the French people were not fit for a republican or representative government, their leaders had the right to re-establish a monarchy. General Bonaparte was "elected" chief because of his distinguished talents and matchless achievements. It was also essential to select a person who, having no ties with the Old Régime, would not desire to take revenge for some of "the mad acts" of the revolution, and who would maintain its gains.[80]

If the right to power was determined by the ruler's contributions to the public weal, no monarch in any age or country ever had a better claim than Napoleon Bonaparte. He had ended the anarchy of the revolution and restored order and tranquillity to France. The personal and social rights of the individual were guaranteed. (Of course, the Napoleonic régime was not a tyranny.) Napoleon had done more to promote national prosperity in a brief period—despite the need to fight the coalitions—than the Bourbon dynasty during its entire history. The arts, science, commerce, industry, and agriculture were promoted. Canals and roads of great public utility were built. No part of France, with the exception of a few seaports, was exposed to the terrors of war. Napoleon's popularity in France was, therefore, almost unparalleled. Here was truly the philosopher-prince.[81]

Henry Banks believed that Bonaparte's foreign policy was in accord with this rôle. Great Britain and her allies had warred against him with the pretense that his ambition and power menaced the world with subjugation. But Napoleon, aware that all previous attempts had failed, was too wise to aim at universal dominion. He had set limits to his unequaled power: the Rhine and the seas. Why not, asked "Pacificator," declare, therefore, that Napoleon's enemies have fought because "the

80 *Sketches,* pp. 73, 83-4. "An American" in the *Virginia Argus,* April 25, 1806; reprinted in the *Lynchburg Star,* May 15, 1806.

81 *Sketches,* 51, 81; "Pacificator" in the *Enquirer,* March 14, 1806; "An American" in the *Virginia Argus,* April 25, 1806.

genius, the talents, the intrepidity and the energy of Bonaparte threaten to produce a new and philosophic aera? An aera, which will restore the rights of free government, and the blessings of civilization, to countless millions?"[82] The French armies came as liberators.[83]

Banks averred that Bonaparte's treatment of Austria disproved the charges of his boundless ambition. Three times that power threatened the peace of Europe and three times the completely victorious Napoleon restored her independence—Campo Formio, Lunéville, Pressburg. In the last treaty, the territories she lost were not added to France but given as rewards to France's German allies. The latter had thus become powerful, independent princes. What unprecedented clemency to a defeated state![84]

Another of the powers that presumed to animadvert on Napoleon's ambition and that joined the Third Coalition was ambitious barbaric Russia. "The Alarics, the Attilas, and the Odoacers, of the nineteenth century, promised to retrace the steps of their predecessors, and once more to overwhelm the south of Europe with barbarism, slavery, and ignorance. Arts, science and social order, were threatened with destruction."[85] If Russia and her allies conquered France, could they not do the same to the United States? Russia, not France, Henry Banks implied at times, was the world's menace. Napoleon was thus the last bulwark against the overgrown power of Russia.[86]

As Napoleon began to speak of "the federative states" of his empire, the gullible Banks became overjoyed. He compared Bonaparte's scheme with that of Henry IV. The purpose of Henry's plan, he asserted, had been war against the Turks;

82 "Pacificator" in the *Enquirer*, March 14, 1806.

83 *Ib.*; also "Pacificator" in same, June 10, 1806.

84 *Sketches*, 98; "Pacificator" in the *Enquirer*, June 10, 1806.

85 *Sketches*, 95.

86 "Pacificator" in the *Enquirer*, March 14, June 10, 1806; *cf.* "Pacificator" in same, September 9, 1807, *infra*, 246.

Bonaparte's was to preserve peace, thereby providing the ruler of each with an opportunity of promoting the arts, science, and civilization. Napoleon, unlike Henry, had the power to apply his project to the most important parts of Europe. His was not a design for world empire but for universal safety and happiness. (Here was to be an early nineteenth century League of Nations.) Had Bonaparte desired to extend his control over those countries which were to be included in the proposed federation, would he have restored their independence? Napoleon's ambition was to become the benefactor of mankind.[87]

The further reduction of the number of petty principalities in Germany with the creation of the Confederation of the Rhine was additional proof of Napoleon's ambition to become the benefactor of Europe. That continent would benefit if the petty principalities, oligarchies, and aristocracies of Germany, Holland, Switzerland, and Italy disappeared.[88]

The expulsion from Europe of the Turks, those "execrable monsters," who were "the scourges of some of the finest portions of the earth," might be another of the noble deeds that Napoleon would perform.[89] In common with other residents of *Respublica Christiana*, Henry Banks detested the infidels.

He asserted that Napoleon looked eastward. The fear of some Americans that Bonaparte, after having realized his schemes in Europe, would attempt to subjugate the United States was unfounded. Unable to invade England at the moment because of the inequality between the British and French navies, Napoleon would turn toward the east. The declining Ottoman Empire almost invited conquest. Turkey was on the high road to British India. The oppressed inhabitants of the Sublime Porte would receive an invading French revolutionary army with transports of joy. A liberated Turkey would aid

87 Anonymous communications to the *Enquirer* on "A federation of European states," July 25, 29, 1806; "Pacificator" in the *Virginia Argus*, August 30, October 1, 4, 1806.

88 "Pacificator" in the *Argus*, September 20, October 1, 1806.

89 *Do*. in the *Enquirer*, October 29, 1805; July 1, 1806.

France in the war against India. The overland trade routes to India would be reëstablished.[90]

The chief obstacle to the execution of Napoleon's beneficent foreign projects, according to Banks, was Great Britain, the power which oppressed Ireland, enslaved India, and organized the three coalitions. It was not the mass of the English people, but the English government—controlled by the king and cabinet in partnership with the opulent "money capitalists"—that was engaged in a war of extermination for the purpose of commercial advantages.

The English were the pirates and tyrants of the ocean. The pamphlet *War in Disguise* proved it. In contrast, Napoleon was fighting for the same principle as the Americans, namely, the freedom of the seas. Since France was not the aggressor, it had the right to prohibit all neutral commerce with Great Britain. The latter, however, had no right of retaliation. Within a few years, Bonaparte would be able to rebuild his navy with the assistance of the continental powers. "Perfidious Albion" would then be compelled to grant peace and the freedom of the seas to a tortured world.[91]

The United States, Banks maintained, should be neutral in the European war. It should under no circumstances ally with tyrannical Britain against the remarkable French leader. Bonaparte had no designs against us. France and the United States favored the same maritime principles. Furthermore, while France was friendly toward us, Britain committed one outrage after another: blockades, commercial restrictions, impress-

90 "Pacificator" in the *Enquirer*, June 27, July 1, 1806, and in the *Argus*, October 11, 18, 1806. Banks even suggested that Napoleon might restore the Jews to Palestine. See my article "Napoleon I As The Jewish Messiah: Some Contemporary Conceptions In Virginia" in *Jewish Social Studies*, vol. VII, no. 3 (July, 1945), pp. 275-280. Permission to reprint portions of this article was granted by the editors of *Jewish Social Studies*.

91 On England *vs.* Napoleon, see especially: *Sketches*, 80, 85-6, 100; "Pacificator" in the *Enquirer*, June 27, 1806, and in the *Argus*, August 9, 13, 16, 23, September 6, 1806.

ment. British aggressions against us were, however, curbed by French victories in Europe.

When a French-directed world commercial blockade of England seemed imminent, Banks urged the United States to support it, his previous insistence on American neutrality notwithstanding. If the United States refused, it would be declaring war against virtually the entire civilized world contending for the freedom of the seas. It would thereby become a tributary of Britain. France would retaliate by having American commerce excluded from every port in every continent where her influence was felt.[92]

Henry Banks concluded his appraisal of Napoleon Bonaparte on one occasion as follows: " No man in any age or clime ever performed so many great actions, in so short a time, as those which have been achieved in the career of Bonaparte. No man was ever more terrible in battle, or more clement in victory. He has been the Saviour of France, the promoter and patron of arts and industry. Thrice has he given peace to the continent of Europe. . . . In all these things, he has proved, that he cherishes the exalted and laudable ambition of becoming, not only the pacificator of Europe, but the benefactor of mankind." [93] The Napoleonic legend was in existence.

. . . .

Though commendation of Henry Banks' scholarship and literary ability could be found in the Republican journals of the Old Dominion,[94] few agreed with his interpretation of the Napoleonic régime. Republican opinion of the French govern-

92 On the American position in the European contest, see especially: *Sketches*, 100; "An American" in the *Virginia Argus*, May 2, 9, 20, 27, 1806; Banks to Jefferson, July 20, August 5, 1806, in *Jefferson Papers*, LC, vol. CLX, pp. 28078, 28152; "Pacificator" in the *Argus*, October 25, 29, 1806.

93 *Sketches*, pp. 98-9. For a more detailed treatment of Banks' opinion of Napoleon see my article "Henry Banks: A Contemporary Napoleonic Apologist in the Old Dominion" in the *Virginia Magazine Of History And Biography*, vol. LVIII, no. 3 (July, 1950), pp. 335-45. Permission to reprint portions of this article was granted by the editor of the *Virginia Magazine Of History And Biography*.

94 *E. g.*, the *Lynchburg Star*, August 14, 1806.

ment, on the whole, remained unaltered during the period May, 1806-February, 1807. Most Republicans continued to castigate Bonaparte for having betrayed the revolution, checked its progress outside of as well as in France, and provided a highly dangerous example for the future.[95] His government was a monarchy—and republicans hated kings.

But when thinking in terms of Napoleon's monarchical enemies, they sometimes charged England and her allies with having created Napoleon. They described how the crowned heads of Europe, hating republican government, had combined to extirpate it in France. This produced extreme suspicion among Frenchmen and, consequently, the reign of terror—equivalent to anarchy in most minds by 1806. This, in turn, paved the way for a military adventurer.[96] Or else, the argument ran: the coalition aroused the military spirit in France, providing the necessary environment for Bonaparte.[97]

There was likewise no change in the Federalists' opinion of France's domestic organization and policy. They continued their vitriolic denunciation of the French régime; but their censure of Bonaparte was coupled with that of the revolution. The Norfolk *Publick Ledger*, commenting on the French decree which established the rules governing the princes of the imperial family, wondered how the bloody regicides—if any of those miserable " wretches " were still left in France—felt on learning of the reëstablishment of an hereditary nobility.[98] The sanguinary revolution had been in vain, concluded another editorial.[99]

That France was under the rule of a " ferocious despot " was common fare in Federalist journals. The Napoleonic despotism

95 *V. Lynchburg Star*, May 15, 1806; *Enquirer*, September 19, 1806.

96 And one despot was better than many. (That was an early Federalist view.) *Enquirer*, October 17, 1806.

97 *Virginia Argus*, December 30, 1806; January 6, 1807.

98 June 9, 1806.

99 July 18, 1806; reprinted from the Charleston *Courier*.

was so absolute, wrote Cowper, that in comparison "the power of the former monarchs of France was the extreme of mildness." [100] There was some hope, however. The Fredericksburg *Virginia Herald* asserted on one occasion that there was a limit to the ill-treatment a people could bear. Despotism would eventually be obliterated in France and the subjugator of Europe would be hurled from the throne he had usurped.[101]

The major interest of Virginians in the period May, 1806-February, 1807, however, was not the French régime but Napoleon Bonaparte's international policies. Was Napoleon a world menace? Was the United States in danger of French conquest? These problems became more acute for Virginians—and Americans in general—as Napoleon's power approached its apogee. The Federalists did not change their opinion; they had made up their minds in 1803. Neither did the small group of Quids. But most of the Republicans wavered and now frequently held views similar to those of their political opponents. Their fluctuating concern about Florida and the dispute with Great Britain was a major determining factor. Party lines were blurred in the ensuing confusion.

The Federalist sounding of the alarm that Napoleon endangered the world became more and more insistent as the months advanced. It filled the columns of their newspapers. The pro-British merchants were endeavoring to divert the attention of the American people from their differences with England toward France, thereby throttling any curbs on Anglo-American commercial relations. The French Emperor provided them with a continuous flow of ammunition. He was marching in seven-league boots. The Federalists convinced themselves of the truth of their propaganda. They appeared to be thoroughly frightened.

Despite Federalist denunciation of the killing of Pierce,[102]

100 December 31, 1806.

101 January 9, 1807; reprinted from a Charleston paper.

102 *Publick Ledger,* May 5, 1806.

opposition to the Non-Importation Act continued. The fact that it was in suspension did not matter. One of the chief and oft-repeated arguments against the measure was that it would trammel Great Britain, the champion of faith, law, and order, and the sole barrier against universal domination. Remove the British navy and the world would be ruled by the tyrant Bonaparte.[103]

The emerging continental system of Napoleon also worried Federalists. Yet they belittled its effects on Europe. Bonaparte's exclusion of British manufactures from Germany, wrote Cowper, would be of no significance, if his armies remained there much longer. What with requisitions, forced loans, and pillage, "the poor devils" would have nothing left with which to purchase British goods. In any case, the Norfolk paper asserted, the system was ineffective. British wares were bought and sold publicly in French cities. Was not the French army clothed with English manufactures? Cowper asked.[104] An editorial in the Fredericksburg *Virginia Herald* declared that the commercial war between France and England would ruin the world's commerce, including our own.[105] Merchants had cause for anxiety.

The Federalists discovered further proof of Napoleon's unlimited ambition in the territorial and constitutional changes he initiated on the continent. The Norfolk *Ledger*, for example, upbraided him for his decision to place his brother Louis upon the new throne of Holland. It is the natural fruit of the Jacobin revolution there, Cowper averred. That wild revolutionary group adopted the ideas of the French regicides and expelled their stadtholder and nobility. Behold the result! Instead of a legitimate prince, they now have an arbitrary ruler, appointed

103 This was the theme of a series of articles taken from the Boston *Repertory* and reprinted in the *Ledger* (*e.g.*, May 2, June 16, 1806). The articles portrayed the evils of French rule in the most lurid colors.

104 May 16, 1806.

105 May 30, 1806; reprinted from the Boston *Repertory*. *Cf.* the editorial in the *Virginia Gazette and General Advertiser*, June 4, 1806.

by a foreign despot. Instead of a native nobility, they will be supplied with foreigners, rapacious members of the Legion of Honor. It has of late become a favorite French maxim that small nations cannot exist without the protection of a great one. Practising this principle, France becomes this great nation and all her neighbors are small and require her protection. The existence and independence of smaller powers was heretofore secured by the balance of power. But, the editor maintained, when a nation seeks protection from another, it ceases to be independent.[106]

Federalists were naturally gratified by the formation of the Fourth Coalition. Prussia had at last been compelled to resist in self-defense, Cowper affirmed on November 10, 1806. Aware of France's might and the celerity and effectiveness with which she wielded that force, the editor stated, the coalition was presumably adequately prepared.

Within a week of the outbreak of hostilities, the Prussian army was in rout. The Norfolk editor at first refused to believe that such a powerful state, as he thought Prussia to be, could be defeated so easily.[107] Even Federalists, however, soon had to admit the Prussian disaster.

Edward Carrington, brother-in-law of John Marshall, and violent Federalist, showed no pity for Frederick William. In a letter on February 25, 1807, to Timothy Pickering of Massachusetts,—perhaps the most prominent Federalist in the country,—Carrington declared that that monarch was paying the just forfeit of his temporizing, dishonest, and pusillanimous policy. It was, however, unfortunate that the brave Prussians had to be involved in his punishment. Russia was no longer to be considered an obstacle to Napoleon's aggrandizement, Carrington asserted. If Russia had been powerful enough to oppose "the Monster," would she have permitted Austria and Prussia to be defeated? The strength of Russia had

106 Editorials on July 23 and August 22, 1806.

107 December 15, 1806.

always been overrated. Her population, though numerous, was—like the American—too widely dispersed to make possible the rapid mobilization of an efficient army. Britain was the only remaining barrier against the overwhelming power of Bonaparte. The American government, in negotiating a treaty with England, ought not, therefore, hamper her too much. In closing, Carrington proposed that the United States build up its navy.[108]

That the defeat of Prussia enhanced the Napoleonic danger to the United States was also the theme of the *Publick Ledger*. On February 11, 1807, it recommended to its readers an article reprinted from the Boston *Repertory*. The writer asserted that if Bonaparte continued his aggrandizement for three more years, and the British navy were destroyed or removed by peace, the conquest of the United States would be a simple matter. Napoleon had enough soldiers for the task. As soon as he conquered a state he enlisted the refuse of the cities to assist him in keeping their countrymen in subjection. He would discover no paucity of French patriots in the United States. Moreover, eighty thousand veterans could easily be transported across the Atlantic, the article affirmed. John Cowper urged Americans to heed the warning of the *Repertory* and arm to resist " the scourge and destroyer of all governments."

Napoleon's Berlin Decree was considered by the *Ledger* as aimed especially against the United States. Bonaparte could not enforce his blockade of Great Britain, the Norfolk paper stated on February 13; but his pirates would capture American ships on the charge that they were bound to blockaded ports. This was his retort to the happy termination of our dispute with England.[109] The French government could not forgive our crime of being independent. The sooner the United States armed in self-defense, Cowper warned, the better. By February 18 the editor could not find any words to express his abhor-

108 *Pickering Papers* (MSS., MHS), XXVIII, 48-9.

109 The Monroe treaty; *v. infra*, p. 217.

rence of such an unheard-of, monstrous atrocity against neutral rights. Prepared as he had been for almost any act of violence and injustice from France, he declared, he did not suppose it possible that she would proceed to such extremes. The Berlin Decree was conclusive proof that the "Imperial Corsican" endangered the United States.

Similar in viewpoint to the Federalists, but for different reasons, was the opinion of John Randolph of Roanoke. He defended his attitude toward the administration's foreign policy under the pseudonym "Decius" in the Richmond *Enquirer*. In an article on November 18, 1806, he criticized the pursuance of an aggressive policy against Britain, with whom the United States was then negotiating and where Pitt, the anti-American, had been replaced by Fox, the great liberal. But the administration, he complained, remained passive to Spanish aggressions. Randolph was, therefore, zealous in the House of Representatives in December, 1806, in carrying out a presidential suggestion [110] that the Non-Importation Act be suspended.

The emotional, pessimistic planter became despondent when tidings of the defeat of Prussia began to arrive. There was no obstacle left to French dominion over the continent, he wrote on December 5, 1806, to James Monroe. If the king of Prussia were to be the only sufferer, Randolph declared, he would not regret the monarch's downfall. But he dreaded the time when the conqueror, no longer finding employment in Europe, would direct his intrigues and arms against the United States. If another Austerlitz—as was very likely—had demolished Prussia, England's destiny was sealed. She would become an appendage to the continent or dwindle into insignificance.[111] By January 2, 1807, Randolph was worried lest Napoleon had already begun to move against America.[112]

When the extent of the Prussian disaster became known, Randolph fell into the depths of despair. He penned the follow-

110 Special message of December 3, 1806.

111 *Monroe Papers*, LC, vol. XIII, pp. 2263-4.

112 *Ib.*, XIV, 2365.

ing statement to Joseph H. Nicholson on February 15, 1807:

> I do, now, believe the destiny of the world to be fixed, at least for some centuries to come. After another process of universal dominion, degeneracy, barbarian irruption & conquest, the character of man may, two thousand years hence|*perhaps*|, [*sic*] begin to wear a brighter aspect. Cast your eyes back to the commencement of the French Revolution—recall to mind our hopes & visions of the amelioration of the condition of mankind, & then look at things as they are. I am wearied & disgusted with this picture, which perpetually obtrudes itself upon me.[113]

Here was expressed in greater intensity the disillusionment with which the nineteenth century had begun its career.[114]

Meanwhile, Monroe, who had been engaged in protracted negotiations in London, had been peppered by Randolph with letters urging him to run for the presidency and informing him that Madison was the administration's choice. The appointment of a joint negotiator—William Pinkney of Maryland—was humiliating to the ambitious ex-Governor. Monroe joined with the disgruntled baron of Roanoke in criticizing the administration's foreign policy but persisted in favoring his own. He reiterated his suggestion for pressure on both Britain and Spain at the same time. Monroe thought that France would now attempt to dishonor the American government and obtain as much money as possible.[115] He could not understand why France did not strive to settle the Spanish affair so as to leave the United States a free hand to defend her neutral rights against Britain. The United States supplied France with the produce of the West Indies. Napoleon, moreover, professed to

113 *Nicholson Papers*, LC, vol. III, pp. 1380a-b.

114 *V.s.*, p. 37.

115 To Jefferson, June 15, 1806; marked "not sent"; *Monroe Writings*, Hamilton ed., IV, 457-8.

vindicate the freedom of the seas. In comparison, the sum which could be expected for Florida was trifling.[116]

Monroe admitted for the first time, in a letter to Randolph on November 12, 1806, that a general despotism overspread most of Europe. The American government, he believed, would survive the wreck. He urged the Quid leader to be more tolerant of the Republican administration, because the American example served the cause of republicanism everywhere.[117] Monroe's enthusiasm for the French Emperor had lessened materially since the failure of the Spanish mission. Communication with Randolph had not helped to revive it.

By December 31, 1806, Monroe and Pinkney had signed a treaty—the so-called Monroe treaty—with the British government.[118] The ex-Governor attempted to convince Jefferson that his accomplishment was extremely significant. He asserted, in a letter to the President on January 11, 1807, that the British government had made concessions in its maritime pretensions at a time when its very existence depended on adhering to them.[119]

President Jefferson, in the meantime, had remained hopeful throughout the period (May, 1806-February, 1807) that there would be a settlement with England. Though the administration continued to be neutral in the European war, Jefferson informed Monroe on May 4, 1806, that the government leaned to the opinion that an English ascendancy on the ocean was safer for the United States than a French.[120] Jefferson did not,

116 To James Bowdoin, June 20, 1806; *ibid.*, 474. To General Armstrong, June 21, 1806; *Monroe Papers*, LC, vol. XIII, p. 2164.

117 *Monroe Writings*, Hamilton ed., IV, 489-90.

118 Samuel Flagg Bemis makes this scathing comment on the treaty: "It is a commentary on the inconsistency of partisan politics and on the political character of James Monroe that he should have signed this instrument so closely resembling the maritime articles of Jay's Treaty which he had once so despised." *A Diplomatic History Of The United States*, revised ed. (New York, 1942), p. 146.

119 *Monroe Writings*, Hamilton ed., V, 2.

120 *Jefferson Papers*, LC, vol. CLVIII, p. 27778. *Cf. s.*, p. 190.

of course, approve of Britain's attempt to control the seas. But as already indicated, the President recommended a suspension of the Non-Importation Act in December in order to permit the satisfactory completion of the negotiations.

Jefferson was also somewhat hopeful for a time about a settlement with Spain-France. He stated in July, 1806, that he believed that reason would probably prevail at Paris and Madrid over the passions which the Quids had attempted to arouse. The uncertain international situation on the continent might further encourage Napoleon to require Spain to grant us justice at least.[121] As the months passed with no apparent results, Jefferson attributed the delay to Spain, not to France.[122]

By December, 1806, the President thought that war with Spain was possible.[123] Yet the Republican leader did not seem to blame Napoleon for the impasse in the negotiations. He informed Senator Plumer in a conversation on December 27 that had Bonaparte been in Paris, the purchase would have been effected promptly.

Jefferson continued to express some agreement with the Emperor's European policy. He asserted, in the same conversation with Plumer, that Napoleon had no designs on us. The victory in Prussia had not altered Jefferson's rational conclusions. Whenever Bonaparte had remodeled Europe in accordance with his plans, the President continued, he would turn his attention to the conquest of San Domingo. It would perhaps be well for Europe if Napoleon conquered the whole continent; for it would undergo changes at his death which would be highly beneficial to itself and the world.[124] The final statement

121 *E. g.*, to Barnabas Bidwell, July 5; *ibid.*, CLX, 27995. To William C. C. Claiborne, July 10; *ib.*, 28027.

122 To T. M. Randolph, November 3, 1806; *Collections Of The Massachusetts Historical Society*, 7th ser., vol. I (Boston, 1900), p. 117.

123 To Caesar A. Rodney, December 5; *Jefferson Writings*, Ford ed., VIII, 497. To John Langdon, December 22; *Jefferson Papers*, LC, vol. CLXIII, p. 28617.

124 Plumer, *Proceedings*, 546.

was in response to Plumer's assertion that most of the Prussian people were indifferent as to who ruled them. It did not mean, therefore, that the philosopher of American liberalism positively approved Napoleonic imperialism. It indicated rather his dislike of the old régimes of Europe. In any case, the idea was spreading among Republicans.[125] Finally, Jefferson, on February 2, 1807, still considered Napoleon to be the champion of the freedom of the seas against British maritime pretensions.[126]

Jefferson's followers in his home state went their individual ways. Most of them oscillated between France and England. The degree of oscillation varied. Unity of opinion in the party concerning world developments was, therefore, lacking. Disunity was especially apparent during the first half of the period, *i.e.*, from May through September, 1806.

One end of the arc of the pendulum of opinion was extreme Anglophobia, combined with Francophilism. Most outstanding were the writings of Henry Banks. In harmony with this interpretation was a poem on the battle of Austerlitz in the *Virginia Argus* of May 9.[127] It depicted the military heroes of France led by the genius Napoleon.

125 *Cf.* the views of Ritchie and Monroe, *supra*, pp. 176-7.

126 Cabinet meeting, in *Anas*; *The Writings of Thomas Jefferson. . . .*, Albert E. Bergh, ed. (Issued under the Auspices of the Thomas Jefferson Memorial Association of the United States; Washington, D. C., 1907), I, 466. If Plumer's reports and Jefferson's cabinet memoranda are reliable, Henry Adams' assertion (*History . . . During The Administration Of Thomas Jefferson*, Bk. III, 422-6) that President Jefferson was angry with Napoleon in the winter of 1806-7 as a result of the second failure of the Spanish negotiations is exaggerated and premature. [*Vide* also Jefferson's memorandum of a cabinet meeting on December 15, 1806 (*Anas*; *Jefferson Writings*, Bergh ed., I, 465). In it he notes that a message urging an appropriation of money for distressed French was not sent, since Turreau had withdrawn his request.] Adams apparently relied largely on Turreau's complaints about the conciliatory policy of the administration toward England during that period. That, however, does not prove that the government was anti-French. Foreign ministers were hypersensitive.

127 Not in the editorial column.

His conq'ring sword the chief does wield,
The freedom of the land to shield
From Russian fetters; and to free
From British tyranny, the sea.[128]

Castigation of barbaric Russia as well as of Britain was becoming a part of pro-Napoleonic opinion.

The two Republican newspapers which oscillated mainly at this end of the arc from May through September were the Richmond *Impartial Observer* [129] and the *Virginia Argus.* The *Observer* of August 2, 1806, doubted whether Bonaparte could do as much evil as England, if he had control of the seas. An article from William Duane's *Aurora*—reprinted in the *Argus* on August 13 and in the *Observer* on the 16th—affirmed that Louis Bonaparte's accession to the newly-created throne of Holland was of no great significance. That country had merely changed masters. The stadtholder had been a puppet of England, the commercial rival and destroyer of Holland; Louis Bonaparte would rule for Napoleon. Whether Bonaparte conquered England or made peace, the article continued, the English people would tamely submit to Napoleon's noose. What difference was it to them who their ruler or tyrant was? Such views were not far from neutrality.[130]

On August 30, however, an *Observer* editorial asserted that the English government, fearful of the ideas of the French

128 Representative John G. Jackson described the European war as a bloody contest to decide whether the ocean was a British or international highway. Jackson to Madison, June 1, 1806; *Madison Papers,* LC, vol. XXX, no. 68.

129 The *Observer* was established on May 1, 1806, with Samuel Brooks as publisher. Beginning with the issue of June 7, 1806, it was published for Brooks by Thomas Pescud Manson, foster nephew of Edward Pescud of the Petersburg *Republican.* From January 19, 1807, till the date of the last issue located, that of July 2, 1807, Brooks published the paper.

130 *Cf.* the editorial in the *Lynchburg Star* of May 22, 1806, which proclaimed Napoleon an unprecedented genius, who, unfortunately, was a usurper. But, the editorial continued, he had chastised the continental powers for their villainy and their leagues, and now threatened the rotten aristocracy of the tottering, corrupt, and despotic government of Britain.

Revolution,[131] had formed a coalition of the royalty, clergy, and aristocracy of Europe to prevent the spread of representative government. The chief to whom France had entrusted the function of putting an end to the coalitions now found it necessary, not only to conquer those powers, but to guarantee their future good behavior and the repose of Europe by transferring their governments to persons whom he could trust. "Pacificator's" conception of Napoleon was spreading.

The *Argus* also shifted to Francophilism. In an editorial reprinted from the *Aurora,* it stated on September 20 that Britain desired to rule the world. Napoleon, on the other hand, would not conclude peace till he had compelled England to acknowledge the neutrality of the ocean.

But on September 27, when the editor of the *Impartial Observer* was apparently concerned about Spanish-American relations, he modified his views slightly. He did assert that Bonaparte's major interests were in Europe, San Domingo, and the Near East. He, nevertheless, warned his countrymen to be prepared for war, either with Spain or France or, what was still more likely, Britain.

Revolving around neutrality, though with a tendency toward the Francophobe end of the arc, were the editorials of Edward Pescud's Petersburg *Republican.* On August 14, Pescud reprinted the *Aurora* editorial which also appeared in the *Argus* and the *Impartial Observer* of August 13 and 16, respectively. Late in August, the *Republican* charged the European monarchs with having caused the transformation of France from a land of liberty to a military despotism, which was now the marauder of Europe.[132] On September 1, Pescud leaned precariously toward Britain. After reprobating Bonaparte for his growing power on the continent, the editor asserted that the only peace terms the French ruler would offer England would

131 See also the editorial of May 1, 1806.

132 Editorial reprinted in the *National Intelligencer* of September 5, 1806. It presumably appeared originally in an issue of the *Republican,* which is not available, *viz.,* that of August 28.

be those which reduced her, like Austria, to a nominal independence. Despite his deprecation of the British form of government, Britain's policy toward neutrals, and, in particular, her hostile and unwarrantable conduct toward the United States, Pescud hoped that Albion's spirit had not become so abased as to accept such humiliating terms. In other words, Pescud, like the Federalists, hoped that Britain would continue the war.[133] Pescud, however, favored a balance between England and France.[134]

Thomas Ritchie of the *Enquirer* voiced opinions from May through September which were more frequently favorable to the British government. Concern about Florida seemed to be uppermost in Ritchie's mind during this period. The *Enquirer* displayed extraordinary tolerance of British impressments on one occasion, justifying them in part by adverting to England's lack of sailors.[135] After all, Fox, the Englishman most admired in American liberal circles, was then Britain's foreign secretary. The editor was, therefore, hopeful of a settlement with England. On the other hand, he thought that France would not aid us in the Spanish question.[136] Ritchie had his doubts about Jefferson's Florida policy.

The *Enquirer* at first maintained and elaborated upon the view of the editorial of August 23, 1805,[137] that the territorial changes instituted by Napoleon might, after his death, redound to Europe's advantage—*e.g.*, the formation of a united Italy.[138] Shortly, however, Ritchie began to recant his indirect approval of Napoleon's foreign policies. He declared that Bonaparte's plan was to fritter the great empires into second-rate powers,

133 See also the issue of September 25, 1806.

134 *V. s.*, p. 201.

135 May 9.

136 May 13, 1806.

137 *Supra*, 176-7.

138 May 13, 1806.

while enlarging his petty neighbors. If he did not gain the latters' loyalty thereby, he appointed members of his family as their viceroys. Since Napoleon was creating small states as his neighbors and as parts of his so-called "federative empire," Italy would not be united. He could be of no benefit to western Europe.[139]

The editor soon introduced an amendment. If Bonaparte destroyed British maritime tyranny and established the rights of neutrals, that action would furnish some justification for his usurpations on the land. Napoleon might also bring civilization—the press, the fine arts, literature, manufactures, and commerce—to the lands under the control of the barbaric Mohammedans: southeastern Europe, the Levant, and north Africa. His object would be to extend French commerce or gain prestige. Though the inhabitants would still be "slaves" under Bonaparte, they would be better off than at present. He would thus resemble the Gothic or Tatar chiefs, who had been profanely called the scourges of God. The sword of France would be chastising the Turkish government for its crimes. These eastern territories would become independent after Napoleon's death. If such were Bonaparte's plans, he would evince less interest in American colonies. Ritchie pointed out that the immediate purchase of the Floridas from Spain might depend on Bonaparte's designs in the east![140]

Although the French Emperor had no serious intention at present of disturbing the peace of the United States, Ritchie wrote in an introduction to an article by "Pacificator" on July 1, 1806, "who will pretend to set bounds to his views on this side of the Atlantic, should he survive but fifteen years longer! Bonaparte hates us, for he hates our government. Thanks too to the friendly *gratitude* of monsieur Talleyrand,[141] who spares no effort to *exasperate* the prejudices of his master against us!"

139 May 27, 1806.

140 June 27, 1806.

141 Reference to Talleyrand's exile in the United States during the 1790's.

"Pacificator's" views angered Ritchie. In answer to an article by Henry Banks on the federative system, the *Enquirer* of July 29 contrasted Napoleon's plan with that of King Henry IV. Henry had desired to erect one great confederation for the whole of Europe with a federal legislature. Bonaparte, on the other hand, was only interested in the states under his immediate control. For them he planned a supreme, irresponsible federal executive in his own person.

Ritchie now wrote as a full-fledged Francophobe. He declared on August 1, 1806, that the British navy was the chief hindrance to Napoleon's ambition! Editorials during August and September castigated Napoleon for having become the new champion of monarchy, imposing a despot upon the degenerate Dutch and planning like changes for Germany and other states.[142] Rumors of an imminent Franco-Spanish invasion of Portugal enraged the Republican politician. Bonaparte did not have the pretext, Ritchie exclaimed, that Portugal had fought against France. If he was chastising Portugal for refusing to shut her ports against England, he was acting like an arbitrary tyrant. Every independent government had the right to regulate its own trade. How would Bonaparte's friends justify this usurpation? the editor asked.[143] He was thinking of the Non-Importation Act which was not yet in operation. Thomas Ritchie did not agree with those Republicans who were justifying French expansion by adverting to British gold and defensive imperialism.

The *Enquirer* stated on September 19 that one group of Republicans,—basing their conclusions on Napoleon's ambitious actions in Europe, his hatred of republics, his desire for "ships, colonies, and commerce," and his opportunity of interfering in our dispute with Spain,—feared an attack on the United States; while another group disagreed, averring that Napoleon looked to the Near East for colonies. The editor reached the fol-

142 August 12, September 12, 1806.

143 September 5, 1806.

lowing conclusion: "*Our own opinion* is, that Bonaparte will not readily relinquish *any* plan of aggrandisement which occurs, whether it is to the East or to the West; that his views are at present turned towards the Turkish Empire in which he will most probably be successful; but that should he be disappointed, he will cast his attention towards America; of course that we ought not neither [*sic*] be so confident as to dismiss all our caution, nor so suspicious as to indulge much apprehension." But it was a conclusion based on vehement distrust of the French Emperor.[144]

The overlapping of Republican and Federalist opinion reached its climax in two articles by "Alcibiades" of Hanover, a Tidewater locality. One was published in the *Enquirer* of September 30,[145] the other in the *Impartial Observer* of October 18. "Alcibiades" proposed an offensive and defensive alliance with Great Britain against France. The aim of American entrance into the war would be to conquer or, at least, to emancipate Spanish America to the Isthmus of Darien. Britain would cede Canada to us in exchange for the West Indies.

The pseudonymous writer attempted to justify his amazing proposition by charging France with being the aggressor in the present war, the reverse of the situation in the preceding decade. Bonaparte's hateful despotism had destroyed all republics. His federative system had scarcely any resemblance to Henry IV's plan. The latter was to have been an alliance of independent states to secure the peace of all; Bonaparte's system, with himself as supreme head, was one of dependence, slavery, and war. In a base sense of the word "peace," the federative system was a peace organization. If all opposition to the Corsican ceased, there would certainly be peace.

144 For other examples of Republican Francophobe opinion, *v.* the July 4 oration of Peter V. Daniel, reported in the *Enquirer*, July 8, 1806. Also see the editorial of the *Petersburg Intelligencer* reprinted in the Fredericksburg *Virginia Herald* of June 13, 1806. It was probably in the *Intelligencer* for June 6 or 10, issues which are not available.

145 This article was also reprinted in the *Petersburg Intelligencer* of October 7 and the *Lynchburg Star* of November 13.

There had been but one ruler on the European continent since Austerlitz, " Alcibiades " continued. Trafalgar, however, had preserved one independent nation in the eastern world. That " ' little bit of land in the ocean ' " still stood as a bulwark against Bonaparte's plan of universal empire. Albion was fighting for her existence.

Although Napoleon had designs on the Ottoman possessions and might even imitate Alexander with an overland expedition to India, the writer averred, he still desired " ships, colonies, and commerce " in the western world. Let the United States, therefore, strike before it was too late. French victories were a consequence solely of the discipline and military skill of the French soldiers. The United States was compelled to become a military nation immediately or be subdued by France. A federal union of republics in the western world must be formed to counteract the federative system of subservient despots in the eastern world. The alternatives were peace and slavery or war and liberty! " Alcibiades " was an extreme exponent of Southern agrarian imperialism.

As a result of " Alcibiades' " articles and other factors the Republican pendulum of opinion on European developments began to swing away from the Francophobe end of the arc. The views of " Alcibiades " seemed to perturb those Republican editors who had been showing dangerous proclivities toward the pro-British Federalist interpretation. Rumors of a Franco-Russian agreement to revive the principles of the armed neutrality seemed to justify Napoleon's posing as the champion of a free sea. Furthermore, the " Decius " letters of John Randolph of Roanoke aroused the Jeffersonians. The President's pacific Spanish policy was reënforced by party loyalty. The retreat of Spanish troops beyond the Sabine [146] also subserved that policy. Most Republicans in the Old Dominion did not at the time really wish to become entangled in the European imbroglio.

146 They had crossed it in the summer of 1806.

The shift in opinion was noticeable in the editorials of Pescud and Ritchie. At first, both—the Richmond *Enquirer* on October 10 and the Petersburg *Republican* on October 16—combined censure of Napoleon with praise. The former journal declared that the establishment of the Confederation of the Rhine in reality violated Napoleon's promise not to extend the boundary of France beyond the Rhine. The latter feared that "the Queen of the Isles" would sooner or later be conquered. Pescud hoped that Bonaparte would be checked on the continent as well as in his war with England. But both Ritchie and Pescud asserted that if Napoleon really planned to emancipate the seas, Americans wished him complete success in that important endeavor.

On October 17, Ritchie revived his idea that Napoleon was "a *scourge* sent into the world to chastise vice into better order." Any change in Europe—*e.g.*, in the organization of Germany, which combined extreme weakness in the executive with petty despotism over the people—would be for the better. If France and Russia agreed to partition Turkey and establish a maritime confederacy for the protection of neutral rights, Napoleon, the most selfish and ambitious man alive, must be applauded. The editor seemed temporarily to have lost his fear of Russia.[147]

The Petersburg *Republican* went farther along the road toward Napoleon on October 20. Pescud, in a review of the events of the year since he became editor, affirmed that, in 1803, England had renewed the war which the kings had begun with the Declaration of Pillnitz. British intrigues and gold incited the formation of a new coalition. At Austerlitz, Bonaparte was the avenger of his country against monarchical aggressors. England, contrary to the law of nations, instituted by mere proclamation a shameful system of blockade against European ports closed to British trade. The editor, nevertheless, lamented the fact that England was plunging headlong to the brink of that yawning gulf which the conspirators at Pill-

147 See his editorial of March 3, 1807. *Cf. supra*, p. 172.

nitz had decided should be the fate of France. Pescud warned Americans to beware of treacherous Europe.

All Republican newspapers in Virginia, consequently, repudiated "Alcibiades'" propositions. For example, the *Republican* warned Americans not to embrace a certain evil, an alliance with Britain, to prevent an imaginary danger.[148] The *Enquirer* proclaimed its unalterable opposition to an alliance with the corrupt English government.[149]

Out of the welter of opinion emerged the underlying repugnance of Republicans to the continuing bloodshed in Europe. They considered it an inevitable concomitant of monarchy. Rumors of a new coalition amazed them. France was invincible, they maintained.[150] The *Enquirer* of October 31, 1806, suggested that the best method of weakening the harmful military propensity of France was to lull it to rest!

Napoleon's swift, decisive, and shattering defeat of the Prussians did not curb the hostility of the Republican editors toward England and the coalition. They characterized the defeat of Prussia as retributive justice for Pillnitz. They pointed to the death of the Duke of Brunswick at the battle of Jena as proof. No one shed any tears for Frederick William of Prussia, considered by Republicans and Federalists alike as dishonest and greedy. Republicans, however, displayed some joy at the discomfiture of the Federalists. To the former, Britain was just as grasping as the Corsican. The only difference between the two powers was in the degree of their success. The French

148 October 27, 1806; see also issue of October 16.

149 October 24. James Graham, editor of the *Lynchburg Star*, doubted whether "Alcibiades" was serious! (November 13, 1806.) Only two articles in the Republican press defended "Alcibiades'" ideas either partially or entirely; in the *Impartial Observer*, October 4, November 8, 1806.

150 *E. g.*, *v.* the *Virginia Argus*, November 11, 1806. Only John Dickson of the *Petersburg Intelligencer*—extremely concerned about the Florida problem (*v.* editorial of September 30, 1806)—believed that Napoleon might be defeated, if Prussia were aided by the other great continental powers; editorials of December 2 and 12, 1806.

advance toward Poland reminded Republicans of their detestation of the partition of that country. That act of gross political immorality, they maintained, was succeeded by others, such as the Declaration of Pillnitz. Now Napoleon was planning to reëstablish Poland, another deed of justice against her despoilers. Republicans could not decide whether the Poles themselves would benefit. But they did agree that Napoleon, the product of the coalitions against republican France, was useful as a scourge for kings, those abominable beings who oppressed mankind.[151]

The Prussian campaign did, however, revive fears of the French Emperor among many Republicans. An original editorial in the Richmond *Argus* declared that that ambitious man might even endanger the United States.[152] John Dickson, editor of the *Petersburg Intelligencer*, was petrified. He was astounded at what he believed to be the immensity of the French victory. The United States, on the verge of war with Spain over Florida, he declared, should not be surprised to discover that its turn was next.[153] It was, nevertheless, the general belief of Republicans that if the Napoleonic despotism attacked the United States, republican patriotism, as in France in 1793, would stand as firm as a rock.[154]

Only the *Impartial Observer* applauded Napoleon wholeheartedly. An editorial on January 5, 1807, averred that the most general and permanent peace in centuries would now

151 *E. g.*, *Virginia Argus*, December 19, 1806, January 6, February 6, 1807; *Lynchburg Star*, January 1, 1807; *Enquirer*, February 20, 24, 1807.

152 February 6, 1807. The journal had presumably hired an editorial writer at the close of 1806 after years of dependence on other newspapers for editorial opinion.

153 December 19, 23, 1806; *v. s.*, n. 150. Thomas Ritchie thought that war over Florida was possible, now that Bonaparte had been victorious in Europe. That was, however, only for a moment (December 27, 1806). Ritchie did not commit himself in an editorial on February 20, 1807, as to whether Napoleon was a threat to the western hemisphere. He merely stated that some thought Bonaparte did endanger this hemisphere.

154 *E. g.*, *Virginia Argus*, February 6, 1807.

come into being. The madness and wickedness of the European despots had elevated Bonaparte to a pitch of power superior to their united strength. The Emperors of Austria and Russia owed their crowns, and even their lives, to his clemency. Napoleon, the article continued, was appointing rulers who would aid him in establishing tranquillity in Europe. The condition of the people could not be rendered worse but, in almost every case, better. Napoleon would then establish the freedom of the seas. How could Federalists in the presence of such facts, asked the writer, describe Napoleon as a menace to the United States? This eulogy of Napoleon Bonaparte, in the style of Henry Banks, was not to be unexpected in a Republican newspaper that was to defend Aaron Burr. Romantic Americans thrilled with delight at both adventurers—the brilliant and successful Corsican as well as his unsuccessful imitator, the American Don Quixote.[155]

From Berlin, Napoleon issued his famous decree against British commerce. The Republican press treated the measure in the same way as other European developments. Criticism of it was tempered with animadversions on British commercial policy. The *Virginia Argus* described it on February 17, 1807, as a stupid and impertinent bravado, which would hurt neutrals. But, the editor affirmed, the English started it in the previous decade in their attempt to starve France.[156] In the same issue, however, the *Argus* reprinted the February 13 editorial of the Federalist *Publick Ledger*.[157] Three days later the *Argus*, adumbrating the embargo, stated that Britain, in violation of neutral rights, might retaliate. In that case, the two belligerents would have declared war against the entire human race. According to the editor, the only possible reply the United States could make would be the cessation of all commerce with them until they returned to sanity. Thomas Ritchie admitted on

155 William Wirt's characterization of Burr. Wirt to Ninian Edwards, February 2, 1807; Edwards, *History Of Illinois*, 422.

156 *Cf. Lynchburg Star*, February 26, 1807.

157 *V. s.*, p. 214.

the same day that Bonaparte had a right to exclude English goods from ports under his jurisdiction. If this ambiguous decree, however, meant that neutrals could not trade with Great Britain, it was the most flagrant violation of neutral principles that the world had ever witnessed. English aggressions, the *Enquirer* concluded, were no justification for French.

At Washington, however, American foreign policy was taking an anti-English form. On February 19, 1807, President Jefferson transmitted to Congress a letter from Decrès, the French Minister of Marine, to John Armstrong, the American envoy to Paris, assuring him that the Berlin Decree would not apply to American commerce, which would still be governed by the Treaty of Mortfontaine. The American government accepted that explanation temporarily, but urged Armstrong to obtain Napoleon's confirmation of that interpretation.[158] Monroe's treaty, which arrived as Congress was about to adjourn, was not even submitted by the President to the Senate. Jefferson declared to a joint congressional committee on March 3 that such a bad treaty could have been signed only under the misapprehension that the Berlin Decree would make war between France and the United States inevitable and that, therefore, the United States had to make common cause with England.[159] To prove his desire for conciliation, however, the President continued the suspension of the Non-Importation Act.[160]

About ten days later arrived the British Order-in-Council of January 7, 1807, cutting short the neutral coasting trade between France and her allies. The Secretary of State wrote a letter on March 31 to James Monroe, castigating this measure. A note appended to the Monroe treaty by the British negotiators had reserved to England the right to retaliate against the

158 Madison to Armstrong, May 22, 1807; *Madison Writings*, Hunt ed., VII, 446.

159 Charles F. Adams, ed., *Memoirs Of John Quincy Adams*, I, 466.

160 See his letter to James Bowdoin, April 2, 1807; *Collections Of The MHS*, 7th ser., VI, 372.

French decree and to refuse the ratification of the treaty, if the United States did not oppose the Berlin Decree to the satisfaction of the British government. In the letter, Madison denounced as unjust the claim to retaliate against the United States for the injury France inflicted upon Great Britain. That injustice, he continued, was aggravated by issuing the retaliatory order even before the British government could know how the American government had reacted to the decree.[161]

Though neutrality was still the lodestar of the administration,[162] it leaned precariously toward France in the next several months. Florida was the constant in Jefferson's foreign policy. The President informed Plumer on March 4 that our negotiation with Spain for the Floridas would make no progress until Napoleon returned to France.[163] The Republican leader, defending his rejection of the British treaty in a letter to the ex-minister Livingston on March 24, made the significant assertion that the Emperor could not be dissatisfied with the new turn in Anglo-American relations. Bonaparte, he wrote, must rather be pleased with our unhesitating rejection of a proposition—the note to the Monroe treaty—to make common cause against him.[164] Jefferson was pursuing his usual policy of playing off France against England for the affections of the American Republic. How little did he realize their current lack of interest! Jefferson, therefore, expressed a hope on April 2 that Napoleon would either compel Spain to do us justice or abandon her to us.[165] The note of impatience at the procrastination was more apparent in Madison's instructions to Armstrong on May 22, 1807.[166]

161 *Madison Writings*, Hunt ed., VII, 405-7.

162 Jefferson to Tench Coxe, March 27, 1807; *Jefferson Papers, Coolidge Collection*, MHS.

163 Plumer, *op. cit.*, 641.

164 *Jefferson Papers, Coolidge Collection*, MHS.

165 To James Bowdoin; *Collections Of The MHS*, 7th ser., VI, 372-3.

166 *Madison Writings*, Hunt ed., VII, 447-9.

President Jefferson's followers in the Old Dominion accepted the shift in foreign policy. They approved the summary disposal of the British treaty. William B. Giles, now a United States senator, expressed the sentiments of the Republican party when he wrote to Monroe on March 4 of his opposition to the treaty and asserted that the only ones in favor of forming an alliance with Great Britain or taking any part in the war whatsoever, before being absolutely forced to do so, were the Anglican party (the Federalists) and a few eccentrics (the Quids). The French decree alone did not justify such concessions on the part of the United States, he concluded.[167]

The original hesitancy among Jefferson's followers with regard to the import of the Berlin Decree continued for a while despite the letter of the French Minister of Marine. There were doubts as to whether Decrès' interpretation was authorized[168] and whether it would be observed.[169] But as anger against Great Britain increased in the succeeding months,—editorials censuring British commercial policy became frequent in the Republican press,—it became customary to accept the statement of the French Minister as definitive.[170] The only hindrance to a positive pro-French attitude with reference to Franco-American relations was the still undecided question of the Floridas.[171]

But John Randolph of Roanoke believed that the administration was already sufficiently pro-French. He wrote on March 7 to his friend Garnett that he was not surprised at Jefferson's action toward England. He charged that the government was fearful that approval of the treaty would affect the Florida

167 *Monroe Papers*, LC, vol. XV, p. 2473. *Cf.* the *Enquirer's* endorsement of the President's attitude, March 13, 1807.

168 Representative William A. Burwell's circular to his constituents, dated March 2, 1807, in the *Lynchburg Star*, March 26, 1807. *Cf.* the *Virginia Argus*, February 27, 1807.

169 *E. g.*, *Enquirer*, March 13, 1807.

170 *E. g.*, *vid. Virginia Argus*, April 14, 1807; *Enquirer*, May 12, 1807.

171 The *Enquirer* stated on April 24, 1807, that war with Spain was possible and that Bonaparte might be bound to assist Spain in that event.

negotiations adversely! The administration was afraid to displease France. No adjustment of our differences with Great Britain was, therefore, to be expected. "Will a Polish diet dispute the commands of a Russian minister?" Randolph asked rhetorically. "In eighteen months (or less) we may be parties to the war, with a French alliance around our necks."[172]

The Federalist *Publick Ledger* expressed more moderate views on the Monroe treaty. But the editor did criticize the President for not submitting it to the Senate. It would be more difficult to obtain a treaty in the future, Cowper maintained, and especially one as beneficial as the Monroe agreement.[173]

Cowper was on the defensive with regard to England's commercial policy. He was chary of comments. But he attempted to justify Britain in a moderate editorial on March 30. The immense carrying trade of the United States, the editor declared, arose during the war as a result of British maritime supremacy. Since this was a war of extermination, Great Britain could not view the advantages France derived from the American flag without great anxiety. France did not respect neutral rights when she could hurt her enemy thereby. France had most extravagantly forced neutrals, whose prosperity depended on commercial intercourse with Great Britain, to exclude British ships and products. She had not attempted such outrageous acts against the United States only because of our geographical situation, which was rendered more secure by the British navy. Cowper, however, concluded these remarks by denying that he intended to pass judgment on the conduct of the belligerents, against whom the United States as a neutral would have abundant and just causes of complaint!

Federalist hatred of Napoleon was, nevertheless, unabated. Partisans continued to berate his character. They animadverted

172 *Letters of Randolph and Garnett*, LC, p. 17.

173 *Vide* the editorials of March 13, 30, and April 20. In his attempt on March 13 to minimize the significance of the appended note to the Monroe treaty, Cowper even accepted at face value the French declaration that the Berlin Decree did not apply to the United States.

on the fraudful policy of which he boasted,[174] on his egotism and self-praise,[175] and on his crimes.[176] They employed the *odium theologicum* against him. Napoleon was identified with the Horned Beast of the Apocalypse (xiii, 11-13) in an article in the Fredericksburg *Virginia Herald*.[177] An article in the *Publick Ledger*, back in October, 1806, had used the last verse of the same Biblical chapter to prove that the name "Napoleon Buonaparte" had three times six letters like that of the Beast. His name, the article averred, also contained that of Apollyon, or Apoleon, the Destroyer.[178]

In the late winter and the spring of 1807, all eyes were focused on the clash of the armed hosts in the swamps of East Prussia. Cowper found a word of praise on March 9 for the "manly determination" of Frederick William to conquer or fall with his people. Europe was becoming aware that its safety depended on resistance to the French, the editor asserted with pleasure. Meanwhile, reports were coming in of diseases afflicting the French troops and of French reverses. Perhaps it was the beginning of the end, Timothy Green's *Virginia Herald* suggested on March 13.[179] The editor of the Norfolk *Ledger* was not yet so sanguine. All he deduced from the news on the same day was that Napoleon's situation was extremely critical. Napoleon was now at the mercy of Austria, the editor stated correctly. But when "his wonderful military talents, the experience of his Generals, and the unexampled discipline of his

174 *Publick Ledger*, May 22, 1807.

175 *Virginia Gazette and General Advertiser*, May 6, 1807.

176 *Ib.*, March 7, 1807.

177 April 10, 1807.

178 Issue of October 22. The article was reprinted from a non-Virginia newspaper. "Y-Z," most probably Henry Banks, had replied to such etymology in the *Virginia Argus* on November 28, 1806. On the basis of the Italian derivation of "Buonaparte," the writer stated that the name meant "a good and beneficent destroyer, or innovator; or, in other words, the friend or benefactor of mankind." "Y-Z," however, declared that he placed no confidence in the etymology of words as a means of judging an individual.

179 Reprinted from the Baltimore *Federal Gazette*.

armies" were taken into consideration, the chances of a Napoleonic victory in a general action were great. Cowper pointed out, however, that the Fabian mode of warfare adopted by the Russians prevented Bonaparte from taking advantage of his disciplined troops.

When complete information of the battle of Pultusk (December 26) reached the Norfolk editor, he affirmed (April 13, 1807) that it amounted to a defeat for the French, since they appeared now to be on the defensive. A defensive war in enemy country would find timid friends converted into bitter enemies. ". . . The impetuous career of Buonaparte is at last checked," John Cowper exulted. What a contrast to the previous war against Austria! If the latter joined the Russians, the editor concluded, Napoleon's ruin was inevitable.

Preussisch Eylau (February 7-8), one of the bloodiest battles in history, was pronounced indecisive by the *Publick Ledger* on April 24. But Cowper affirmed that the Russians had shattered the belief in Napoleon's invincibility. The difficulties of the French were greater than at any other period. The problem of drawing recruits from distant France was not diminished by the use of soldiers from conquered countries, for such men were not reliable in case of disaster. By May 4 the Norfolk journal seemed convinced that Napoleon had been defeated. Immediately, however, a new worry arose; but it was promptly quashed. Cowper thought that Bonaparte would attempt to frighten Austria by adverting to the Russian menace. ". . . Surely it must be acknowledged that if the Russians can ruin the army of Buonaparte, that Europe must rely much on he[r] moderation. At the same time Russia can only be *suspected* whilst France is *known*." Here was the attachment to the balance of power concept so dear to British diplomacy. The *Ledger* of June 10, nevertheless, poked fun at the decimation of Napoleon's so-called invincible legions. Napoleon was, after all, the archvillain in the Federalist drama.

Republican opinion in Virginia concerning Bonaparte's relations with Europe, on the other hand, became more favorable to the Corsican. The new turn in American foreign policy swung the pendulum of opinion. Except for the small group of Napoleonic partisans, however, there was no love anywhere for Bonaparte.

The Republicans were becoming more consistent on the question of Napoleon's orientation. Thomas Ritchie, modifying his previous opinion, stated categorically that Bonaparte's ambition lay to the east, not the west. He maintained that Bonaparte could obtain "ships, colonies, and commerce" more easily from the rich and defenseless provinces of Turkey.[180]

Samuel Pleasants' *Virginia Argus* now reversed its position on the problem of Napoleon as a possible danger to the United States. The editor termed it remote and possibly imaginary. In contrast, British enmity was already manifest. Though he admitted that Napoleon seemed to threaten the inhabitants of Europe with subjugation, he asserted that the Emperor's power on the land might compel the tyrant of the ocean to give us justice.[181] Such was the practical factor creating the pro-French tendencies in the Republican party.

Is it any wonder that Republican editors, far more readily than the Federalist, tended to believe the French war bulletins? The English reports were considered unreliable. The Republican press, generally, expected a French victory. In nearly all Republican newspapers, therefore, Napoleon won the battles of Pultusk and Eylau.[182]

There was some Republican rejoicing over the discomfiture and disappointment of the "Royalists and Anglo-Federalists." [183] How could the Federalists, an *Argus* editorial asked,

180 April 17, 24, 1807.

181 May 13, 1807.

182 *E. g.*, *Virginia Argus*, April 14, 1807. Only Dickson's *Petersburg Intelligencer* thought that Bonaparte had lost the battle of Eylau. The situation of the French army, an editorial on June 5 stated, was extremely critical now. Dickson affirmed that if the allies maintained their unity, the French mastery of the continent would be ended.

183 *E. g.*, the Petersburg *Virginia Apollo*, April 18, 1807.

support the horrible members of the coalition: Russia, the most barbarous; Prussia, the most atheistic; and England, the most oppressive and bloody government in modern Europe?[184] The English régime was especially singled out for criticism by the Republican press.[185]

The opinion of most Republicans, however, continued to be that the war was, on the whole, a struggle of ambition, a conflict between kings and emperors, almost completely extraneous to the cause of freedom.[186] As a result of the bloody battle of Preussisch Eylau the Republican journals of the Old Dominion were replete with anti-war editorials. "Such," declared the *Virginia Argus*, "are the fruits of monarchy, and of those dreadful playthings of mighty monarchs, large standing armies." [187]

A decidedly pro-Napoleonic approach was, in contrast, taken by a writer "X" in the *Enquirer* of June 20, 1807. The friendly relations which Napoleon had established with the Ottoman and Persian rulers opened the prospect, the writer believed, of an overland expedition through those territories to India. By liberating India, Napoleon would ensure the freedom of the seas, the repose of Europe, and the long-violated rights of humanity. Europe and Asia might thenceforward be united by principles of common justice and mutual interest. Such views were of the school of Henry Banks.[188]

Two days later, on June 22, 1807, the British man-of-war *Leopard* committed an act of war off the Virginia coast against

184 May 20, 1807.

185 *E. g.*, *Argus*, May 13, 1807; *Enquirer*, May 15, 1807.

186 *Vide, e. g.*, the *Enquirer*, April 17, 1807.

187 April 21, 1807. Dickson wept bitterly in a lengthy editorial; *Petersburg Intelligencer*, May 8, 1807. The *Lynchburg Star* suggested as the best means of preventing future wars that the king, the nobility, the prominent generals, and all the other war-makers be placed in the front rank of the order of battle (April 2, 1807; reprinted from a non-Virginia newspaper).

188 See also the article signed "Z" on the battle of Pultusk in the *Virginia Argus*, March 27, 1807.

the American frigate *Chesapeake*. The Old Dominion rose up in a burst of nationalism. Party lines were temporarily forgotten. Mass meetings were held in towns and court-houses from Tidewater to Trans-Alleghany, offering the lives, fortunes, and sacred honor of the participants to the national government.[189]

Some Republicans believed that a war, under the circumstances, would have a beneficent influence upon the young republic. Representative John G. Jackson of the Trans-Alleghany wrote to his brother-in-law Madison on July 5 that a tame submission to such an outrage would disgrace the government and the Republican party. It would be a signal for every species of insult until the national spirit was broken. America would then take refuge from such wrongs in a military despotism under a Bonaparte or a Burr.[190] Wilson Cary Nicholas, now a representative, wrote to the President on July 7 that war would destroy that deadly party spirit that endangered the republic. Nicholas was still fearful of an American Napoleon.[191] He declared that he favored war despite his having wished for British success in her contest with France.[192] He could not have meant that he had desired a complete British victory.[193] Nicholas was a stanch Jeffersonian.

Even John Randolph of Roanoke allowed himself to be swept into the anti-British current. His first reaction to the *Chesapeake* affair, however, was anger at the administration. He expected it, he insisted, because of the change in the British

189 *E. g.*, the Richmond meeting on June 27, dominated by Spencer Roane, Ritchie, and other Republican party bigwigs; reported in the *Enquirer*, July 1, 1807.

190 *Madison Papers*, LC, vol. XXXII, no. 68.

191 *V. s.*, p. 166.

192 *Jefferson Papers*, LC, vol. CLXVIII, pp. 29669-70.

193 *Vide* Nicholas to ——, May 16, 1808; *Wilson Cary Nicholas Papers* (MSS., LC), vol. III, p. 663.

ministry and the administration's rejection of the British treaty. It was the result of the foolish policy of 1805-6.[194] Now that his endeavors to maintain peace, especially with Great Britain, had failed and the rupture had taken place, Randolph wrote to Garnett on August 31, he favored the most determined action against the enemy. It was to the interest of both countries to be at peace. " But that of England is *immediate* & urgent; of the U.S. [*sic*] (comparatively) *remote* & *contingent*." He was thus softening his previous warnings of the Napoleonic menace to the United States.

Randolph asserted that Britain was now paying the price of her sins; but the United States was not exempt from a partial penance for its follies. British tyranny and corruption begot the dismemberment of her empire, which in turn was the immediate cause of the French Revolution and of the gigantic power that now threatened destruction to the liberties of man and to the very existence of Great Britain as a nation. The destiny of Europe was sealed. France would become another Rome. The language and literature of England would be indebted to North America for their preservation. Good Lord, Randolph prayed, deliver us from a French alliance! That would be the forerunner of our subjugation. The day was not far distant when Americans would owe their exemption from the French yoke to their own valor, the planter of Roanoke again warned. Of what folly and villainy mankind was capable! All wars, murders, and robberies were the effects of human wickedness, Randolph concluded his letter to Garnett. The misanthropist—who excluded women from his hatred—was ready for evangelical religion.[195]

In spite of his fears of France, however, Randolph continued to express jingoish sentiments toward Britain.[196]

194 To Nicholson, June 25, 28, 1807; *Nicholson Papers*, LC, vol. III, pp. 1398a, 1398c.

195 *Letters of Randolph and Garnett*, LC, pp. 22-5.

196 See his addresses to the House during November and early December; *e. g.*, November 10, 1807 (*Annals of Congress*, 10th Cong., 1st Sess., I, 834-8).

Federalists also joined the anti-British clamor. The Norfolk *Publick Ledger* and the Richmond *Virginia Gazette and General Advertiser* demanded war. John Cowper and Augustine Davis entered military service temporarily.

But President Jefferson delayed the session of Congress until October 26. He hoped thereby to allow passions to subside, to permit American vessels to return home, and to give the British government an opportunity to disavow and make reparation for the attack.[197] He preferred non-intercourse—a pacific means of redressing injustice, he called it,—to war.[198] Though he soon doubted whether Britain would make ample reparation, and declared that hostilities might be forced upon the United States, on the whole, he did not change his preference for peace.[199]

As passions cooled, many Republicans began to prefer peace, if suitable reparation was forthcoming.[200]

John Taylor of Caroline supported those who urged caution. He criticized Randolph's attitude in a pacifistic letter to Garnett. Whether the war began rightly or wrongly, Taylor maintained, it would transform the government. If England continued to stand against French attacks, our war would lead to a Federalist or, rather, a monarchical administration in the United States. If France conquered England, he continued, our entrance into the war would be followed by a revolution and end in a despotism. In any case, it would be a war for honor, a "metaphysical war." It would terminate in the destruction of the last experiment in free government. No metaphysical war, Taylor continued in his abstruse vein, had ever benefited man-

197 To the Vice-President, July 6, 1807; to Governor Cabell, July 16, 1807; *Jefferson Papers, Coolidge Collection,* MHS.

198 To Cabell, June 29; to the Vice-President, July 6, 1807; *ibid.*

199 *E. g.*, to J. W. Eppes, July 12, 1807; *Jefferson Writings,* Ford ed., IX, 108. To Thomas Mann Randolph, July 13, 1807; *Jefferson Papers,* LC, vol. CLXVIII, p. 29718.

200 *E. g., vide* John Love's speech in the House of Representatives, December 3, 1807; *Annals of Congress,* 10th Cong., 1st Sess., I, 1034.

kind. How had all the wars for the balance of power ended? In the same way that this proposed war for a balance of power on the water would end. Taylor, therefore, proposed that the government temporize.[201]

Meanwhile, the Federalists had, chameleon-like, resumed their original colors. Henry Lee, the famous general of the revolution, offered military advice to Secretary of State Madison on July 19, but hoped that war could be avoided honorably.[202] By August, the Norfolk *Publick Ledger* was hedging on the need for war, and September found the editor turning against a war with Great Britain.

During the summer and fall of 1807 relations between the United States and Great Britain were in a state of suspension. Americans waited anxiously for England's reply to the demands of their government. Under the circumstances, the relations between the United States and France took on added significance. President Jefferson declared on July 10 that cordial friendship with France and peace, at least, with Spain were now more important.[203] The annual message (October 27)—delivered before Britain's reply was known—condemned Albion's outrages against the United States, but remarked indirectly on the friendly relations with France. Yet the President was still waiting for Napoleon's intercession in the Florida dispute.

The Republican leader thought that the British reply would be determined by the military developments in Europe. He wrote to his son-in-law, Thomas Mann Randolph, on July 13: "I suppose our fate will depend on the successes or reverses of Buonaparte. It is hard to be obliged to wish successes so little consonant with our principles."[204] Napoleon, after all, was a pariah in the eyes of the liberal leader. Furthermore, Jefferson

201 December 14, 1807; *Virginia Magazine Of History And Biography*, vol. LII, no. 2 (April, 1944), pp. 122-4.

202 *Madison Papers*, LC, vol. XXXII, no. 78.

203 To Bowdoin; *Jefferson Papers*, LC, vol. CLXVIII, p. 29690.

204 *Ibid.*, p. 29718. *Cf.* his letter to John Taylor, August 1, 1807; *Jefferson Papers, Coolidge Collection*, MHS.

had never positively approved Napoleon's continental imperialism.[205] French procrastination in the Florida negotiation might also have had its effect. French victories, nevertheless, were beneficial to the United States. Every time the President voiced such opinions, he felt compelled to apologize. He explained on August 21: "But the English being equally tyrannical at sea as he is on land, & that tyranny bearing on us in every point of either honor or interest, I say, 'down with England' and as for what Buonaparte is then to do to us, let us trust to the chapter of accidents. I cannot, with the Anglomen, prefer a certain present evil to a future hypothetical one." [206]

The Napoleonic victory at Friedland (June 14), Jefferson wrote to Madison on August 20, would be followed by peace on the continent, an army dispatched through Persia to India, and the main army brought back to its former position on the channel. This would compel England to withdraw everything home and "leave us an open field." [207] The Secretary of State replied that the French victory would act as a stimulus to an Anglo-American settlement.[208] Jefferson asserted on September 3 that only if the British were excluded from the Baltic area, would they be disposed to peace with the United States.[209] The President was thinking not only of England's need for the Baltic markets but also of her dependence on Prussian grain. With the latter source closed, American grain and flour would be especially essential.[210]

Despite the possibility of war with England, neither the Republican federal administration nor its following in the Old

205 His statement to Senator Plumer on December 27, 1806 (*v. s.*, pp. 218-19), is explicable by the character of the conversation.

206 To Thomas Leiper; *Jefferson Papers*, LC, vol. CLXX, p. 30007.

207 *Ibid.*, 29996.

208 September 3, 1807; *ib.*, 30080.

209 To Madison; *ib.*, 30079.

210 *Vide* Madison's instructions to Monroe and Pinkney, May 20, 1807; *ASP, FR*, III, 172.

Dominion thought of forming an alliance with the French Emperor.[211] Toasts were still offered to General Moreau, who was in exile in the United States.[212] The influential Richmond *Enquirer* even proposed on July 24, 1807, that Moreau be given the command of the American army of freemen in the impending war against Great Britain. No repudiation of Napoleon Bonaparte could have been more definitive.

Virginia Republicans, nevertheless, shared the administration's recognition of the usefulness of Napoleon to American foreign policy. There was no further talk of a war over Florida. There was no more concern about England's fate in the European conflict. The pendulum of opinion on European developments had now swung over to the Francophile end of the arc.

A series of articles by " A Citizen of Richmond " in the *Enquirer*, probably expressing Ritchie's opinion too, was typical of the new trend. The writer asserted that if France were defeated, English aggressions against the United States would increase.[213] If, on the other hand, Napoleon defeated Britain, and acted on the seas as tyrannically as the Federalists expected, he still could not treat the United States as outrageously as England had.[214] Bonaparte had not applied the Berlin Decree to us, the "Citizen" continued. France claimed to be fighting for the freedom of the seas. Until there was proof to the contrary, she merited our approbation. The United States and France had the same maritime goals. If France ended the war victoriously, the writer concluded, we would obtain better terms than in the recent British treaty.[215]

211 *Cf.* Turreau's complaints to the Minister of Foreign Affairs, September 4, 1807; *Affaires Étrangères, États-Unis*, LC, vol. LX, pt. 3, fols. 199-200.

212 See the toast by General John Minor at a Fredericksburg July 4 celebration; Fredericksburg *Virginia Herald*, July 10, 1807.

213 June 27, 1807.

214 July 11, 1807.

215 July 28, 1807. *Cf.* the *Virginia Argus* editorial of November 13, 1807, reprinted from the Salem *Essex Register*, refuting the Federalist charge that Napoleon was a danger to the United States.

Napoleon's victories were, consequently, acclaimed by Republicans. News of an armistice pleased even John Dickson of the *Petersburg Intelligencer*. Bonaparte, having won a decisive victory, would dictate the terms of peace, the editor affirmed. (No one realized that Tilsit was to be a negotiated peace.) England would better beware. John Bull, Dickson concluded, would have enough to do now without waging war on the American people. No more the old concern about the Napoleonic danger! [216]

Two days before learning of the *Chesapeake* affair, James Monroe, still negotiating in London, had also expressed the belief that French victories would aid American diplomacy.[217] On August 4, however, he informed the Secretary of State that there was a strong party in Britain eager for war with the United States—*viz.*, the shipowners, the East and West India merchants, the navy, and certain politicians, implying, *e.g.*, Canning. The disasters on the continent, instead of inspiring moderation in the British government, he complained, seemed to have had the opposite effect. Monroe pointed out that a powerful fleet had been sent to the Baltic to take possession of the Danish navy and, probably, the Russian also.[218]

Republicans at home were apparently unanimous in their interpretation of Albion's rôle in world history. That corrupt and perfidious country, they maintained, had formed four coalitions with her gold and wantonly sacrificed " hecatombs of human victims " for her maritime usurpations.[219] When the British navy bombarded Copenhagen and took possession of the Danish fleet, Republican condemnation was bitter and universal.[220]

216 September 8, 1807. In contrast, see his views in December, 1806; *supra*, p. 229.

217 Monroe and Pinkney to Madison, in Monroe's handwriting, July 23, 1807; *Monroe Papers*, LC, vol. XV, pp. 2633-4.

218 *Ib.*, 2653-4.

219 "A Citizen of Richmond" in the *Enquirer*, July 24, 28, 1807. See also, *e. g.*, Petersburg *Republican*, September 9, 1807.

220 *E. g.*, *Virginia Argus*, November 6, 1807; *Enquirer*, December 17, 1807.

Most Republicans now thought that Bonaparte's victory on the continent would redound to the benefit of Europe as well as the United States. That Napoleon had checked the forces of vandalism and barbarism by defeating Russia was the view of "A Citizen of Richmond" [221] and of Henry Banks in a "Pacificator" article in the *Enquirer* of September 9. Banks accused Russia of being the aggressor and described Napoleon as the avenger of Europe and Asia against expansionist Russia. Notwithstanding his "power without former example," the incomparable Napoleon would display clemency to the vanquished. Europe would now have peace.[222]

But Henry Banks was no longer in a small minority in his eulogy of Bonaparte's foreign policy. Circumstances had converted most Republicans, at least, temporarily. This, despite the fact that Napoleon had not changed an iota. Thomas Ritchie did not criticize "Pacificator" now. Edward Pescud, in his annual review of the news in the Petersburg *Republican*, declared on September 30 that English influence, bribery, and corruption had been permanently extinguished on the continent! The editor maintained that Napoleon had finally secured "that peace for which Europe [had] sighed. . . ." John Dickson was now writing about "the valor, the genius, and the imperishable energies of the French Emperor." [223] The *Virginia Argus* of October 7, 1807, reprinted from the *Aurora* an article by "A Christian," which depicted Napoleon as a favorite of God. The writer claimed that Napoleon's treatment of foreign countries was marked by unequalled moderation and goodness. Could Henry Banks have asked for more? [224]

Federalist opinion of Napoleon, however, had not altered in the slightest; criticism of Great Britain had been short-lived.

221 *Enquirer*, June 27, July 28, 1807.

222 *Cf.* the article by "X" in the *Enquirer*, August 25, 1807.

223 September 22, 1807.

224 Even Bonaparte's domestic policy received some praise. *V.*, *e. g.*, the reprint in the *Virginia Argus*, November 20, 1807, from the Boston *Independent Chronicle*, applauding the economic progress of France.

Bonaparte was still the archfiend. John Cowper attempted in the Norfolk *Publick Ledger* of August 26 to refute the Republican belief that French victories subserved the foreign policy of the United States. Russia and Prussia, he stated, would most probably have to make peace on the best terms they could obtain under the circumstances. Great Britain would again be left to contend single-handed with the gigantic power of France. England, fighting for her very existence,[225] would permit no weakening of her navy, the bulwark of her safety. She would, therefore, never consent to the principle that the flag protects all that sails under it. This would probably be the demand of our government, if the French were completely victorious on the continent. We would thus have a war in spite and because of the French victories. Preparedness was the best means of preserving peace, the editor maintained. The world was in turmoil. If we were unprepared, we should deserve the fate of those nations, who were now groaning under horrible oppressions. The implication was almost clear. The United States had to be prepared against England *or* France.[226]

Continental developments continued to be interpreted by Federalists in an anti-Napoleonic vein. The *Publick Ledger* declared on September 7 that the armistice would probably be followed by a continental peace. Prussia was lost; she would probably receive a new dynasty. Poland would not be restored. Cowper asserted that Kosciusko and the deluded Polish patriots, who had flocked to Poland when Bonaparte entered it, would be disillusioned. Bonaparte had used them as long as he had needed them. He was not the man to bestow any portion of the fruits of his labors on patriots. On the twenty-first, the Norfolk paper stated that the Treaty of Tilsit might be considered " a prelude to the downfall of the Prussian monarchy, whose fate if the cause of nations was not involved, we should contemplate without regret." Federalists could not forgive the

225 *Cf. Winchester Gazette*, September 22, 1807.

226 Editorial reprinted in the Fredericksburg *Virginia Herald*, September 1, 1807.

Prussian King for his vacillation. When they learned that Russia was becoming hostile toward Britain, they directed their wrath against her. Green's Fredericksburg *Virginia Herald* of December 1 declared that it was a fundamental policy of the Russian government to finish its wars by fighting against its allies.

Federalist opinion of the Anglo-French commercial war as well as of continental developments was Francophobe. The Norfolk *Ledger* even attempted—though some hesitation was to be found—to justify the British attack on Copenhagen.[227] On November 2, Cowper characterized the Order-in-Council of January, 1807, as a measure of self-defense, while, on November 9, he asserted that French commercial policy was proof of her aim of world rule.

Rumors that France had applied the Berlin Decree to the United States and that the British government had issued a new order prohibiting all commerce with its enemies reached the United States in November. The Federalists immediately believed the rumor about France to be true.[228] According to the *Enquirer,* the Federalists were endeavoring to arouse our animosity against French commercial policies in order to divert our just indignation from the corrupt British government.[229]

There were, however, some Republicans who also believed the reports about France. Wilson Cary Nicholas wrote to the governor of Virginia, William H. Cabell, on November 20, ". . . It is not impossible that there exists at this very moment sufficient cause to justify this country in going to war with that nation as well as G.B. [*sic*] and every reason to believe that the effect of the regulations of the two nations will be to . . . deprive us of all commerce." The United States could not war with the whole world, he continued. The choice of enemies would create a risk of serious dissension. A considerable por-

227 See the editorials of October 7, 16, and November 16, 1807.

228 *Vide* the *Virginia Gazette and General Advertiser*, November 27, 1807.

229 December 17, 1807.

tion of Americans, he stated with exaggeration, would prefer a war with France and would willingly change our discussions with Great Britain into arrangements for an alliance against the former. Nicholas, however, opposed an alliance with any European power. He had no respect, he declared, for the honor or good faith of either England or France. France hoped to force us into the war as her ally by her hostile acts toward us. If we went to war with England, Nicholas concluded, the French decree would be inoperative, since all commerce with Britain would cease.[230]

More Republicans disagreed with the Federalists concerning the authenticity of the news. President Jefferson thought that the rumor about the English measure was almost probable, considering the known principles of the British government.[231] But he described the report of the extension of the Berlin Decree as a Federalist fabrication.[232] Though the basis of that conclusion was the character of the news report, the fact that the President still believed Napoleon to be interested in neutral rights [233] undoubtedly had its influence.

Ritchie of the *Enquirer* was apparently in accord with the leader of his party. An editorial on December 4, 1807, assumed that the interpretation of the Berlin Decree by the French Minister of Marine was still correct. Ritchie defended the edict as a justifiable municipal regulation, which did not violate the Convention of 1800. France did not construe the decree as a blockade of Great Britain or her empire. France did not stop, seize, and confiscate every neutral vessel bound to or from her enemy's ports. An American ship that touched at a British port and then went to Bordeaux, for example, was not con-

230 *Nicholas Papers,* LC, vol. II, pp. 562-3.

231 To Thomas M. Randolph, November 16, 1807; *Jefferson Papers,* LC, vol. CLXXII, p. 30466.

232 To Colonel Minor, November 25, 1807; *Jefferson Writings,* Washington ed., V, 215.

233 To William Duane, July 20, 1807; *ibid.,* 140.

fiscated but refused admission to Bordeaux. That was a municipal policy and, therefore, did not violate the rights of neutrals. England, the editorial concluded, consequently had the right to retaliate only with a similar municipal decree but not with a blockade of France.

But within a fortnight the United States found itself in the midst of the commercial war. The young republic was a part of Western Europe.

CHAPTER VII

WHO IS THE ENEMY? AN AGRARIAN REPUBLIC IN THE VORTEX OF COMMERCIAL WAR

(December, 1807-March, 1809)

ON December 18, 1807, President Thomas Jefferson submitted a special message to the United States Congress which was the beginning of a chain of events culminating in the War of 1812. The President's decision to propose an embargo was precipitated by a series of unpalatable occurrences. There was no hope of a treaty with Britain; Monroe was finally returning home.[1] On December 16, 1807, arrived the official information concerning the royal proclamation of October 17, which required all British naval officers to exercise impressment against neutral ships to the limit. Rumors that the English government was about to issue a new Order-in-Council aimed at American commerce became more persistent in December. Finally, it was learned on December 17 that the Berlin Decree was now being enforced against the United States in spite of the Convention of 1800. Commercial warfare was now the order of the day in the western world.

The situation, however, was not completely dark. An opportunity for solving America's external difficulties without resort to war had apparently arisen.

The embargo, which the Republican leader proposed on December 18, had a dual character. In one sense, it meant virtual economic isolation. In another, it represented a policy of economic sanctions against the two major European belligerents. Though the embargo was apparently to be impartial, depriving Great Britain of American produce and a market, and France of her West Indian produce as well as a market, the former would bear the brunt of the economic pressure. England's

1 A special British envoy, George Rose, was, however, on his way to Washington to settle the *Chesapeake* affair. The mission came to naught.

closer commercial relations with the United States and her mastery of the seas ensured that result.[2]

The need for the embargo was confirmed by the receipt in 1808 of the new British Orders-in-Council of November, 1807,[3] and of the Milan Decree. By means of the first the British mercantile oligarchy hoped to acquire a monopoly of the commerce with the European continent. Neutral trade with the continent was permitted only on condition that the neutral vessel stop *en route* at an English port. It was the " old colonial system " in another guise. The Milan Decree of December 11, 1807, was Napoleon's method of retaliating against the latest English orders. This decree definitely extended the application of the Continental System to the sea. Every ship which submitted to the Orders-in-Council was now lawful prize at sea as well as in port.[4] Neither Britain nor France hereafter recognized any neutrals.

Jefferson's whole moral fibre was aroused. To the philosopher of the Age of Reason Europe was now in a " paroxysm of . . . insanity." [5] " Those moral principles and Conventional usages," he wrote to a Virginia Baptist association, " which have heretofore been the bond of civilized nations, which have so often preserved their peace by furnishing common rules for the measure of their rights, have now given way to force, the law of Barbarians, and the nineteenth century dawns with the Vandalism of the fifth." [6] Under the circumstances, it was best to sever all intercourse with Europe.[7]

2 Besides, the Non-Importation Act had gone into effect on December 14.

3 The most important was that of the eleventh.

4 *Vid.* Heckscher, *Continental System*, pp. 90-1, 123-4.

5 To Kosciuszko, May 2, 1808; *Jefferson Papers*, LC, vol. CLXXVII, p. 31380.

6 To the members of the Ketocton Baptist Association, October 18, 1808; *ibid.*, CLXXXI, 32233.

7 Such views were repeated in numerous public and private letters justifying the embargo.

The President yearned for peace. There was no sense in fighting maniacs, he wrote.[8] The embargo might bring the belligerents to terms with us or, at least, postpone war till peace came to Europe. Peace in Europe would remove all our difficulties.[9] If, however, the international situation continued materially unchanged, the next Congress would have to decide whether a continuation of the embargo would not be a greater evil than war.[10] Madison, who was in reality the acting president by the close of 1808,[11] agreed wholeheartedly with the alternative of embargo or war, though hoping beyond hope that the belligerents would recede.

But opposition to the embargo, led by the commercial interests of New England, caused its replacement by a weaker measure in the last days of the Jefferson administration, much to the chagrin of the retiring President and of his successor. Jefferson reluctantly signed the sham Non-Intercourse Bill on March 1, 1809.

In the Old Dominion, the embargo as well as the commercial restrictions of the ensuing years was opposed by all those whose pockets and/or hearts were bound to Albion. The majority of the bourgeoisie—and their dependents—were reënforced by segments of the planting and farming groups. "Those of whose politics the price of wheat is the sole principle," to use Jefferson's terminology,[12] became hostile to the Republican administration. Great Britain, no longer able to rely upon the European continent for its grain, looked with

8 To David B. Warden, July 16, 1808; *Jefferson Papers,* LC, vol. CLXXIX, p. 31699.

9 See, *e. g.*, to John Taylor, January 6, 1808; *Jefferson Writings,* Washington ed., V, 227.

10 *E. g.*, to Major Joseph Eggleston, March 7, 1808; *Jefferson Papers,* LC, vol. CLXXV, p. 31085.

11 Jefferson did not wish to impose his opinions on the new administration. *Vide* to Levi Lincoln, November 13, 1808; *Jefferson Writings,* Washington ed., V, 387.

12 To Madison, April 27, 1809; *Jefferson Papers,* LC, vol. CLXXXVII, p. 33276.

hungry eyes at the American wheat fields. The needs of the British armies in the Iberian peninsula bolstered the pro-British proclivities of many wheat growers. British areas became the chief consumers of American wheat and flour.[13] Fine quality tobacco with a market in England likewise did its share in creating opposition to the administration. For such merchants and agriculturists the Orders-in-Council did not seem so evil. What was evil in their opinion was Washington's commercial restrictions which closed or curtailed the British market.

Their discontent was expressed through the Federalist party and the minority Republicans, most of the latter being the Tertium Quids. The four Virginia representatives who voted against the embargo on December 21, 1807, were Garnett, Randolph, Edwin Gray,[14] and the Federalist from the northern Piedmont, Joseph Lewis, Jr. The dissatisfaction in the Old Dominion with the embargo culminated in the attempt to prevent the election of Jefferson's chosen successor and to place the disgruntled James Monroe—humiliated by the rejection of his treaty—in the presidential chair. The area which was most strongly represented at a caucus of state legislators for Monroe held on January 21, 1808, was the Tidewater, with the Trans-Alleghany and Valley close behind.[15] Four representatives from the state likewise expressed their support for Monroe. They were Randolph, Garnett, Gray, and Abram Trigg.[16] The Federalists of Virginia split in the elections, with some voting for Monroe and others for the official Federalist candidate, C. C. Pinckney.[17] As has already been indicated, the Monroe

13 *V. s.*, pp. 15-16.

14 *V. s.*, p. 17.

15 *Vide Enquirer*, January 26, 1808, for the list of names; and Earl G. Swem and John W. Williams, *A Register Of The General Assembly Of Virginia, 1776-1918, And Of The Constitutional Conventions* (Richmond, 1918) for the counties represented.

16 *Enquirer,* March 11, 1808.

17 *Ibid.*, October 18, November 1, 1808. The Norfolk *Publick Ledger* supported Monroe; *v.* issue of September 30, 1808.

ticket received most of its votes from the Tidewater.[18] Pinckney's meager strength was in the central Valley.[19]

A vote for Pinckney or Monroe was, in a sense, a vote against Napoleon Bonaparte. Both Federalists and dissident Republicans had continuously repeated the charge that the administration was Francophile. Both had condemned the French Emperor.

The Federalists especially were Francophobe. Now that their pockets were deeply hurt by the commercial restrictions on the trade with Great Britain and a war with England was impending, their blood pressure reached the bursting point.

Though Federalist denunciation of France was a handy propagandistic technique to divert American attention from the aggressions of the government of " the sea-girt isles," there is no doubt that the venom truly reflected the profoundest sentiments.

Federalists found no difficulty in developing a one-sided picture of the commercial warfare of the western world in the final year and a quarter of the Jefferson administration. Imperial France was *the* enemy of the United States. Though there was occasional criticism of British acts against the United States,—for example, by grouping England and France together as culprits,[20]—the general tendency was either not to mention English policy or to minimize and defend it.

According to Federalists, France had begun the commercial war in 1793 and renewed it with the " monstrous " Berlin Decree. That decree, besides violating America's neutral rights, was a serious infraction of the Treaty of Mortfontaine.[21] In contrast, the British Order-in-Council of January 7, 1807, merely prohibited a trade to which neutrals had a doubtful right.[22]

18 *V. s.*, p. 38.

19 He received only 435 votes; Ambler, *Sectionalism in Virginia*, pp. 89-90.

20 *E. g.*, *Publick Ledger*, December 28, 1807, June 27, 1808.

21 *Ib.*, February 6, 1808.

22 *Ib.*, November 16, 1808.

The Milan Decree, John Cowper claimed, was directed against the United States. If a British ship-of-war boarded an American vessel, the latter would be considered a prize by a French cruiser. The Norfolk editor maintained, however, that a belligerent had the right to board and examine neutrals. If we paid duties in an English port, our ships would be forfeited. "In the name of all that is just and reasonable, how can we enter a British port or possession without being subjected to the payment of duties? Do not British ships pay duties in our ports?"[23] This was truly an ingenious way of defending the Orders-in-Council of November, 1807! The Milan Decree prohibited all trade with British possessions, the *Publick Ledger* pointed out, but the British orders permitted the lucrative trade with enemy holdings in the West Indies.[24] Cowper's contention was that the United States must not submit to the tyrannical decree of the French Emperor.[25]

The French practice of burning American ships on the high seas—caused by the former's maritime weakness—came in for proper castigation by the party's press. Editorials called the attention of their readers to French burnings and confiscations, but rarely mentioned or minimized English admiralty action.

Federalists noted sardonically that Napoleon nevertheless posed as the champion of a free sea and that Republicans applauded him. The only reason the French pretended to favor the principle "free ships make free goods" was that it was the means of counteracting British supremacy on the seas. The tyrant and plunderer of Europe was eager to make the seas as free as he had made the land.[26]

Federalists animadverted bitterly on the insulting tone of the French government toward the United States. They pointed to the letter of the French foreign minister, Champagny, to General Armstrong, dated January 15, 1808, which declared that

23 *Ib.*, February 19, 1808.

24 *Ib.*, March 30, July 8, 1808.

25 *Ib.*, February 19, 1808.

26 *Ib.*, May 30, 1808; reprint from the Baltimore *Federal Gazette*.

the Emperor had no doubt that the United States would retort to England's aggressions with a declaration of war and that, therefore, those American vessels which had been brought into French ports would merely remain sequestered until the American government had made its decision.[27] In other words, the Norfolk *Ledger* exclaimed, Bonaparte insolently informed us that he would restore American property only if we went to war with Great Britain.[28]

From the time of the American Revolution, France had designs of making the United States subservient to herself, Cowper reiterated in a number of editorials in 1808. Napoleon was no exception.[29]

Federalist newspapers occasionally attempted to frighten their readers even more with stories of French spies. For example, the Fredericksburg *Virginia Herald* of June 17, 1808,[30] suggested that Moreau might be a Napoleonic spy. Was it not Bonaparte's custom to compel his enemies to commit suicide? Why did Bonaparte permit Mme. Moreau to return to France? Had not Talleyrand, posing as a refugee in the preceding decade, commanded immense sums of money belonging to the French government? The government of France, the editorial maintained, could not be trusted.

Hints of Federalist editorials that the United States should engage in hostilities with France, consequently, became frequent.[31] France was America's enemy.

English policy toward the United States was, in contrast, painted by the party with an entirely different brush. Anglophile Timothy Pickering's words were treasured and repeated by Virginia Federalists from Chief Justice John Marshall[32]

27 For the letter *v. ASP, FR,* III, 249.

28 May 4, 1808.

29 March 9, 11, May 4, 1808.

30 Editorial reprinted from the Baltimore *Federal Gazette.*

31 *V., e.g., Ledger,* February 19, July 20, 1808.

32 *E.g.,* Marshall to Pickering, December 19, 1808; *Pickering Papers,* MHS, vol. XXVIII, p. 412.

to the anonymous author of a campaign pamphlet in the fifth congressional district.[33] The pamphlet declared that the able Massachusetts Senator had refuted Madison's opinion of the Rule of 1756. That rule was not exclusively British; it was a common practice of belligerents. The anonymous author also defended the right of impressment.[34]

Great Britain's attitude toward the American government continued friendly, Federalists averred. She did not demand that the United States declare war against France. Her Orders-in-Council were products of necessity and self-defense.[35] Henry Lee, the Light-Horse Harry of the revolution, now sick and impoverished, wrote to the President-elect on February 11, 1809, that England was still disposed to settle all our differences amicably. Lee asserted that Britain treated our ministers respectfully and had greatly curtailed the licentious demeanor of her naval commanders.[36]

Besides, Federalists affirmed, Great Britain was America's best market. She bought our wheat and flour, for example, while France was our competitor in the field. England, furthermore, found markets for most of those American commodities that she did not consume.[37] "Nothing is more impolitick," John Cowper declared, "than to compel a nation who is dependent [the United States], to endeavour to become independent." [38]

Yet the Republican administration had imposed an embargo against England. The embargo was supposed to have kept us

33 *An Address To The Freeholders Of The Congressional District Composed Of The Counties Of Greenbrier, Botetourt, Rockbridge, Monroe, Giles, Kanawha, and Mason* By A Citizen Of The District; printed at the office of the *Staunton Political Censor* (March, 1809) [NYPL]. The circular is dated February 24, 1809.

34 *Ib.*, pp. 6-7.

35 *E. g.*, *Publick Ledger*, February 6, 1808.

36 *Madison Papers*, LC, vol. XXXVI, no. 42.

37 *E. g.*, *Publick Ledger*, August 15, 1808.

38 February 17, 1808.

out of war, wrote the Norfolk organ on June 13, 1808. It possibly did; if the United States and Britain had reached a friendly settlement, France would have declared war against us!

The Federalists accused their opponents of constantly condemning England, but never France. The administration and its party were under French influence. That charge became shriller and more persistent with the years. The "dambargo," [39] Federalists affirmed, was laid at the behest of Napoleon. The United States, like Napoleon's European allies, was coöperating with his nefarious plans against Albion.[40] Thus Jefferson, Madison, and the whole caboodle of "Jacobinic aristocrats" were nothing but tools of the "Imperial Jacobin." [41]

References to Napoleon in the Federalist press as the "Imperial Jacobin," identifying him completely with the detestable anarchic revolution, showed that the lines between the revolution and Bonaparte were becoming blurred by time. Federalists, nevertheless, continued to reiterate that anarchy inevitably resulted in despotism.

They continued to characterize the Napoleonic régime as the worst military despotism in history. "In France, legislation is mockery," stated the *Publick Ledger* on May 25, 1808. "There is no party but the party of the Emperor, who by a nod creates and destroys. . . . There is no such thing as trial by jury. The Emperor appoints the judges, and the judges . . . decide. As to the press, which is licenced and superintended by licencers, its office is approbation and eulogy. Add to this awful spectacle an army in France of six hundred thousand men, and then let the reader ask whether the mind can admit of an idea of tyranny more complete?" [42]

39 *Publick Ledger*, January 20, 1808.

40 *E. g.*, *ib.*, July 29, 1808.

41 See the hysterical article signed "Firelock" in the Fredericksburg *Virginia Herald* of October 4, 1808.

42 Reprint from the New York *American Citizen*.

The Republicans, Federalists maintained, were, nevertheless, tools of this fiend who menaced the world with an extension of his monstrous despotism to all peoples. This destroyer of republics as well as monarchies found as many friends among Republicans as did the " bloody republick " he had destroyed.

Mankind was rapidly approaching a doom like that of the ancient world that fell under the sway of Rome. So wrote Cowper on March 4, 1808. True, the Roman Empire brought peace, but it was a peace of slavery, of abasement, and of declining civilization.

There was still but one effective barrier, according to the Federalists. England was the only power, John Marshall wrote to Pickering on December 19, 1808, which protected any part of the civilized world from the tyrant's despotism.[43]

How could a patriotic American under the circumstances desire to harm Great Britain? That was the core of all Federalist arguments. It was becoming monotonous. Yet, the Federalists declared, the Republicans had imposed the embargo. The Republicans were Anglophobes. They would—horror of horrors—even go to war with England. Were the latter subdued as a result of American intervention, the United States would become a French province.[44]

In any case, an alliance with France would be disastrous. Did not Republicans know what happened to the allies as well as the defeated enemies of Bonaparte? Look at the events in Europe and beware!

Bonaparte's rule of Europe brought the Continental System in its train. Napoleon was bent upon ruining commerce, the Norfolk *Ledger* asserted. It was the only means of destroying his enemy, whose power, he correctly conceived, was derived principally from commerce.[45] This anti-commercial system was creating poverty for all, including France.[46]

43 *Pickering Papers*, MHS, vol. XXVIII, p. 412.

44 See Pickering's letter to his constituents, February 16, 1808, published and endorsed by the *Publick Ledger* of March 23, 1808.

45 December 12, 1808.

46 *Ib.*, March 25, June 13, 1808.

The Federalists still dilated on the alleged terror and injustice as well as the economic ruin that Napoleon brought to the countries under his control.[47] An article in the editorial column of the *Virginia Gazette and General Advertiser* noted, however, that each European state, thinking itself safe, had successively stood by while another had been conquered by the Corsican. The lesson for the United States was clear.[48]

Napoleon's annexation of part of the Papal States to the Kingdom of Italy provoked John Cowper to another exhortatory editorial.[49] How could America trust Bonaparte? He was a member of the Catholic Church and was, therefore, bound by his conscience to respect the spiritual rights of the pope. Common justice obliged him to respect the temporal rights as well. Yet he disregarded both by depriving the pope of his territory.

The editor of the *Norfolk Gazette and Publick Ledger* had, however, commented on the French invasion of Portugal with mixed emotions. There was another victim for the insatiable ambition of "*the destroyer of nations,*" Cowper lamented. But Cowper's admiration for the Prince Regent was unlimited. The Regent, the royal family, and many nobles had sailed for Brazil! The Portuguese fleet would reënforce the British![50] Brazil would become commercially dependent on Great Britain, the newspaper indicated. Napoleon had thereby benefited England.[51]

Napoleon's attempt to plug the leaks in his Continental System precipitated the insoluble Peninsular War. Taking advantage of palace intrigues at Madrid, he engineered the abdication of the Bourbons. It was the beginning of his troubles.

These and the ensuing events in the Iberian peninsula aroused Federalists in the Old Dominion—and elsewhere in

47 *Vide, e.g.*, the articles in the *Ledger* of August 5 and 8, 1808, taken from the New York *Evening Post.*

48 October 4, 1808; article signed "A. B."

49 September 16, 1808.

50 February 2, 1808.

51 February 17, 1808.

the United States—as had no other European event for some time past. Spain, they exclaimed, had been a submissive ally of Bonaparte for years, obeying his mandates implicitly. See her reward! She will soon become another province of the mighty empire. " Such baseness, such tyranny, were never exhibited in the annals of civilized man." Napoleon had thrown off his mask. He no longer came as a friend and protector of the people against the tyranny of the English merchants. He came avowedly to oppress. Americans, Federalists warned, beware of French friendship![52]

As the Spanish rising became a reality, Federalist enthusiasm knew no bounds. ". . . Every real friend to the freedom and happiness of mankind," wrote John Cowper in his paper on July 29, 1808, must wish for the success of the Spaniards. William G. Lyford, editor of the *Staunton Political Censor*, declared on August 24, 1808, that the prayers of the whole Christian world were for a Spanish victory. After all, what mattered to Federalists was that the Spanish rising was not a revolution but the reaction of traditional nationalism to foreign rule.

Yet it had a popular character. All to the better! exclaimed conservative Federalists. They, who had felt the deepest revulsion at the popular phase of the French Revolution, who feared the common man in America, saw no paradox in lauding the Spanish " War of Independence." If the common man was a conservative, he was acceptable.[53]

Federalists stressed the popular character of the Spanish war. They even compared it with the struggle of the French revolutionists against the First Coalition.[54] More frequently, they compared it with the American Revolution. It was so

52 Quotation from *Publick Ledger*, August 10, 1808; *vide* also the *Virginia Herald*, May 27, 1808, and the *Ledger*, August 3, 1808 (editorial reprinted from the New York *Evening Post*).

53 *Cf.* the English Tory attitude; Maccunn, *op. cit.*, 112-113.

54 See, *e. g.*, *Publick Ledger*, July 29 (*infra*, p. 264), and September 9, 1808 (reprint from the New York *American Citizen*).

much like 1776, they asserted. The Supreme Junta resembled the Continental Congress, the juntas of the Spanish provinces were equivalent to the provincial congresses of the several colonies, and the juntas to be formed in the large cities to our committees of correspondence.[55]

The *Publick Ledger* admitted that the object of the Spanish rising, as the Republicans indicated, was not a republic. But the Spanish people, like the French, were not fit for republican government. They were, nevertheless, fighting for freedom—the freedom to select their own form of government.[56]

The interests of the United States, furthermore, were involved in the Peninsular War, Federalists asserted. The Spaniards were fighting our battles against the world menace.[57] Moreover, as the nations of Europe were liberated from the yoke of Napoleon, American commerce with those countries became free and unshackled. If not for the embargo, partisans pointed out, we could have been selling our produce in the Iberian peninsula since the beginning of the war.[58] Despite all of these factors, they maintained, the Republicans opposed the Spanish "War of Independence."

But, according to many Federalists, Republican hopes would be shattered.[59] The Spanish affair was the dawn of better times. The Almighty could not permit the righteous cause in the Iberian peninsula to be defeated. John Cowper of the *Ledger* was among those who tended to believe in a Spanish victory. After all, Bonaparte was contending for the first time with a

55 *E. g., Virginia Herald,* September 2, 1808, reprinted from the Boston *Columbian Centinel.*

56 *Publick Ledger,* September 9, 1808, reprinted from the New York *American Citizen.*

57 Edward Carrington to Pickering, December 23, 1808; *Pickering Papers,* MHS, vol. XXVIII, pp. 421-2.

58 *V. Publick Ledger,* July 29, August 10, 1808.

59 There were, however, voices of gloom among Federalists in 1808. For example, "Scaevola" in the Richmond *Virginia Gazette* of September 6, basing his conclusions on "the martial genius of the modern Caesar" and the supine state of the rest of Europe, mourned the inevitable doom of Spain.

people, not with mercenaries.[60] "When a *whole people* resolve to be free," the editor wrote enthusiastically, "it is [*sic*] only to will it, and they will be free." Had not the enthusiasm of liberty, he asked, inspired France's undisciplined volunteers at the *beginning* of the revolution? [61] Had not the veteran legions of Europe, as a result, been driven from the field in disgrace? [62]

Napoleon's embroilment in Spain, the *Publick Ledger* affirmed, would diminish the severity of France's military régime in the countries under its control. The example of Spain, moreover, proved that the only possible chance of escaping slavery was through resistance. Cowper declared hopefully that the Spanish war might rouse the nations of Europe to emulate the Spanish people, to rise *en masse* and "'break their chains upon the head [*sic*] of their oppressors.'" Spain might thus set the *ne plus ultra* to the "greatest conqueror of modern times." [63] The Federalists had discovered a new weapon—a people's war—to beat the inveterate foe of England.

Cowper warned, however, that "the Spanish patriots" would sustain many severe defeats before they could expect to expel the invaders.[64] A defeat in a battle, nevertheless, would be insignificant. As during the American Revolution, a defeat involved only a small loss, for the militia either returned home or joined other corps.[65]

The Spanish victories in 1808, the flight of Joseph Bonaparte from Madrid, and the surrender of General Junot, the commander of the army that invaded Portugal, threw John Cowper into a state of ecstasy. It was unbelievable, he wrote on October 10. France's reverse in fortune exceeded anything

60 November 30, 1808.

61 An intentional error?

62 July 29, 1808.

63 July 29, August 13 (reprint from the Baltimore *North American*), and August 15, 1808.

64 September 7, 1808.

65 September 28, 1808.

that had occurred since the beginning of the revolution. Spain and Portugal were free, he exclaimed prematurely. Austria, it seemed, would soon go to war and another coalition would be formed. If the eastern powers grasped the opportunity, they would succeed in regaining their independence. If the other European nations did not follow the example of Spain and Portugal, the *Publick Ledger* continued on the 17th, they deserved to wear their chains. " The people have discovered that Napoleon is not invincible, a discovery fatal to the tyrant's power." Napoleon had found his *ne plus ultra*.

The French Emperor's personal intervention in the Spanish campaign late in 1808 and his victories did not seem to disconcert the Norfolk editor. Even the capitulation of Madrid was minimized in the issue of February 20, 1809, with the remark that those who remembered the American Revolution would not consider a nation conquered, merely because the enemy had taken its capital. It was a people's war!

. . . .

The opinion of American foreign policy and of European developments held by the dissident Republicans was not too different from that of the Federalists.

When President Jefferson's embargo message reached the House of Representatives, John Randolph of Roanoke immediately proposed an embargo, in the belief—according to his sympathetic biographer William C. Bruce—that it was merely a method of securing the safety of American vessels and seamen. But the Senate version, which the House debated secretly in the next few days, was a general embargo, unlimited in time and space. Randolph, consequently, turned against the proposal, becoming one of its most virulent critics.[66] In any case, the master of Roanoke explained his change of position to his friend Joseph H. Nicholson of Maryland by asserting that the administration, by laying such an embargo, was submitting to

66 *V.* Bruce, *Randolph,* I, 319-20. *Cf.* the similar explanation of Hugh A. Garland, *The Life Of John Randolph Of Roanoke,* 2 v. in 1, 11th ed. (New York, 1857), I, 266-7.

Bonaparte's insolent mandate that there should be no neutrals. The United States, he concluded, had thus been dragooned to adopt a measure that must lead to immediate war with England.[67]

Randolph's jingoism against Great Britain had suddenly dissipated. The Quid faction was now unanimously opposed to a war. It endeavored thereafter to prevent the United States from becoming embroiled in Europe.

The Tertium Quids fought bitterly against commercial restrictions. Their goal, like that of the Federalists, was "free trade." Since Britain controlled the Atlantic, that meant trade with Great Britain. Randolph described the allegedly disastrous effects of the embargo on the Virginia countryside. Not only was the market for Virginia produce closed, he pointed out, but the prices of industrial commodities had risen.[68] He maintained that while the embargo was ruining the United States, it was completely ineffective against the two belligerents.[69] Randolph criticized the Non-Intercourse Bill almost as vehemently, denouncing it as a measure that might produce war.[70]

One of the chief arguments against the policy of the administration and of the majority was the charge of French influence. After all, as Randolph interpreted it, the administration did not wish to come to any accommodation with England for fear of French resentment.[71]

How could the Republicans be pro-French, the Republican minority asked, despite the fact that France was as hostile as

67 Randolph to Nicholson, December 24, 1807; *Nicholson Papers,* LC, vol. IV, p. 1422a.

68 Addresses in the House, November 30, December 3-5, 1808; *Annals of Congress,* 10th Cong., 2nd Sess., 597-8, 675-88.

69 Randolph to Nicholson, November 13, 1808; *Nicholson Papers,* LC, vol. IV, p. 1514a.

70 *Vide* his address of February 23, 1809; *Annals of Congress,* 10th Cong., 2nd Sess., 1509.

71 Randolph to Nicholson, March 28, 1808; *Nicholson Papers,* LC, vol. IV, p. 1459a. *Cf.* his explanation of the rejection of the Monroe treaty, *supra*, pp. 233-4.

Great Britain toward the United States? ". . . The injustices received from both," Representative James M. Garnett informed his constituents, "are limited only by the power and the policy of inflicting them." [72] Monroe, though not a member of the Quids, was their candidate for election and held views during 1808 and 1809 which were very similar. He wrote on February 2, 1809, that "both those powers wish our overthrow or at least that of our free system of government. . . ." [73]

Notwithstanding its apparent impartiality between the two belligerents, the minority affirmed that the Jefferson administration was as much to blame as England for the latter's hostile acts. It was the erroneous policy of 1805-6 and the rejection of the treaty with Britain, they maintained, that had caused the present crisis in American foreign relations.[74] On occasions, in a discussion of foreign aggressions against the United States, the faction listed England second and France first.[75]

How could the Republicans be Francophile, the Quids asked further, when France was no longer revolutionary but under a military despotism? [76] Besides condemning the French

72 April 12, 1808; in the *Publick Ledger*, May 9, 1808.

73 To Jefferson; *Monroe Writings*, Hamilton ed., V, 94.

74 Both Randolph and Monroe, though differing as to what the policy of 1805-6 should have been, agreed on this type of criticism. Both were vain men. The former, therefore, harped on the policy which precipitated the schism in the party as the beginning of America's foreign difficulties, while the latter emphasized the rejection of the treaty. *E. g.*, Randolph to Nicholson, March 28, 1808; *Nicholson Papers*, LC, vol. IV, p. 1459a. Monroe to John Taylor, January 9, 1809; "Letters of John Taylor of Caroline County, Virginia," *The John P. Branch Historical Papers of Randolph-Macon College*, vol. II, nos. 3 and 4 (1908), William E. Dodd ed., pp. 296-7.

75 *E. g.*, *v.* circular of the Monroe Corresponding Committee, September 24, 1808; in the *Publick Ledger*, September 30, 1808. Sometimes one obtains the impression that the Quid criticism of England was preëminently a form of political strategy. *Vide* the lashing John Randolph gave to Barent Gardenier, the New York Federalist, for his indiscretion in averring that the United States had few complaints against Great Britain. Address in the House, February 20, 1809; *Annals of Congress*, 10th Cong., 2nd Sess., 1464-5.

76 *E. g.*, such were the implications of Randolph's address, April 4, 1808; *ibid.*, 10th Cong., 1st Sess., vol. II, 1910-11.

régime, the minority called attention to the lessons of recent French history. On September 13, 1808, Edward C. Stanard, in the prospectus to his newly-established Quid newspaper, the Richmond *Spirit of 'Seventy-Six,* justified dissent by the minority Republicans from Jefferson's opinion by adverting to the dangers of idolatry in politics. The editor pointed to the tyranny in France as an example of the effect of the unbounded popularity of an individual.

Garnett and Randolph, opposing the allegedly Francophile characteristics of the Jeffersonians and the concomitant tendencies toward war with England, attempted to prove that such a war was dangerous as well as unnecessary. While Garnett's above-mentioned letter to his constituents criticized England for its desire for commercial monopoly, France was reprobated for its "lust of universal dominion." Garnett maintained that the destruction of either power by the other would probably be attended with disastrous consequences for the United States.[77] It would, therefore, be best, he affirmed, if the United States could avoid a conflict with both.

John Randolph, arguing on April 4, 1808, against a bill to increase the regular army, denied that there was any immediate danger of invasion from either Great Britain or France.[78] While the British navy held the trident, he declared, France could not send an army of any appreciable size against the United States. Even when France would crush Great Britain —as was probable—and the might of the former would become colossal, there would still be enough spirit and virtue in America to hurl the enemy back into the sea. "France, in better days, set us the example how to meet an invading enemy. . . ." There was no danger, on the other hand, Randolph continued, that Bonaparte's death would permit England to acquire an ascendancy on the continent and, consequently, the power to dominate the earth. Had Caesar's death liberated Gaul? Or had the contemptible Augustus, even after a civil

77 April 12, 1808; in the *Publick Ledger,* May 9, 1808.

78 *Cf.* his speech of March 5, 1806, *supra,* p. 196.

war,—which might also occur in France to determine who shall be the head of the Empire,—succeeded to the undivided dominion of his adopted father? The baron of Roanoke concluded that the modern Roman Empire—more dangerous to the liberties of the world than any combination of despots that had ever been seen—would last.[79]

Other dissident Republicans were more outspoken than Randolph or Garnett during the final year and a quarter of the Jefferson administration in stressing the French danger to the United States and to the world at large. For example, a member of the Monroe Corresponding Committee, though favoring peace, wrote to a Madison supporter that an American war with Great Britain would be more injurious to the United States than a war with France. American entrance into the war against Britain would complete the world combination against her. England would fall. If Bonaparte, already in control of the European continent, acquired the British navy, the Americans would become the slaves of France.[80]

Under the circumstances, the Tertium Quids were extremely sympathetic with the cause of the "Spanish patriots." Their interpretation of the character of the Peninsular War was identical with that of the Federalists. On September 13, 1808, Stanard's *Spirit of 'Seventy-Six* condemned Napoleon's treatment of his Spanish ally. The editor concluded with this moving statement: "It is more honorable for Spain and better for the world, that one half of the nation should be exterminated in so glorious a contest than that they should prostrate themselves at the foot of a despot who would trample them as he has already trampled Italy, Switzerland, Holland, and indeed almost all Europe, in the dust." [81]

79 *Annals of Congress*, 10th Cong., 1st Sess., II, 1905-12.

80 Unsigned, unfinished, and undated draft of a letter; Monroe Papers (MSS., NYPL), 1806-8 Box. See also John Taylor's letter to Ritchie, published in the *Enquirer*, March 14, 1809; Monroe to Jefferson, February 2, 1809, *Monroe Writings*, Hamilton ed., V, 99-100.

81 The editorial was reprinted in the Federalist Norfolk *Publick Ledger* of September 16, 1808.

The dissident Republicans abhorred and feared Napoleon Bonaparte.

. . . .

Defenders of the policy of commercial restrictions and critics of "perfidious Albion" in the Old Dominion were to be found among those planters and farmers who raised second-grade quality tobacco. They resented the arrogant and insulting commercial policy of the middleman England. It was the English government that placed curbs on the route to their markets in continental Europe. The declining real income after 1807 of such Virginia agriculturists especially, resulting from the increasing divergence between prices for agricultural produce and the higher level of prices for industrial products, intensified the discontent.[82] They were reënforced by independent merchants and by nascent industrial interests, which might come into full bloom behind the protective walls of non-importation, embargo, and non-intercourse.

The opinions of these groups were expressed through the Republican party. Notwithstanding the charges of "French influence" which were reiterated *ad nauseam*, Republicans not only took a defensive position but also counter-attacked with vigor and success.

Republicans maintained that conditions in the United States were ripe for the influence of Britain but not at all for that of France. The channels of British influence included the following: language, literature, jurisprudence, Tories and their descendants, intermarriage, mercantile capital, and the press.[83]

82 *V. s.*, pp. 17-18. G. R. Taylor in "Agrarian Discontent In The Mississippi Valley preceding the War of 1812," *Journal of Political Economy*, vol. XXXIX (February-December, 1931), pp. 471-505, has rightly called attention to the agriculturist's interest in maritime policy. Opinions of Virginians prove it. It seems to the present author, however, that Taylor's thesis should not only be applied to the entire United States but also that the disparity of interests between different agrarian groups with different markets should be taken into consideration.

83 *E. g.*, William B. Giles, December 2, 1808; *Annals of Congress*, 10th Cong., 2nd Sess., 229. *Cf.* Jefferson to Alexander McRae, February 8, 1809; *Jefferson Papers*, LC, vol. CLXXXVI, p. 32990.

In contrast, there were few Frenchmen in the United States. Their language and habits were so foreign as to prejudice Americans against them.[84]

The tale of "French influence," United States Senator William B. Giles declared, was originally invented by the British cabinet and transmitted through the governor of Nova Scotia to British partisans in Boston.[85] "The truth," wrote William Wirt, now prospering as a lawyer in Richmond, "is that the Federal opponents of the embargo are, in their political principles and feelings, as truly British as if we had already gone back to the darkest ages of our colonial servitude."[86] Republicans pointed out that Federalists magnified and harped on French aggressions against America, while minimizing, palliating, or remaining silent about the English.[87] The Federalist program, they declared, involved submission to British tyranny. The Federalists desired a British alliance.[88] The more ardent Federalists even preferred the reëstablishment of the rule of the mad George III over his former colonies to a continuation of the Republican administration.[89]

Such were the traitors, Republicans affirmed, who deceitfully declaimed about "French influence." William Pope, zealous Republican member of the state House of Delegates, warned the President that millions in British gold were probably being circulated freely by British spies and Tories among the people of New England.[90]

84 *Virginia Argus*, November 18, 1808; editorial reprinted from a non-Virginia journal.

85 November 24, 1808; *Annals of Congress*, 10th Cong., 2nd Sess., 122-3.

86 To N. Edwards, November 26, 1808; Edwards, *History of Illinois*, 435.

87 *E. g.*, Giles' address, December 2, 1808; *Annals of Congress*, 10th Cong., 2nd Sess., 222-3.

88 *E. g.*, *Virginia Argus*, August 16, 1808.

89 *Vide, e. g.*, Wirt to Edwards, November 26, 1808; Edwards, *op. cit.*, 433-7.

90 October 14, 1808; *Jefferson Papers*, LC, vol. CLXXXI, p. 32213.

The time was well-nigh at hand, Wirt stated, when American patriots would have to tar and feather the Tories as during the revolution.[91] Judge Archibald Stuart wrote to Jefferson on December 23, 1808, that a war with England would have the beneficial effect of destroying British influence in the United States once and for all.[92] Larkin Smith, collector of the port of Norfolk, declared more bluntly that during the war the Republicans could purge the country of monarchists, aristocrats, and British emissaries and partisans.[93]

The Quids were grouped with the Federalists in these Republican countercharges. The powerful Republican politician Judge Spencer Roane characterized John Randolph's sentiments as "Anglican" and claimed that they would lead directly to submission.[94]

Republicans denied that the embargo proved their French character. That measure placed all nations on an equal footing, Chairman Thomas Newton, Jr., of the House Committee on Commerce and Manufactures asserted.[95] Senator Giles admitted on November 24, 1808, that the embargo was less injurious to France, since her commercial connection with the United States was less important than Britain's. Yet it might have caused the French army's lack of provisions in Portugal, which was one of the grounds given for the recent evacuation of that country. The French West Indies too had felt the pressure of the embargo, Giles stated.[96]

91 To Edwards, November 26, 1808; Edwards, *op. cit.*, 437.

92 *Jefferson Papers*, LC, vol. CLXXXIV, p. 32618.

93 To W. C. Nicholas, August 30, 1808; *Nicholas Papers*, LC, vol. III, p. 681.

94 To W. C. Nicholas, January 5, 1809; *ibid.*, III, 704. The letter begins on pp. 703-4 of vol. III and is continued in vol. VI, pp. 1222-3. A study of the calligraphy and contents of both parts led to this conclusion.

95 January 11, 1808; *Annals of Congress*, 10th Cong., 1st Sess., I, 1387.

96 *Ibid.*, 10th Cong., 2nd Sess., 110-111.

The opposition was charged by the Republicans with being the prime factor causing the English government to persevere in the Orders-in-Council. As a result of Federalist opposition to the embargo, Virginia planters became vehemently anti-bourgeois. Denunciations of the avarice and cupidity of

Federalists cried "French influence"; yet England's aggressions were ten times, nay, a hundred times worse than those of France, Republicans generally affirmed.[97] Great Britain began the war upon neutral rights back in 1793—before the French [98] —and renewed it with the first paper blockade, the Order-in-Council of May, 1806.[99] The retaliatory Berlin Decree was not enforced against the United States until the case of the *Horizon*, adjudicated in October, 1807. The British government did not know of this event when it issued the November Orders-in-Council. Since the Berlin Decree was not applied against the United States until October and since the American government did not learn of the *Horizon* affair until after November, the British government had no right to retaliate against the United States, even granting the unjustifiable pretension of retaliation against an innocent bystander for submitting to the other belligerent.[100]

Republicans asserted that the purpose of the British orders was not to blockade France but to establish a British global commercial monopoly.[101] The Americans were being treated as

---

the mercantile class, the class which allegedly endangered American society and government, became common. *V.*, *e.g.*, John G. Jackson to Madison, July 17, 1808; *Madison Papers*, LC, vol. XXXIV, no. 105. Thomas Gholson, Jr., address in the House of Representatives, December 6, 1808; *Annals of Congress*, 10th Cong., 2nd Sess., 711. On Jefferson, *v.s.*, p. 34.

97 *E. g.*, J. G. Jackson, December 2, 1808, February 6, 1809; *Annals of Congress*, 10th Cong., 2nd Sess., 645, 1406.

98 *E. g.*, communication by the President and Secretary of State to Congress, December 28, 1808; *ASP, FR*, III, 263-94.

99 *E. g.*, that was Madison's opinion. Erskine to Canning, November 10, 1808; *Great Britain, F. O. 5*, LC, vol. LVIII, pt. 2, fol. 149.

100 Madison to David M. Erskine, March 25, 1808; *ASP, FR*, III, 210-13. John W. Eppes, address before the House of Representatives, April 7, 1808; *Annals of Congress*, 10th Cong., 1st Sess., II, 2039-46. *Enquirer*, August 2, 1808.

101 Addresses of William A. Burwell, December 1, 1808, J. G. Jackson, December 2, 1808, and W. B. Giles, February 13, 1809; *Annals of Congress*, 10th Cong., 2nd Sess., pp. 614-5, 635, and 358, 371, respectively.

if they were colonists again. They were forced to stop in Britain and pay tribute before trading with the continent. Americans were again being subjected to "taxation without representation." As in 1776, American independence was at stake.[102]

Republican politicians and newspapers placed much stress on the fact that the British orders forced upon second-grade tobacco and other American produce an indirect route to their continental markets. Moreover, they stated, the duties which had to be paid in Britain would reduce the profits of American planters and farmers. In any case, if Napoleon could enforce his decrees, stopping at an English port would automatically close the continent to American produce. In such an event, the market would be limited exclusively to Great Britain. The result would be falling prices for American agriculture. No matter what happened, submission to the Orders-in-Council would entail ruin for the agrarian republic.[103]

Besides the violation of American neutral rights, England was guilty, according to Republicans, of many other insults and aggressions. The attempt to enforce the Rule of 1756 was not forgotten.[104] The horrible practice of impressment, Jef-

102 Giles to Creed Taylor, March 27, 1808; *Copies of the Letters and Writings of Creed Taylor*; from the originals in the possession of A. T. Howard of Farmville, Va. (MSS., Virginia State Library), pp. 64-5. Senator Andrew Moore, address, November 22, 1808; *Annals of Congress,* 10th Cong., 2nd Sess., 62. Resolutions adopted by the Virginia General Assembly early in 1809 by an overwhelming vote; *Journal Of The House Of Delegates Of The Commonwealth Of Virginia,* Session beginning December 5, 1808, pp. 30-32 (NYPL). The resolutions were allegedly written by Wirt; John Kennedy, *Memoirs Of The Life Of William Wirt, Attorney General Of The United States* (Philadelphia, 1849), I, 260.

103 *E. g.,* Burwell to a merchant of Bedford William Dickenson (?), November 20, 1808; Miscellaneous Papers of William A. Burwell (MSS., LC). Burwell's address, December 1, 1808; *Annals of Congress,* 10th Cong., 2nd Sess., 618. Giles' address, February 13, 1809; *ib.,* 364. *Enquirer,* June 7, 1808.

104 *Vide* the satirical article by "Solomon Sneaking" in the *Enquirer,* January 9, 1808.

fersonians insisted, was followed exclusively by "perfidious Albion." Remember the *Chesapeake*! [105]

Demands for war against Great Britain as the only alternative to the embargo became frequent by the beginning of 1809. Yet the more bellicose Republicans permitted themselves to be led by the more peaceable. One of the important factors which made that possible was the conduct—sometimes incomprehensible—of the French Emperor toward the American Republic.[106]

No Republican, even when considering war against Albion, desired an alliance with Emperor Napoleon.[107] The French ruler was censured in varying degrees at different times for his treatment of the United States. Republican politicians tended to be more critical of Bonaparte than Republican editors. The former—subject to removal from office—had to be more cautious. Republicans frequently classed both England and France as wanton violators of international law. Both belligerents, they said, were so eager to harm each other that they trampled on any neutral rights which curbed their destructive course.[108] Napoleon's aggressions were as great as France's maritime power made possible, Republicans sometimes admitted.[109] Re-

105 *V.*, *e.g.*, Eppes' address, April 7, 1808; *Annals of Congress*, 10th Cong., 1st Sess., II, 2039 f. *Enquirer*, April 8, 1808.

106 See the suggestive article in the editorial column of the *Enquirer*, August 18, 1809.

107 Only Henry Banks wrote an occasional article reiterating his hackneyed idealization of Napoleon and suggesting coöperation with France's Continental System against English tyranny on the seas. But even Banks declared—though incongruously—that he desired that the United States keep out of the European imbroglio by remaining neutral. (*E. g.*, an article in the Richmond *Virginian* for May 27, 1808. The article was one of a series entitled "Truth Without Guile, or Political Discussions For 1808." This insignificant, short-lived newspaper was published by Henry's brother Gerard in conjunction with others.)

108 *E. g.*, *Enquirer*, November 11, 1808.

109 *E. g.*, *Virginia Argus*, February 12, 1808. Representative Wilson Cary Nicholas went further and declared on May 16, 1808, that there was now little difference between the two with regard to the indignities and insults they had perpetrated against the United States. (To ——; *Nicholas Papers*, LC, vol. III, p. 663.)

publicans, in general, were more critical of France's policies toward the United States than Federalists of Great Britain's.

Occasional talk of a triangular war—a war by the United States against the two belligerents simultaneously—should, however, be largely discounted. Spencer Roane implied in a letter to W. C. Nicholas on January 5, 1809, that if such action were taken, it would be merely a face-saving gesture for the Republicans. No contact with France was possible; peace with her would follow shortly. The triangular war would thus be transformed into what had really been desired all the time: a war with "perfidious Albion." [110]

Despite some criticism of Napoleon Bonaparte's acts against the United States, Republicans generally considered Britain as the chief enemy. They, consequently, frequently extenuated Napolon's acts.

At first, some Republicans continued to cling to the belief that Bonaparte was leading the continent in a struggle for the freedom of the seas against tyrannical Britain.[111] That interpretation, however, was disappearing.

Republicans, following Madison's line of reasoning, distinguished between the municipal and international aspects of the Berlin Decree, the latter part of which—*i.e.*, its application to the high seas—was not enforced against the United States until the case of the *Horizon*. Municipally, every government had the sovereign right to exclude any goods or vessels it chose. Such action was not a violation of neutral rights.[112] Moreover, because of France's maritime weakness, the Berlin and Milan Decrees were innocuous in contrast with the British

110 *Ibid.*, VI, 1223. *V.s.*, n. 94.

111 Besides Henry Banks, see, *e.g.*, John Tyler to Thomas Newton, March 13, 1808 (*William and Mary College Quarterly Historical Papers*, I, no. 3, January, 1893, p. 173); *Enquirer*, April 8, 1808. President Jefferson no longer considered Napoleon a champion of neutral rights; *e.g.*, to Short, August 29, 1808, *Jefferson Papers*, LC, vol. CLXXX, p. 31973.

112 *E.g.*, Madison to Armstrong, February 8, 1808; *Madison Writings*, Hunt ed., VIII, 12-15. Madison to Erskine, March 25, 1808; *ASP*, *FR*, III, 210-13.

orders against which they had retaliated. The French decrees were " a dead letter." [113]

Champagny's communication of January 15, 1808, might almost be considered an amelioration of the Milan Decree, the *Enquirer* stated on April 8, 1808, since American property would be held in sequestration instead of being confiscated as the decree had threatened.[114] In contrast, Erskine's letter of February informing the American government of the November orders [115] offered no proposition for restoring our captured property. In a like vein, Representative John Love asked the opposition why it condemned Champagny's letter but did not even mention Erskine's equally insulting communication.[116]

Some Republicans even attempted to palliate the Bayonne Decree of April, 1808, providing for the seizure of all American vessels entering France, Italy, or the Hanseatic towns subsequent to the embargo. While Napoleon was helping us enforce the embargo, Thomas Ritchie declared on July 12, 1808, the English government was inciting to violation of our laws. The decree was really aimed against Great Britain, not the United States, exclaimed the *Virginia Argus* on July 15. Why then all the Federalist clamor?

How could Federalists, Republicans asked rhetorically, accuse *republicans* of being under " French influence " when France was a despotism? Jeffersonians admitted that during the French Revolution American Republicans had been enthusiastic about France—and Napoleon too. " How did all America," wrote William Wirt on July 2, 1808, " stand on tiptoe, during his brilliant campaigns in Italy at the head of the army of the republic! With what rapture did we follow his

113 Madison to Pinkney, February 10, 1809; *Madison Writings*, Hunt ed., VIII, 46. *Cf. Enquirer*, June 3, 1808.

114 *Cf.* the similar viewpoint of the *Virginia Argus*, April 12, 1808.

115 For the letter of February 23, 1808, to Madison, *v. ASP, FR*, III, 209-10.

116 Address of April 13, 1808; *Annals of Congress*, 10th Cong., 1st Sess., II, 2105-6.

career, and how did our bosoms bound at the prospect of an emancipated world!" But alas! see its end: France was "buried beneath the darkness of despotism." [117] How could a Republican, Representative Thomas Newton, Jr., asked, be the pander or puppet of despots? [118]

There was thus no affection for the French régime among Virginia Republicans.[119] France was under a military despotism. According to Thomas Ritchie on January 12, 1809, a defeat for Bonaparte in Spain would deprive him of the diadem of France. Napoleon's power was thus considered based on continued military success. Ritchie described Napoleon on another occasion as "one of the most ardent foes of liberty that ever existed." [120] The *Petersburg Intelligencer* classed him with the "despot" George III.[121] Republican and Federalist opinions of the French régime were very similar.[122]

Yet the Republican picture of France was not all black. In the same editorial which characterized Napoleon as an ardent foe of liberty, Ritchie affirmed that Napoleon did evince some wisdom. The Emperor encouraged industrial improvements. Roads and other useful public works were constructed. Moreover, the editor stated, parts of the new code of laws were

117 Wirt, now a firm believer in revealed Christianity, even bewailed in this letter the instability of earthly hopes of any kind. To Benjamin Edwards; Edwards, *History of Illinois*, 461-2.

118 February 22, 1808; *Annals of Congress*, 10th Cong., 1st Sess., II, 1667.

119 Henry Banks, writing in 1808 in the Richmond *Virginian*, was almost the sole exception. He repeated his views about the origin and character of the Napoleonic régime. The latter, in his opinion, was still the best order of things for France. *V.* especially the series of articles "Truth Without Guile"; in the *Virginian*, May-July, 1808. *Cf.* the article signed "Lucian" in the *Virginian*, January 26, 1808.

120 *Enquirer*, April 12, 1808.

121 October 21, 1808.

122 Journals of both parties occasionally published the same editorials on it. *E.g.*, on June 3, 1808, the Charles Town *Farmer's Repository*, a stanch Republican newspaper, reprinted the defamatory article from the New York *American Citizen* which had appeared in the *Publick Ledger* of May 25, 1808. *V.s.*, p. 259.

wise. The *Virginia Argus* applauded the Napoleonic legislation on the Jews as ending the persecution of "this illiberally despised people" and emancipating them.[123] Republicans also occasionally recalled that certain abuses of the Old Régime were no longer in existence in Napoleonic France.[124]

Nevertheless, as Thomas Jefferson charmingly expressed it in his farewell address to the citizens of Washington, the United States was "the sole depository of the sacred fire of freedom & self-government," from whence sparks would emanate to rekindle liberty in other quarters of the globe.[125]

But Federalists were accusing the administration of endangering the United States by attempting to harm Great Britain, the barrier against a universal French despotism. Republican rejoinders to this argument were varied.

England, Republicans maintained, was fighting for maritime despotism. She had refused to make peace, Wilson Cary Nicholas stated on May 16, 1808, because she was afraid that peace would provide France with the opportunity of rebuilding its naval strength. England was thus determined on perpetual war, Nicholas concluded.[126] Not England really, but the English oligarchy. Every Republican expressed loathing for Albion's régime at every possible opportunity.[127]

Republicans[128] affirmed that both Britain and France were stimulated by a lust for "lawless domination." The only difference was the element to which each could apply its power. Great Britain was the tyrant of the seas; hence, she was America's immediate enemy. Bonaparte, on the other hand,

123 May 13, 1808; reprint from the New York *Oracle*.

124 *V.*, *e. g.*, the July 4 oration by a Samuel Acres, reported in the *Petersburg Intelligencer*, July 19, 1808.

125 March 4, 1809; *Jefferson Papers*, LC, vol. CLXXXVII, p. 33168.

126 To ———; *Nicholas Papers*, LC, vol. III, p. 663. *Cf.*, *e. g.*, the article by "Timoleon" in the *Virginia Argus*, August 26, 1808.

127 *E. g.*, John Love, March 11, 1808; *Annals of Congress*, 10th Cong., 1st Sess., II, 1794. "Patriotic Odes For The Year 1808," Ode VI, in the *Argus*, September 6, 1808.

128 Except Henry Banks.

was merely the despot of Europe. It was unfortunate for Europe; but the French despotism was less injurious to the United States than the British.[129]

A combination of military and naval predominance in the hands of either nation, Republicans maintained, would be dangerous for the United States.[130] It was likewise dangerous to ally with either. William Wirt asserted that it seemed to be the wretched destiny of every state that intermeddled with either of them to fall sooner or later under the tyranny of the Corsican. Bonaparte's friendship as well as his hostility was perilous, Wirt concluded.[131]

The extreme Francophile tendencies of Republicans after the *Chesapeake* affair had been curbed by Napoleon's commercial policy. Unfortunate Republicans! Since Napoleon's appearance on the stage of history they had yearned to idolize him; instead the " Little Corsican " always disappointed and angered them.

For Republicans, therefore, France and England served as a counterpoise to each other.[132] Republicans desired a balance of power between the two major belligerents.

In answer to the Federalists, some Jeffersonians claimed that England was safer at that period than at any previous one during the entire revolutionary era. Senator Giles declared on February 13, 1809, that there was no anxiety about the security of England in that country, but only in the United States! Britain's government was stable, her navy unchallenged, her resources great. The French Empire, on the other hand, was

129 *E. g.*, Giles, November 24, 1808, February 13, 1809; *Annals of Congress*, 10th Cong., 2nd Sess., 122, 357, 378. *Enquirer*, June 28, 1808; *Argus*, August 16, 1808.

130 *E. g.*, Giles, February 13, 1809; *Annals of Congress*, 10th Cong., 2nd Sess., 378.

131 To N. Edwards, December 26, 1807; Edwards, *History of Illinois*, 430. *Cf.* Nicholas to ——, February 28, 1808; *Nicholas Papers*, LC, vol. III, pp. 620-1.

132 *E. g.*, *Enquirer*, June 17, 1808.

probably dependent on the life of a mortal. Therefore, he concluded, Great Britain even had a better prospect of ultimate success.[133]

When Napoleon's health and vigor failed him or when he died, Representative Nicholas stated, his empire would disintegrate. Upon the first appearance of a favorable opportunity, all the enslaved nations of Europe would not only assert their independence but would seek revenge for the injuries they had received. Aided by Great Britain, they would endanger France's existence.[134] How prophetic!

A few Republicans, however, did believe that England's fall was imminent. But no Republican desired it.[135] John Daly Burk, the Irish refugee, hoped that Britain would avert the disaster—decreed by the Almighty for her crimes—by a change in the form of her government and the principles of her morality.[136]

Was the United States in danger of a French attack? Representative William A. Burwell, in an address before the House on April 5, 1808, admitted that France might menace the American Republic. Though Napoleon was more interested in lands other than the United States, Burwell stated, France was, after all, a despotism, and personal resentment "to a man of his [Napoleon's] irritable and despotic character, may mark us for his vengeance and the weight of his power."[137] Some Re-

133 *Annals of Congress*, 10th Cong., 2nd Sess., 378. *Cf.* Burwell, December 1, 1808; *ib.*, 619-20.

134 Undated article, speech, or letter, probably *c.* December, 1808; *Nicholas Papers*, LC, vol. VI, pp. 1306-7.

135 Except Banks; *v.*, *e.g.*, "Truth Without Guile" in the *Virginian*, June 10, 1808.

136 March 4 oration, in the *Enquirer*, March 11, 1808. Ritchie still believed on April 8, 1808, that Bonaparte was the champion of the freedom of the seas against England. The editor, therefore, desired his success in the struggle against British maritime tyranny but hoped that Britain itself would not be destroyed.

137 *Annals of Congress*, 10th Cong., 1st Sess., II, 1956. The *Petersburg Intelligencer* of March 15, 1808, accepted the possibility that Moreau might be a French spy.

publicans, like William Wirt, portrayed Napoleon in their theoretical analyses as a menace to the liberties of the entire world. In practice, however, they proceeded to consider England as the chief enemy of the United States.[138]

Even admitting that Britain was a useful bulwark against Bonaparte, Jeffersonians argued, must the United States submit to English tyranny now to prevent a future, contingent evil? Under these circumstances, French conquest would be of no significance. The United States, already enslaved, would have nothing to defend. That Federalist argument was inane, Republicans concluded.[139]

Burwell pointed out that the Federalists were inconsistent. Americans were warned not to resist Great Britain, lest, by so doing, they overturned or jeopardized her and thereby destroyed the barrier between the United States and France. Yet Federalists maintained that a war with England would result in a swift British victory![140]

Many Republicans, however, still believed that the French Emperor's orientation was eastward, not toward the United States.[141]

In any case, Napoleon could not conquer the United States.[142] The Peninsular War was conclusive proof in President Jefferson's mind. He wrote on October 27, 1808:

138 *E. g.*, compare Wirt's theoretical analysis of European developments, July 2, 1808 (to Benjamin Edwards, in Edwards, *History of Illinois*, 461-2), with his treatment of Anglo-American relations, November 26, 1808 (to Ninian Edwards, *ibid.*, 434-7).

139 *E. g.*, a statement by Burwell, *c.* 1808, in his *Private Memoir written at the request of a friend* (MSS., LC), p. 44; also Burwell's address, February 1, 1809; *Annals of Congress*, 10th Cong., 2nd Sess., 1286. Giles, February 13, 1809; *ib.*, 379. *Enquirer*, March 4, 1808; *Argus*, February 28, 1809.

140 Burwell's address, February 1, 1809; *Annals of Congress*, 10th Cong., 2nd Sess., 1286.

141 *E. g.*, *Enquirer*, April 8, 1808.

142 *E. g.*, Burwell's address, February 8, 1808; *Annals of Congress*, 10th Cong., 1st Sess., II, 1581.

> If, in a peninsul[a], the neck of which is adjacent to him & at his command where he can march any army without the possibility of interception or obstruction from any foreign power, he finds it necessary to begin with an army of three hundred thousand men, to subdue a nation of 5. millions, brutalized by ignorance, & enervated by long peace, and should find constant reinforcements of thousands after thousands necessary to effect at last a conquest as doubtful as deprecated, what numbers would be necessary against 8. millions of free Americans spread over such an extent of country as would wear him down by mere marching, by want of food, autumnal diseases, &c.? How would they be brought, & how reinforced across an ocean of 3000. miles in possession of a bitter enemy whose peace, like the repose of a dog, is never more than momentary? And for what? For nothing but hard blows.[143]

No matter what the character of the European war and its potentialities, Britain was the chief enemy of the United States according to Republicans. They believed that English defeats in the war with Napoleon might make her less arrogant toward America.[144] Under the circumstances, Republicans—especially partisan newspapers—applauded and derided British defeats [145] and frequently presented an exculpatory, if not sympathetic, account of France's rôle in European developments.

Albion, the *Enquirer* asserted on April 8, 1808, was the author of Pillnitz [!] and of all the coalitions against France. "British gold has converted Europe into a *slaughter-house,*" exclaimed the Charles Town *Farmer's Repository*, a Valley journal, on August 5.[146] France's overgrown power—of which

143 To Dr. James Brown; *Jefferson Papers*, LC, vol. CLXXXII, p. 32278. *Cf. Virginia Argus*, October 25, 1808.

144 *E. g.*, Jefferson to T. M. Randolph, January 2, 1809; *Jefferson Papers, Coolidge Collection*, MHS.

145 *E. g.*, *Enquirer*, February 21, 1809.

146 Sometimes, however, Republicans depicted the continental monarchies as equal partners with England in the crime against France. *Vide* the Petersburg *Republican*, August 3, 1808.

Republicans usually did not approve in this period—was the result, they said, of Britain's policy.[147]

John D. Burk, in his last March 4th oration celebrating Jefferson's inauguration, about a month before his fatal duel with a Frenchman, described Napoleon as a divine scourge sent to mete out retribution to the evil crowned heads, "who madly and impiously blasphemed against the most glorious phenomenon [the French Revolution] by which the moral horizon had been irradiated. . . ." [148] That was in essence the conception of Napoleon Bonaparte's rôle in history now held by Republicans generally.

"The combining monarchs," wrote William Wirt, "thought that they were in danger of nothing but the propagation of the doctrines of liberty; but ruin has come upon them from another quarter." [149] Bonaparte's easy conquests in Europe were attributed by Republicans to the existence of "mouldering monarchies" which tumbled at "the tyrant's touch." [150] A Napoleonic victory, consequently, might not be so harmful. Ritchie of the *Enquirer* averred on April 8 and 12, 1808, that Bonaparte was spreading the revolutionary spirit into other countries, whose "hoary institutions . . . are so bad that no change can scarcely make them worse. . . ." [151]

Napoleon's treatment of his Spanish ally, however, threw confusion into the ranks of Republicans. Napoleon, who had some connection with the revolution, was faced with a popular rising. But the popular rising was of a conservative cast. Yet the right of national self-determination, so dear to Republican

147 *E. g.*, "Pacificus" in the *Enquirer*, March 8, 1808; also *Enquirer*, April 8.

148 Reported in the *Enquirer*, March 11, 1808.

149 To Benjamin Edwards, July 2, 1808; Edwards, *History of Illinois*, 462.

150 *V.* toast no. 11 at a Richmond celebration of July 4; *Enquirer*, July 5, 1808.

151 Henry Banks was still writing enthusiastically about Napoleon's federative scheme for Europe. Banks still believed that the Corsican had introduced the best order of things in Europe as well as in France. *E. g.*, "Truth Without Guile," *Virginian*, June 14, July 22, 1808.

hearts, was involved. Whom should the American liberal support?

The Spanish affair was, however, another aspect of the Anglo-French war. And England was *the* enemy of the United States. In a conflict between *realpolitik* and ideology—which was uncertain of itself anyway—the former had to win. Federalist enthusiasm for the Spanish cause facilitated this result. Out of the welter of ideas in 1808 consequently emerged a more uniform Republican approach in 1809. Anglo-Spain generally became the enemy.

But the Spanish imbroglio revived President Jefferson's thoughts of Florida. He, therefore, had little difficulty in reaching a decision. He was delighted with Napoleon's new tribulations. Here was an opportunity of closing his presidency with éclat. If England reëstablished amicable relations with the United States while Bonaparte was at war with Spain, he wrote in August, 1808, in an optimistic vein to the members of his cabinet, the moment might be favorable for taking possession of "our territory held by Spain, and so much more as may make a proper reprisal for her spoliations." [152]

Still fearful of a powerful neighbor, the President was opposed to the replacement of Spanish control of Cuba or Mexico by British or French rule. It was, therefore, decided at a cabinet meeting on October 22 that if such a possibility arose, the United States would not only offer moral encouragement to a movement for independence by those colonies, but, if the circumstances warranted, might even "make common cause" with them.[153]

The Peninsular War, however, was of more immediate concern. Jefferson's sympathy for the Spanish cause seemed unlimited in 1808, despite his admission that the new turn in European affairs might make the English government more

152 *E. g.*, to Secretary of the Navy, August 12, 1808; *Jefferson Papers, Coolidge Collection*, MHS.

153 Cabinet memoranda in the *Anas*; *Jefferson Writings*, Bergh ed., I, 484-5.

arrogant toward the United States.[154] He wrote to T. M. Randolph of Bonaparte's " murderous purposes on Spain & Portugal." [155] The President's belief in the right of self-determination reënforced his practical politics.

The Republican leader was at first sanguine as to the possibility of Spanish success.[156] " Altho' the Spanish government is a wretched one," he wrote to his Secretary of State in the first flush of news, " the people there have not, like the Germans, been rendered by oppression indifferent to the master they serve." [157] Baylen, Saragossa, the flight of Joseph from Madrid, and the French defeat at Vimiero greatly reduced Napoleon's military prestige in the President's opinion. His resultant belittling of the Napoleonic danger to the United States has already been noted.[158]

Jefferson realized, however, that if Bonaparte were determined to put forth all efforts to conquer Spain, the Spaniards would ultimately be defeated.[159] The apparent settlement of Napoleon's differences with Alexander, as exemplified in the Erfurt conference, decreased the Virginian's hopes. Bonaparte was now free to conquer Spain.[160]

Thomas Jefferson accepted the ensuing turn in the tide with resignation, though his sympathies continued to be with the Spanish " patriots." [161] He asserted on January 2, 1809, that

154 To Thomas Digges, August 10, 1808; *Jefferson Papers*, LC, vol. CLXXIX, p. 31853.

155 December 13, 1808; *Jefferson Papers, Coolidge Collection*, MHS.

156 *E. g.*, to Madison, September 13, 1808; *Jefferson Writings*, Washington ed., V, 367.

157 August 9, 1808; *Madison Papers*, LC, vol. XXXIV, no. 122.

158 *V. s.*, pp. 282-3.

159 Erskine to Canning, November 5, 1808, report of a conversation with the President; *Great Britain, F. O. 5*, LC, vol. LVIII, pt. 2, fols. 138-138ᵛ.

160 To T. M. Randolph, December 13, 1808; *Jefferson Papers, Coolidge Collection*, MHS.

161 To Monroe, January 28, 1809; *Jefferson Papers*, LC, vol. CLXXXV, p. 32910.

Joseph had undoubtedly resumed his throne before then. Parts of Spain would hold out for a while, he continued, but the end would soon be in sight.[162] England, he declared on March 2, was nevertheless still a barrier to a French conquest of the Spanish colonies.[163]

Despite the French victories, the President still thought that the United States might benefit. Britain, excluded from the commerce of the continent, might consider the American market more important than her Orders-in-Council. France, turning to the conquest of the Spanish colonies, might endeavor to purchase American neutrality by a repeal of the " illegal " parts of the decrees, " with perhaps the Floridas thrown into the bargain." [164] The United States loomed too large in the retiring President's eyes.

Followers of Jefferson in the Old Dominion, in contrast, were bewildered by the Spanish affair. Most of them, apparently, were not preoccupied with Florida at that time. The commercial war was for them the immediate and pressing problem. Yet the Spanish question was not a simple one.

All Republicans condemned Napoleon in varying degrees for acting so shamefully toward a loyal ally,[165] though some added harsh criticism of the rule of the Spanish Bourbons.[166] But Republican opinion of the merits of the Spanish rising at first ran the entire gamut from pro-Spanish to anti-Spanish reactions. Moreover, it vacillated.

Thomas Ritchie had remarked in the *Enquirer* of May 24, 1808, upon the reforms introduced in Portugal by the French

162 To T. M. Randolph; *Jefferson Papers, Coolidge Collection,* MHS.

163 To Du Pont de Nemours; *Jefferson Writings,* Washington ed., V, 432.

164 To Monroe, January 28, 1809; *Jefferson Papers,* LC, vol. CLXXXV, p. 32910.

165 *E. g., Enquirer,* July 29, 1808; *Virginia Argus,* August 2, 1808; Petersburg *Republican,* August 3, 1808. The latter two justified Bonaparte's acts against the constant members of the coalitions, but reprobated his treatment of Spain.

166 *Petersburg Intelligencer,* August 2, 1808.

army and added that a similar development in Spain would be equally beneficial. Upon receiving news of the abdication of the Bourbons, he expressed a desire for a French victory. The *Enquirer* averred on July 29 that Spain was in such a bad condition that no change could possibly make it worse. Nothing could be worse than the corrupt rule of Godoy, the queen's lover, the "unbounded despotism" of the clergy over the consciences and purse of the people, the pride and wealth of the grandees, and the sloth and ignorance that pervaded the nation. A rebellion by the Spaniards would result only in fixing the French fetters more firmly upon them. The Spanish people, the editor concluded, should, therefore, submit.[167]

How could the undisciplined, inexperienced Spaniards expect to subdue "the first warrior of the world" who had all the prerequisites for success? Ritchie asked on August 12. Spain, not ripe for revolution, had no means of extricating herself from her difficulties. There was, moreover, no probability of aid from any other source than the corrupt and selfish English cabinet.

Other Republican newspapers reacted differently. In contrast to the *Enquirer* was the Petersburg *Republican's* initial unstinted support of the Spaniards.[168] The editor of the Richmond *Virginia Argus*, however, frankly discussed the conflict that was tearing his vitals. He proclaimed his sympathy on August 9 with the Spanish struggle for national independence, but doubted its success unless it was aided by a new continental coalition. The Spanish colonies, the editor continued, now had the opportunity to become independent. (Republicans generally favored such an outcome.) [169] Unfortunately, the *Argus* stated, there was too much degeneracy, ignorance, and superstition in the colonies to make such an effort possible. The editorial writer affirmed that despite his profound sympathy for

167 *Cf. Petersburg Intelligencer*, August 2, 1808.

168 August 3, 1808.

169 *Cf. Enquirer*, August 12, 1808.

Spain, as well as for the other oppressed powers of Europe,—including France,—the fact that Great Britain would benefit from the Peninsular War had to be taken into consideration. After all, the possibility of the emancipation of Europe was a chimera. As a result of the Spanish developments, Albion would become more obstinate in her course of injustice toward the United States. England might even direct her attention to the acquisition of the Spanish colonies, the editorial warned.[170]

On August 12, the *Argus* criticized those Republicans who justified a French conquest of Spain with the argument that no change could be for the worse. The newspaper affirmed that the lower classes were, in varying degrees, badly off in every country. If the aforementioned argument were consistently adhered to, Bonaparte would be justified in conquering every state. What would then become of the right of national self-determination? Was Napoleon to be the judge of the happiness of nations? [171]

In answer to Federalist beliefs, on the other hand, the editorial asserted that a French victory in Spain would not harm the United States, for France had in reality controlled that country for some time. But an Anglo-Spanish victory would open a new market for English wares, thereby weakening the effect of the embargo. The editorial writer now openly declared that a good American ought to wish for a Spanish and British defeat!

The latter view tended to become uppermost in the mind of the *Argus* editor. The journal, consequently, began to retreat from its bold stand on the right of self-determination. Federalist enthusiasm for the Spanish "patriots" made the retreat more pronounced. On September 9, the *Virginia Argus* launched a frontal attack on the doctrine. For what were the Spaniards fighting? the editor asked. For a mere choice of tyrants. How could Americans, therefore, feel much sympathy

170 Editorial reprinted in the *Petersburg Intelligencer*, August 12, 1808. *V.* also the editorial in the *Intelligencer* of August 26, 1808.

171 Similar views were presented on August 30.

for them? It was nonsensical to compare the Spanish war with the American Revolution, as the Federalists did. Did the Federalists remember their attitude toward the French Revolution and their execration of the Irish struggle for independence? Why the inconsistency? The answer, the editorial concluded, was not the ardent attachment of the Federalists to the Spanish cause, but their secret love for Great Britain![172]

This Richmond newspaper now began to find other faults with the Spanish cause. An editorial on September 20, 1808, called attention to the persecuted Jews of Spain. Now was their opportunity, the writer declared, to rise against the hated Spanish rule and in support of Napoleon, whose policy toward them had been comparatively beneficent. Such a development would entail certain defeat for the so-called "Spanish patriots." The writer concluded: "A great deal of sensibility has been affected in their [*i.e.*, the Spaniards'] behalf, but surely under the abstract influence of philanthropy, the mind will be very nearly balanced between the condition of the Jews and that of the Spaniards."

Though the editorial writer could on December 9 again display some enthusiasm for the "people's war" in Spain, *realpolitik* had won. In 1809 the Spanish war was generally described by the *Virginia Argus* as an Anglo-French war.[173] In that case, Republicans knew where to stand.

The *Enquirer's* irresolution had taken a different road. In the fall of 1808, Ritchie stopped writing about the usefulness of a change in Spain. Instead, he harped on criticism of Napoleon's conduct toward his Spanish ally.[174] He began to refer to the Spanish "patriots." By January 12, 1809, Thomas Ritchie was averring that the Spanish people must feel something of that fire and enthusiasm which animated the Ameri-

172 Editorial reprinted in the Petersburg *Republican*, September 10, 1808. See also the *Argus* for September 16, and the Charles Town *Farmer's Repository*, August 12, 1808.

173 *E. g.*, January 20.

174 *E. g.*, October 28.

cans and French during their revolutions, though the Spaniards were merely contending for the privilege of selecting their own species of despotism. Bonaparte, faced with a popular uprising, had the most difficult undertaking of his career. The editor, nevertheless, concluded that the Emperor would win because of France's military superiority in all respects.

On January 24, however, *realpolitik* won in the *Enquirer* office too. An editorial of that day noted the connection between the Spanish market and the American embargo. Thereafter Ritchie interpreted the Peninsular War in the light of American national interests. He again became anti-Spanish.[175]

When Republicans thought in terms of national interest, they stressed the ignoble objects of the Spanish rising—*i.e.*, its conservative character. Ambrosius Henkel, member of a famous family of Lutheran ministers and later a minister himself, the publisher of the first German weekly in the South,[176] *Der Virginische Volksberichter und Neumarketer Wochenschrift*, did not find it difficult to detest the Spanish cause. On February 22, 1809, his Valley newspaper reprinted an editorial from the Boston *Chronicle*, which declared that the Spaniards had been misled to take up arms, not in order to defend their freedom, but to further the malicious intentions of the instigators of the Inquisition. The Republican attitude toward the Spanish struggle thus became generally hostile in 1809.

Many Republicans recognized that the future of the Napoleonic Empire was at stake in the Peninsular War. Secretary of State Madison had written to Jefferson on August 14, 1808, that " a protracted check even may produce a general reflux of the tide agst [*sic*] him." [177] Thomas Ritchie went so far as to declare on January 12, 1809: ". . . If he [*i.e.*, Napoleon] be vanquished in this enterprise, there is every reason to believe

175 *E. g.*, February 21, 1809.

176 Lester J. Cappon and Ira V. Brown, eds., *New Market, Virginia, Imprints, 1806-1876, A Check-List* (University of Virginia Bibliographical Series, No. 5; Charlottesville, Va., 1942), pp. ix-x.

177 *Jefferson Papers*, LC, vol. CLXXX, p. 31882.

that his unpopularity and loss of military renown will deprive him of the diadem of France."

Spain was in truth to become the grave of the Napoleonic Empire.

. . . .

By the time Thomas Jefferson retired from public service on March 4, 1809, the pattern of partisan thinking in the Old Dominion concerning Napoleon Bonaparte had been generally fixed. Federalists and dissident Republicans abhorred the very name Napoleon. Majority Republicans, though, in general, disliking Napoleon Bonaparte, hated "perfidious Albion," *the* enemy of America, much more. Sympathy for Napoleon, under the circumstances, could not be eradicated. French victories subserved American foreign policy.

CONCLUSION

AFTER March 4, 1809, American foreign policy took the most circuitous road to war. Yielding to the pressure of pro-British interests, the movement toward "free trade" was at first precipitate. But Napoleon's compliance with the form of the so-called Macon's Bill No. 2 left the United States apparently with one enemy. The Madison administration was slowly but surely drawn to a war with the former mother country.

In general, partisan opinion during these years continued to follow the trends already indicated. Though the displeasure of Republicans with Bonaparte's hostile commercial policy increased, their anger toward Great Britain grew even more. They, therefore, tended to support Napoleon's foreign policy in Europe. Quids and Federalists, in contrast, continued to condemn this as well as all other aspects of Napoleonic policy.[1]

The War of 1812 did not affect Federalist and Quid opposition to the "French" administration and to Bonaparte. Members of both groups were, in general, "at war" with the French Emperor. They usually stood aloof from "Mr. Madison's War." [2] England was their champion and ally against the Antichrist.[3] On the other hand, the War of 1812 confirmed most Republicans in their support of Napoleon's war effort.

1 As the clamor for war against Great Britain increased, John Randolph again became hysterically anti-Napoleon. *Vide, e. g.*, his address in the House of Representatives on December 10, 1811; *Annals of Congress*, 12th Cong., 1st Sess., I, 441-55.

2 However, the British depredations and arming of slaves in the Chesapeake region combined with the fall of Napoleon to influence John Randolph to begin supporting the war effort. *Vide* his "Letter to a Gentleman in Boston," dated December 15, 1814, in the *Enquirer*, December 31, 1814. Likewise, the Chesapeake campaign while Bonaparte was at Elba aroused some animosity against England among Virginia Federalists. *V., e.g.*, the Richmond *Virginia Patriot*, October 15, 1814. The *Patriot* was the successor to the defunct *Virginia Gazette and General Advertiser*.

3 See John Randolph's address in the House of Representatives, January 13, 1813; *Annals of Congress*, 12th Cong., 2nd Sess., 803-4.

The fall of the French Emperor in 1814 was met with sighs of relief on the part of Federalists. "The long agony is over. . . ."[4] Though Republicans, on the whole, cared little about the fate of Napoleon Bonaparte as a person, they regretted the reënforced strength that England could now bring to bear on the American campaign.

The Hundred Days, however, found America at peace and able to examine European developments with somewhat less partiality. But long-held opinions could not be eradicated so easily. Federalists, though less hostile toward the Corsican than for many a year, consequently, continued to sympathize with the coalition. Napoleon regained in Republican eyes some of the glamor that he had had during the nineties. They believed that he was now fighting for the right of national self-determination. Moreover, Britain, the ex-enemy of the United States, and the Anglo-Federalists were discomfited thereby.

But after Napoleon was expelled from the center of the stage of history Virginian interest in him naturally waned. It was not Napoleon Bonaparte the individual that had interested them, but Napoleon Bonaparte the general of the French Republic and then the ruler of consular and imperial France.

. . . .

This study in opinion has demonstrated that the Virginian of the late eighteenth and early nineteenth centuries could not examine the European scene as an abstract problem in history, for he was involved in the developments overseas.

Fundamental factors created a division of opinion which, in general, coincided with the political party alignments. Any sectional manifestations that occurred in the history of this opinion were incidental.

Bitter partisan rivalry sometimes compelled loyal adherents of a party to assume attitudes concerning Napoleon—at least in public—for reasons of political expediency. But partisan

4 From Gouverneur Morris's July 4 oration; available in the *Virginia Patriot*, July 9, 1814.

opinion and the trends of opinion within the political parties were generally produced by more significant factors.

The political conservatism of the Federalist party, on the one hand, and the liberal tendency in the Republican party, on the other, greatly influenced partisan attitudes toward the domestic policies of the Man on Horseback. The Federalist party, whose nucleus was a middle class dependent on the British economy, found the problem of forming opinions concerning the international as well as the domestic policies of Napoleon Bonaparte simplified by the almost continuous hostilities between England and France. In contrast, the Republican party, not based upon a single economic group bound to a single European country, but primarily upon heterogeneous agricultural interests, frequently found it more difficult to decide upon its attitude toward the international policies of Napoleon. The latter's peculiar relation to liberalism and the revolution, at home and abroad, added to the difficulty. The foreign policy pursued by the Jefferson administration—steering a course between the Scylla and Charybdis of the European war—intensified the uncertainty of the Republicans for a number of years. Furthermore, the commercial war which engulfed the United States after 1805 precipitated a schism within the party. But thereby the way was paved for the Republican party to become a more cohesive group. Agriculturists raising crops which sold in continental markets [5] tended to approve of Bonaparte's foreign policies in Europe. The other planters and farmers provided recruits for the dissident Republicans and the Federalists. Such were some of the basic factors—as this study has shown—which molded Virginian opinion of Napoleon Bonaparte.

The majority of Virginians, the Republicans, had applauded General Bonaparte prior to Brumaire; for many he was an exemplar of the republican hero. The coup d'état sufficed to make him a pariah for some Republicans; others continued to hope that the Consulate was purely of an emergency character. It was not until the establishment of the Life Con-

5 Except wheat growers provisioning British armies in the Iberian peninsula.

sulate that Bonaparte lost most of the remaining sympathy of the liberals in the Old Dominion. Yet the Consulate was not as bad as a Bourbon restoration. But Napoleon's decision to wear a crown was the final blow to Republican hopes. Thereafter, when considering the domestic policy of Napoleon,—though they recognized on occasions that the Empire was not equivalent to a Bourbon régime and that Bonaparte was an enlightened despot,—the Republican countenance was fixed in anger toward the liberticide, the betrayer of the French Revolution. Henry Banks' eulogy of the "philosopher-prince" was decidedly not the norm.

The Federalists had followed a different road with regard to the Napoleonic régime. Though criticizing it in its early years and warning Americans that democracy led to despotism, Federalists believed the Consulate to be better than the horrible French Revolution. Not diverted in 1802 by an Anglo-French war, American conservatives applauded Napoleon's assumption of the Consulate for life. Soon, however, domestic American politics and the renewal of the European war created a predominantly hostile attitude toward the government of Bonaparte. Federalist condemnation of France as a vicious military despotism became the keynote of the party's attitude.

The opinion held by Federalists concerning Napoleon's foreign policy generally ran parallel to their attitude toward the Napoleonic régime. Though they had expressed some enthusiasm in the latter half of 1802 for Napoleon's foreign policy in Europe, from 1803 on Bonaparte became for them the world-danger and England the bulwark of the United States against that menace. With regard to American foreign relations, the Federalist tendency was to take an anti-French position. A hostile attitude after 1802 toward all phases of Napoleonic history—domestic and foreign—was generally the characteristic feature of the average Federalist.

Opinion of French foreign relations on the part of Republicans, on the other hand, was to a considerable degree independent of their evaluation of Napoleon's domestic organization and policies. The pro-French proclivities of Republicans with reference to Franco-American relations were continually restrained by Bonaparte's actions toward the United States beginning with the retrocession of Louisiana. With regard to international developments in Europe, Republican sympathy with the French "republican" arms continued until the establishment of peace between Britain and France. The renewal of the war, however, found most Jeffersonians neutral. Though neutrality continued to be the Republican lodestar for several years, oscillation between France and Britain developed. From February, 1807, however, Republican opinion was weighted on the side of France. The tendency was to recognize the usefulness of "the Corsican scourge" for the implementation of American foreign policy.

In contrast, dissident Republicans reprobated the French Emperor. They maintained that Napoleon Bonaparte endangered the world.

Despite the existence of a division of opinion in Virginia generally based on party lines, overlapping of views was frequent, especially after 1803. Affection for Napoleon Bonaparte as a person was, on the whole, not current after the coup d'état. His "inordinate ambition" became the major characterization after the Louisiana affair. Virginians, moreover, usually disliked the Napoleonic monarchy. Criticism of its foreign policy was heard in Republican as well as Federalist ranks. Most Virginians, nevertheless, recognized the efficiency of the French régime. Equally, if not more, widespread was appreciation of Napoleon's military ability.

Bonaparte the overambitious warrior: such might be considered the judgment of contemporary Virginians as to the core of the history of France in the age of Napoleon. From the viewpoint of the American of that period, were they far from the truth?

SELECT BIBLIOGRAPHY

Abbreviations for libraries:

- AAS: American Antiquarian Society (Worcester, Mass.)
- BA: Boston Athenaeum
- BPL: Boston Public Library
- BU: Brown University Library
- CU: Columbia University Library
- DU: Duke University Library
- HU: Harvard University Library
- LC: Library of Congress
- MHS: Massachusetts Historical Society
- NA: National Archives
- NYHS: New York Historical Society
- NYPL: New York Public Library
- VHS: Virginia Historical Society
- VSL: Virginia State Library
- YU: Yale University Library

I. Bibliographical Guides

A. TO MANUSCRIPTS

Bullock, Helen D. "The Papers of Thomas Jefferson," *The American Archivist*, vol. IV, no. 4, October, 1941, pp. 238-249.

Leland, Waldo G., Meng, J. J., and Doysié, A. Guide to Materials for American History in the Libraries and Archives of Paris, vol. II: Archives of the Ministry of Foreign Affairs. Washington, D. C., 1943.

LC: Handbook of Manuscripts in the Library Of Congress (United States, Library of Congress, Division of Manuscripts). Washington, 1918.

Garrison, Curtis W. List of Manuscript Collections in the Library of Congress to July, 1931 (United States, Library of Congress, Division of Manuscripts). Washington, 1932.

Powell, C. Percy. List of Manuscript Collections Received in the Library of Congress, July, 1931 to July, 1938. Washington, 1939.

Annual Reports of the Librarian of Congress, 1939 to date.

Ford, Worthington C. Papers of James Monroe. Listed in chronological order from the original manuscripts in the Library of Congress. Washington, 1904.

NYPL: "Manuscript Collections in the New York Public Library," *Bulletin of the New York Public Library*, vol. V, January–December, 1901, pp. 306-336.

Paltsits, Victor H. "The Manuscript Division in the New York Public Library," *Bulletin of the New York Public Library*, vol. XIX, January–December, 1915, pp. 135-165.

Paullin, Charles O. and Paxson, F. L. Guide to the Materials in London Archives for the History of the United States since 1783. Washington, D. C., 1914.

VHS: Catalogue of the Manuscripts in the Collection of the Virginia Historical Society and also of some printed papers. Richmond, 1901.

B. TO NEWSPAPERS AND PERIODICALS

Beer, William. "Checklist of American Periodicals," *Proceedings of the American Antiquarian Society*, n. s., vol. XXXII, April 12, 1922–October 18, 1922 (Worcester, 1932), pp. 330-345.

Brigham, Clarence S. "Bibliography of American Newspapers, 1690-1820, Part XVIII: Virginia-West Virginia," *Proceedings of the American Antiquarian Society*, n. s., vol. XXXVII, April 13, 1927–October 19, 1927 (Worcester, 1928), pp. 63-162.

——. History and Bibliography of American Newspapers, 1690-1820. Worcester, 1947. 2 v.

Gilmer, Gertrude C. Checklist of Southern Periodicals to 1861. Boston, 1934.

Gregory, Winifred, ed. Union List Of Serials In Libraries Of The United States And Canada. New York, 1927. Supplements: New York, 1931; New York, 1933.

Haskell, Daniel C. Checklist of Newspapers and Official Gazettes in the New York Public Library. New York, 1915.

Parsons, Henry S. A Check List of American Eighteenth Century Newspapers in the Library of Congress. Originally compiled by John Van Ness Ingram. New ed., revised and enlarged. Washington, 1936.

Slausson, Allan B. A Check List of American Newspapers in the Library of Congress. Washington, 1901.

Swem, Earl G., Minor, K. P., and Harrison, S. B. A list of newspapers in the Virginia State Library, Confederate Museum and Valentine Museum (Virginia State Library Bulletin, October, 1912, vol. V, no. 4). Richmond, 1912.

Wescott, Mary and Ramage, A. A Checklist of United States Newspapers (And Weeklies Before 1900) In The General Library [of Duke University], Part VI, Virginia-Wyoming. Durham, 1937.

C. GENERAL AND MISCELLANEOUS

American Imprints Inventory (The WPA Historical Records Survey Program. Division of Professional and Service Projects), no. 14: A Check List of West Virginia Imprints, 1791-1830. Chicago, 1940.

Bemis, Samuel F. and Griffin, G. G. Guide to the Diplomatic History of the United States, 1775-1921. Washington, 1935.

Cappon, Lester J. and Brown, I. V., eds. New Market, Virginia, Imprints, 1806-1876, A Check-List. Charlottesville, 1942. (University of Virginia Bibliographical Series, No. 5).

Clemons, Harry. A Survey of Research Materials in Virginia Libraries, 1936-7 (University of Virginia Bibliographical Series, No. 1). Charlottesville, 1941.

Davis, Innis C., with the assistance of Johnston, Emily, *et al.* West Virginia. Biennial Report of the State Department of Archives and History, including A Bibliography of West Virginia in two parts. For the period ending June 30, 1938. n. p., n. d.

Evans, Charles. American Bibliography, vol. XII (1798-9). Chicago, 1934.

McMurtrie, Douglas C. West Virginia Imprints. Being a first list of books, pamphlets, and broadsides printed within the area now constituting the state of West Virginia, 1791-1830. Charleston, W. Va., 1936.

Peterson, C. Stewart. Bibliography of County Histories. Typescript; December, 1935. CU

Phillips, P. Lee. Virginia Cartography, A Bibliographical Description. Washington, 1896. (Smithsonian Miscellaneous Collections, 1039, vol. 37).

Swem, Earl G. A Bibliography of Virginia, 2 Parts (Virginia State Library Bulletin, April, July, October, 1915, vol. VIII, nos. 2-4; January-October, 1917, vol. X, nos. 1-4). Richmond, 1916-1917.

——. Virginia Historical Index, 2 v. Roanoke, Va., 1934, 1936.

Union List of Microfilms, A Basic List of Holdings in the United States and Canada (Philadelphia Bibliographical Center and Union Library Catalogue, Committee on Microphotography). Philadelphia, 1942. Supplements 1-3. Philadelphia, 1942-4.

Wegelin, Oscar. Early American Plays, 1714-1830. A Compilation of the titles of Plays and Dramatic Poems written by authors born or residing in North America previous to 1830. 2nd ed. revised. New York, 1905.

——. Early American Poetry. A Compilation of the titles of volumes of verse and broadsides by writers born or residing in North America north of the Mexican border, 2 v. in 1. 2nd ed., revised and enlarged. New York, 1930.

II. Primary Sources

A. MANUSCRIPTS

HU: A few scattered Thomas Jefferson and John Marshall items.

LC: Henry Adams Transcripts: French State Papers, 1798-1814. 5 v.

John Ambler Papers.

Materials on William A. Burwell:

(1) Private Memoir written at the request of a friend by William A. Burwell.

(2) Miscellaneous Papers.

(3) Papers of William B. Randolph. Boxes 1, 3, 4.

Campbell-Preston Papers. Vols. III-V.

Dabney Carr: Letters to Peachey R. Gilmer.

Sir Augustus John Foster. Notes on the United States of America Collected in the Years 1804-5-6-7 and 11-12. 5 v. (each with a different title); vol. V is entitled: Part of Journal in the United States of America, 1811-12, containing allusions to the declaration of war.

France. Affaires Étrangères, Correspondance Politique, États-Unis. Vols. LI-LXXII, January, 1799-March, 1816. Photostats.

Great Britain. Public Record Office, London. Foreign Office 5. Vols. XXV, XXIX, XXXII, XXXV, XXXVIII, XLI, XLII, XLV, XLVIII, XLIX, LII, LVI, LVII, LVIII, LXII-LXIV, LXIX, LXX, LXXIV, LXXVI, LXXVII, LXXXIV-LXXXVIII, CVI, CVII. Despatches of the British Minister to the United States to the Foreign Office, 1799-1815. Vols. XXV-XLIX are Carnegie Institute transcripts; the remaining volumes are photostatic copies.

Harry Innes Papers, vol. XXI.

The Papers of Thomas Jefferson. Vols. XCIX-CCVII, September 7, 1795-August 9, 1816. (Also available in microfilm, CU, NYPL).

Thomas Jefferson's Memorandum Book, Record of the Weather, 1776-1820.

Jones Family Papers. Vols. XXXI-XXXIII. [The Jones Family of Northumberland County].

The Papers of Richard Bland Lee, 1700-1825.

Materials on James Madison:

(1) Papers of James Madison. Vols. XIX-LXII, January 5, 1796-August 5, 1816.

(2) Papers of James Madison. Autobiography and Miscellaneous Papers. 1 v.

(3) Notes on Government.

(4) Papers of James Madison found in the collection of William C. Rives. (Passim).

Materials on John Marshall:

(1) John Marshall, Transcripts and Photostats. Vols. I-III, 1776-1835 and undated.

(2) Photostat of "General Marshall's Journal In Paris From September 27, 1797 to April 11, 1798."

(3) Box of various accessions, including letters to his wife.

(4) Box of Robert Goodloe Harper items.

(5) Box of Rufus King items, 1784-1800.

(6) Papers of Charles Dabney, 1769-1809, Miscellany and Letters.

Garret Minor-David Watson Correspondence. 3 boxes.

Materials on James Monroe:

(1) Papers of James Monroe. Vols. IV-XXIII, September 26, 1795-June 25, 1816.

(2) Memoranda And Accounts. James Monroe; 1795-1801.

(3) James Monroe Papers. Letter Book. 2 v.

(4) A few Monroe letters in Henry Clay Papers, vols. I, II, and in Genet papers.

Papers of Hugh Nelson, 1808-1833.

Wilson Cary Nicholas Papers. 7 v. Vols. I-IV, 1765-1831; vols. V-VII, undated.

Joseph H. Nicholson Papers. Vols. I-VI.
Materials on John Randolph of Roanoke:
(1) John Randolph Papers, 1742-1835.
(2) Letters of John Randolph of Roanoke, Charlotte County, Va., and James M. Garnett of Elmwood, Essex County, Va., 1806-1832. (Transcripts).
(3) Letters of John Randolph of Roanoke to Josiah Quincy, 1812-1826.
(4) Box of Letters of John Randolph to T. M. Forman and T. F. Bryan.
(5) Letters to Jeremiah Evarts, 1781-1831.
William Short Papers. Vols. XXX-XXXVIII, September 4, 1795-January 22, 1818.
[Andrew] Stevenson Papers. Vol. I, December 8, 1809-June 21, 1833.
John Tyler Papers. Vol. I, 1710-1834.
William Wirt Papers. Vol. I, April 8, 1802-May 8, 1825; vol. VI, undated.

MHS: Jefferson Papers. Coolidge Collection.
Jefferson Papers, 1801-1808, Not printed by Paul Leicester Ford in his *Writings of Thomas Jefferson*. Given by Worthington C. Ford, April 20, 1916.
John Quincy Adams MSS., 1794-1816.
Levi Lincoln Papers.
Pickering Papers. Vols. XXI-XXIII, XXVI, XXVIII, XXIX.
T. Pickering Manuscripts. Letters From Correspondents. Vols. XXIII-XXV, XXX.
Sargent Papers. 4 boxes.
Taft Papers, vol. I.
Washburn Papers. Vols. II (Jefferson Papers), IV, IX, XVI.
Winthrop Papers. Vol. XXV (Bowdoin Papers, 1801-1813).
Some unbound letters by Virginians.

NA: Dispatches of James Monroe from France, Spain, and Great Britain, 1803-7; in the volumes for the respective countries.

NYHS: A few Thomas Jefferson, James Madison, and James Monroe items.

NYPL: MSS. Division: James Barbour Papers. Box, 1792-1828.
Expense Accounts of Thomas Jefferson. 1791-1803.
Account Book of Thomas Jefferson. 1804-26. (Photostats).
Jefferson Letters. Letters subsequent to the Revolution. Transcripts; Ford collection. 5 v., 1784-1826.
2 boxes of the Presidential Papers, Thomas Jefferson.
Madison Papers. 2 boxes, 1773-1842.
Monroe Papers. 6 boxes, 1796-October, 1817.
Some stray letters by Virginians.

VSL: Copies of the Letters and Writings of Creed Taylor. From the originals in the possession of A. T. Howard of Farmville, Va.
Fredericksburg Personal Property Rolls.
Land Tax Book, Norfolk City, 1806-15, Auditor's Office Of Virginia.
Petersburg Personal Property Rolls.
Richmond City Licenses.
Richmond City Personal Property and Land Books.

B. CONTEMPORANEOUSLY PUBLISHED SOURCES (NON-GOVERNMENTAL)

An Address To The Freeholders Of The Congressional District Composed Of The Counties Of Greenbrier, Botetourt, Rockbridge, Monroe, Giles, Kanawha, and Mason. By A Citizen Of The District. Printed At The Office Of The Staunton *Political Censor*. March, 1809. NYPL

The Annual Register And Virginian Repository For The Year 1800. From The Blandford Press. Sold by Ross and Douglas, Petersburg, [1801]. LC

Banks, Henry. Propositions To Establish A Mechanic's Bank In The City of Richmond, Connected With Some Objects of Benevolence And Public Utility. Richmond, 1812. NYPL

——. A review of political opinions, published for the benefit of the people of Kentucky. Frankfort, Ky., 1822. LC

——. (Under the pseudonym of "An American":) Sketches Of The History Of France, From The Earliest Historical Accounts, To The Present Time—1806: With Some Remarks Concerning The Life And Achievements Of The Celebrated Napoleon Bonaparte, Now Emperor Of France. By An American. Sola Stat Veritas. Richmond, February, 1806. LC

——. Sketches & propositions, recommending the establishment of an independent system of banking; permanent public roads, a new mode for the recovery of interest on private loans, changes at the penitentiary, and a general system of defence, with some observations necessary to illustrate these several topics. Read before you condemn. Richmond, [1811?]. LC

Broadsides in LC, NYPL.

Burk, John [D.]. Bethlem Gabor, Lord Of Transylvania, Or, The Man Hating Palatine; An Historical Drama In Three Acts. Petersburg, 1807. NYPL

——. Bunker-Hill; Or The Death Of General Warren: An Historic Tragedy. In Five Acts. New York, 1797. NYPL

——. Female Patriotism, Or The Death Of Joan D'Arc: An Historical Play, in V. Acts. New York, 1798. NYPL

——. History Of The Late War In Ireland, With An Account Of The United Irish Association From The First Meeting At Belfast, To The Landing Of The French At Kilale. Philadelphia, 1799. NYPL

——. The History Of Virginia, From Its First Settlement To The Present Day. 4 v.: vol. IV; Commenced by John Burk, and continued by Skelton Jones and Louis Hue Girardin. Petersburg, 1804-5, 1816. NYPL

—— An Oration, Delivered On The Fourth Of March, 1803, At The Court-House, In Petersburg: To Celebrate The Election Of Thomas Jefferson, And The Triumph Of Republicanism. T. Field, Printer. NYPL

Callender, James T. The Prospect Before Us. Richmond, 1800-01. 2 v., with vol. II in two parts. NYPL

——. Sedgwick & Co. Or A Key To The Six Per Cent Cabinet. Philadelphia, 1798. NYPL

[Carey, Matthew.] Carey's General Atlas, Improved And Enlarged: Being A Collection Of Maps Of The World And Quarters, Their Principal Empires, Kingdoms, &c.... Philadelphia. Published by M. Carey, 1814.

Duke De La Rochefoucault [*sic*] Liancourt. Travels Through The United States Of North America, The Country Of The Iroquois, And Upper Canada, In The Years 1795, 1796, And 1797; With An Authentic Account Of Lower Canada. [Trans., H. Neuman]. London, 1799. 2 v.

Gray, Edwin. [No title page; apparently a letter to his constituents.] n. p., n. d. of publication; but letter is dated Southampton, July 11, 1808. NYPL

[Harper, Robert G.] Correspondence Respecting Russia, Between Robert Goodloe Harper, Esq. And Robert Walsh, Jun., Together With The Speech of Mr. Harper Commemorative Of The Russian Victories. Delivered at Georgetown, Columbia, June 5th, 1813. And An Essay on the Future State of Europe. Philadelphia, 1813. NYPL

——. Speech of Robert Goodloe Harper, Esq., at the Celebration of the Recent Triumphs of the Cause of Mankind in Germany. Delivered at Annapolis, January 20, 1814. Alexandria, n. d. LC

Jones, Thomas, A Citizen of Frederick County. An Address To The People Of Virginia In Two Parts. Shewing The Danger Arising From The Unbounded Influence Of Lawyers, And The Impolicy Of Confiding To Them The Legislation Of Our State. Winchester. Printed by Isaac Collett [1807]. NYPL

Julap, Giles, of Chotank, Va. The Glosser; A POEM In Two Books. n. p., March, 1802. BU

Love, Charles. A Poem On The Death of General George Washington, Late President Of The United States. In Two Books. Alexandria, Va., 1800. BU

Marcus [Pseudonym of Oliver Wolcott]. British Influence On The Affairs Of The United States, Proved and Explained. Boston, 1804. LC

Marshall, John. The Life Of George Washington... Vol. V. Philadelphia, 1807.

Munford, William, of the County of Mecklenburg, and State of Virginia. Poems, And Compositions In Prose On Several Occasions. Richmond, 1798. NYPL

An Address From Wilson C. Nicholas, A Representative In Congress From Virginia To His Constituents. Together With A Speech Delivered By Him On The Bill To Interdict Commercial Intercourse With France, England, &c. Richmond, 1809. NYPL

Speeches Delivered By Alexander Smyth, In The House Of Delegates And At The Bar. Richmond, 1811. LC

Tacitus [Pseudonym of Thomas Evans of Virginia according to LC catalogue]. A Series Of Letters Addressed To Thomas Jefferson, Esq., President Of The United States, Concerning His Official Conduct And Principles: With An Appendix Of Important Documents And Illustrations. Philadelphia, 1802. NYPL

Tatham, William. An Historical And Practical Essay On The Culture And Commerce Of Tobacco. London, 1800.

Taylor, John. Arator; Being A Series Of Agricultural Essays, Practical & Political: In Sixty-One Numbers. 2nd ed., revised and enlarged. Georgetown, D. C., 1814.

[Taylor, John.] Definition Of Parties; Or The Political Effects Of The Paper System Considered. Philadelphia, 1794.

Taylor, John. An Inquiry Into The Principles And Policy Of The Government Of The United States. Fredericksburg, 1814.

A Virginian. Odes, And Other Poems. Printed by Augustine Davis. Richmond, 1812. LC

Winterbotham, W. An Historical, Geographical, Commercial, And Philosophical View Of The American United States And Of The European Settlements In America And The West-Indies. Vols. I, III. London, 1795.

Wirt, William. The Letters of the British Spy. 10th ed., revised and corrected. New York, 1832.

[Wirt, William.] The Old Bachelor. Printed At The Enquirer Press, Richmond, Va., For Thomas Ritchie & Fielding Lucas, 1814.

Wirt, William. An Oration Delivered In Richmond On The Fourth Of July, 1800; The Anniversary Of American Independence. Richmond, 1800. LC

[Wirt, William, *et al.*] The Rainbow; First Series. Originally Published In The Richmond Enquirer. Richmond, 1804.

Warren [Pseudonym of James Cheetham]. An Antidote To John Wood's Poison. New York, 1802. NYPL

C. SUBSEQUENTLY PUBLISHED WRITINGS

Adams, Charles F. Memoirs Of John Quincy Adams, Comprising Portions Of His Diary From 1795 To 1848. Vol. I. Philadelphia, 1874.

Bergh, Albert E. The Writings Of Thomas Jefferson... Issued under the Auspices of The Thomas Jefferson Memorial Association of the United States. Washington, 1907. 20 v.

Betts, Edwin M. Thomas Jefferson's Garden Book, 1766-1824, With relevant extracts from his other writings. Philadelphia, 1944. (Memoirs of the American Philosophical Society. Vol. XXII.)

Brown, Everett S. William Plumer's Memorandum Of Proceedings In The United States Senate, 1803-1807. New York, 1923.

Burke, Edmund. Reflections on the Revolution in France... (1790). In: The Works Of The Right Honorable Edmund Burke, 7th ed., vol. III, pp. 231-563. Boston, 1881.

Chinard, Gilbert. The Commonplace Book Of Thomas Jefferson. A Repertory Of His Ideas On Government. Baltimore, 1926. (The Johns Hopkins Studies in Romance Literatures and Languages. Extra vol. II.)

——. "La correspondance de Madame de Staël avec Jefferson," *Revue de littérature comparée*, Année 2 (Paris, 1922), pp. 621-40.

——. The Correspondence of Jefferson and Du Pont de Nemours, with an introduction on Jefferson and the Physiocrats. Baltimore, 1931. (The Johns Hopkins Studies in International Thought.)

——. Jefferson Et Les Idéologues D'Après Sa Correspondance Inédite Avec Destutt De Tracy, Cabanis, J-B. Say, et Auguste Comte. Baltimore, 1925. (The Johns Hopkins Studies In Romance Literatures And Languages. Extra vol. I.)

——. The Letters Of Lafayette And Jefferson, With an introduction and notes. Baltimore, 1929. (The Johns Hopkins Studies in International Thought.)

——. The Literary Bible Of Thomas Jefferson. His Commonplace Book Of Philosophers And Poets. Baltimore, 1928.

Collections Of The Massachusetts Historical Society. 7th Series. Vol. I, The Jefferson Papers (Boston, 1900). Vol. VI, Bowdoin and Temple Papers, Pt. II (Boston, 1907).

Diamond, Sigmund. "Some Jefferson Letters," *Mississippi Valley Historical Review*, vol. XXVIII, no. 2, September, 1941, pp. 225-42.

[Dodd, William E.] "Letters of John Taylor, of Caroline County, Virginia," *The John P. Branch Historical Papers of Randolph-Macon College*, vol. II, nos. 3 and 4 (Richmond, 1908), pp. 253-353.

Donnan, Elizabeth. Papers Of James A. Bayard, 1796-1815. Washington, 1915. (Annual Report Of The American Historical Association For The Year 1913, vol. II.)

Early History Of The University Of Virginia, As Contained In The Letters Of Thomas Jefferson And Joseph C. Cabell, Hitherto Unpublished... Richmond, 1856.

Edwards, Ninian W. History Of Illinois, From 1778 To 1833; And Life And Times Of Ninian Edwards. Springfield, 1870.

Fitzpatrick, John C. The Writings Of George Washington from the Original Manuscript Sources, 1745-1799. Prepared under the direction of the United States George Washington Bicentennial Commission and published by authority of Congress. Vol. XXXVII, November 1, 1798-December 13, 1799. Washington, 1940.

Ford, Paul Leicester. The Writings Of Thomas Jefferson. New York, 1892-9. 10 v.

Ford, Worthington C. "Letters of Joseph Jones of Virginia to James Madison," *Proceedings Of The Massachusetts Historical Society*, 2nd ser., vol. XV, 1901-02 (Boston, 1902), pp. 116-161.

——. "Letters of James Monroe," *ib.*, vol. XLII (3rd ser., vol. II, 1908-09) (Boston, 1909), pp. 318-41.
——. Thomas Jefferson Correspondence Printed From The Originals In The Collection Of William K. Bixby. Boston, 1916.
——. The Writings Of George Washington. Vols. XIII-XIV, 1794-9. New York, 1891.
"Glimpses Of The Past. Correspondence Of Thomas Jefferson," *Missouri Historical Society*, vol. III, nos. 4-6, April-June, 1936, (St. Louis, 1936), pp. 77-133.
Hamilton, Stanislaus M. The Writings Of James Monroe... Vols. I-V, 1778-1816. New York, 1898-1900.
Hammond, Hans. "Letters of John Taylor of Caroline," *Virginia Magazine Of History And Biography*, vol. LII, nos. 1-2, January, April, 1944, pp. 1-14, 121-134.
Hunt Gaillard. The Writings Of James Madison... Vols. I-VIII, 1769-1819. New York, 1900.
Lamont, Hammond. Burke's Speech On Conciliation With America. Boston, 1898.
Letters And Other Writings Of James Madison, Fourth President Of The United States. Published By Order Of Congress. Vols. II, IV. New York, 1884.
"Letters of Reverend James Madison, President of the College of William and Mary, to Thomas Jefferson," *William and Mary College Quarterly Historical Magazine*, 2nd ser., vol. V, nos. 2-3, April-July, 1925, pp. 77-95, 145-58.
"Letters of James Monroe," *Bulletin of the New York Public Library*, vol. IV, 1900, pp. 41-61; V, 1901, pp. 371-82, 431-3; VI, 1902, pp. 210-30; XII, 1908, pp. 527-30.
"Letters of James Monroe," *Tyler's Quarterly Historical and Genealogical Magazine*, vol. IV, no. 2, October, 1922, pp. 96-108; IV, no. 4, April, 1923, pp. 405-11; V, no. 1, July, 1923, pp. 11-28.
"Letters Of John Randolph, Of Roanoke, To General Thomas Marsh Forman," *Virginia Magazine Of History And Biography*, vol. XLIX, no. 3, July, 1941, pp. 201-16.
"Letters of Spencer Roane," *Bulletin of the New York Public Library*, vol. X, 1906, pp. 167-80.
"Letters of Thomas Jefferson to William Short," *William and Mary College Quarterly Historical Magazine*, 2nd ser., vol. XI, nos. 3-4, July, October, 1931, pp. 242-50, 336-42; XII, nos. 2, 4, April, October, 1932, pp. 145-56, 287-304; XIII, no. 2, April, 1933, pp. 98-116.
"Letters from John Marshall to his wife," *William and Mary College Quarterly Historical Magazine*, 2nd ser., vol. III, no. 2, April, 1923, pp. 73-90.
Lodge, Henry Cabot. Life And Letters Of George Cabot. Boston, 1877.
McGuire, J. C. Selections From The Private Correspondence Of James Madison, From 1813 To 1836. Washington, 1858.

Malone, Dumas. Correspondence between Thomas Jefferson And Pierre Samuel Du Pont De Nemours, 1798-1817. Translations by Linwood Lehman. Boston and New York, 1930.

Marraro, Howard R. "Unpublished Correspondence Of Jefferson And Adams To Màzzei," *Virginia Magazine Of History And Biography,* vol. LI, no. 2, April, 1943, pp. 113-33.

Mason, Frances N. John Norton & Sons, Merchants Of London And Virginia. Being the Papers from their Counting House for the Years 1750 to 1795. Richmond, 1937.

Mayo, Bernard. Thomas Jefferson and his unknown brother Randolph. Twenty eight letters exchanged between Thomas and Randolph Jefferson... during the years 1807 to 1815... Charlottesville, 1942.

Moffat, L. G. and Carrière, J. M. "A Frenchman Visits Norfolk, Fredericksburg and Orange County, 1816," *Virginia Magazine Of History And Biography,* vol. LIII, nos. 2-3, April-July, 1945, pp. 101-23, 197-214.

Norflett, Fillmore. "Norfolk, Portsmouth, and Gosport As Seen By Moreau de Saint-Mery in March, April, And May, 1794," *Virginia Magazine Of History And Biography,* vol. XLVIII, nos. 1-3, January-July, 1940, pp. 12-30, 153-64, 253-64.

Oster, John E. The Political and Economic Doctrines of John Marshall... New York, 1914.

Padgett, James A. "Letters of Thomas Newton, Jr.," *William and Mary College Quarterly Historical Magazine,* 2nd ser., vol. XVI, no. 1, January, 1936, pp. 38-70.

——. "Letters from Thomas Newton," *ib.,* 2nd ser., vol. XVI, no. 2, April, 1936, pp. 192-205.

"Papers of Archibald Stuart," *William and Mary College Quarterly Historical Magazine,* 2nd ser., vol. V, no. 4, October, 1925, pp. 285-99; VI, no. 1, January, 1926, pp. 80-85.

Pendleton, Edmund. "The Danger Not Over. October 5, 1801," *The John P. Branch Historical Papers of Randolph-Macon College,* vol. IV, no. 2, June, 1914, pp. 80-85.

"The Leven Powell Correspondence," *The John P. Branch Historical Papers of Randolph-Macon College,* vol. I, no. 3, 1901, pp. 217-55.

Richardson, James D. A Compilation Of The Messages And Papers Of The Presidents, 1789-1908. Vol. I, 1789-1817. New York, 1908.

"Some Letters of John Preston," *William and Mary College Quarterly Historical Magazine,* 2nd ser., vol. I, no. 1, January, 1921, pp. 42-51; II, no. 3, July, 1922, pp. 187-93.

Tyler, Lyon G. The Letters And Times Of The Tylers. Vol. I (Richmond, 1884); III (Williamsburg, 1896).

Washington, H. A. The Writings Of Thomas Jefferson... New York, 1857. 9 v.

D. PUBLISHED RECORDS, STATISTICS, AND LEGISLATIVE DEBATES

1. *National*

American State Papers. Documents, Legislative And Executive Of The Congress Of The United States... Selected and edited under the authority of Congress, by Walter Lowrie & Matthew St. Clair Clarke. Class 1, Foreign Relations, vols. II-IV; Class 4, Commerce And Navigation, vols. I-II. Washington, 1832-4.

Annals Of The Congress Of The United States. The Debates And Proceedings In The Congress Of The United States... Fourth Congress, 1st Session-Fourteenth Congress, 1st Session. Washington, 1849-54.

Congressional Directory For The Second Session Of The Fourteenth Congress Of The United States. Washington City. Printed by Daniel Rapine, 1816.

Coxe, Tench. A Statement Of The Arts And Manufactures Of The United States Of America, For The Year 1810. Philadelphia, 1814. (United States Treasury Statement.)

Pitkin, Timothy. A Statistical View Of The Commerce Of The United States Of America... 2nd ed., with additions and corrections. New York, 1817.

Seybert, Adam. Statistical Annals: Embracing Views Of The Population, Commerce, Navigation... Of The United States Of America... Philadelphia, 1818.

[United States.] Second Census Of The United States. Return Of The Whole Number Of Persons Within The Several Districts Of The United States... Washington, 1801.

United States. Census Office. Third Census. Aggregate Amount Of Each Description Of Persons Within The United States Of America... In The Year 1810. Washington, 1811.

2. *State*

Calendar Of Virginia State Papers And Other Manuscripts... Arranged, edited under the direction of H. W. Flournoy. Vols. IX, X. Richmond, 1890, 1892.

A Collection Of All Such Acts Of The General Assembly Of Virginia Of A Public And Permanent Nature As Are Now In Force... Vol. I. Richmond. Printed by Samuel Pleasants, Jun., and Henry Pace, 1803.

Documents Containing Statistics Of Virginia Ordered To Be Printed By The State Convention Sitting In The City Of Richmond, 1850-51. Richmond, 1851.

Hening, William W. The Statutes At Large; Being A Collection Of All The Laws Of Virginia, From The First Session Of The Legislature, In The Year 1619. Vols. XII, XIII. Richmond, 1823.

Journal, Acts, And Proceedings Of A General Convention Of The Commonwealth Of Virginia, Assembled In Richmond, On Monday, The Fifth Day of October, In The Year Of Our Lord, 1829. Richmond, 1829.

Journal Of The House Of Delegates Of The Commonwealth Of Virginia... [Sessions from November 8, 1796, through the one beginning November 11, 1816.] Richmond. LC, NYPL, VSL

Journal Of The Senate Of The Commonwealth Of Virginia... [Sessions beginning December 1, 1800; December 7, 1801; December 3, 1804; December 1, 1806; and sessions from December 5, 1808, through the one beginning November 11, 1816.] LC, NYPL, VSL

The Norfolk Directory for 1806. Printed by Chs. H. Simmons. Norfolk, 1806. LC

Summers, Lewis P. Annals of Southwest Virginia, 1769-1800. Abingdon, Va., 1929.

Supplement, Containing The Acts Of The General Assembly, Of A Public And Generally Interesting Nature, Passed Since The Session Of Assembly Which Commenced In The Year One Thousand Eight Hundred And Seven. Richmond. Printed by Samuel Pleasants, 1812.

Swem, Earl G. and Williams, John W. A Register Of The General Assembly Of Virginia, 1776-1918, And Of The Constitutional Conventions. Richmond, 1918.

E. NEWSPAPERS

Newspaper titles are those which represent the basic name used throughout the particular period. C. S. Brigham's *Bibliography* has generally been followed in this respect. Asterisks denote years or periods for which a majority or more of the issues of the newspaper were available. The issues are scattered throughout the indicated libraries.

1. *Virginia*

Alexandria

Alexandria Advertiser. December 8, 1800-February, 1801.* Complete file. AAS

Columbian Mirror and Alexandria Gazette. 1796,* 1797-February, 1800. AAS, HU, LC, NYPL, NYHS

Times. 1797,* 1798,* 1799-February, 1801. AAS, HU, LC, NYPL

Charlestown (later Wellsburg, Brooke County)

Charlestown Gazette. April 1, 1814. AAS

Charles Town (Jefferson County)

Farmer's Repository. 1808-March, 1816.* AAS, HU, LC, NYPL

Clarksburg

Bye-Stander. February 1, 1814. AAS

Dumfries

Republican Journal. 1796. HU

Fincastle

Fincastle Weekly Advertiser. 1801. AAS, LC

Herald of Virginia. December 5, 1800. LC

Fredericksburg

Apollo. 1803-04. AAS, HU
Courier. 1800-01. AAS, LC
Fredericksburg News-Letter. May 25, 1801. HU
Genius of Liberty. 1798. AAS, LC
Impartial Observer Or The Rights Of Man. February 5, 1811. NYHS
Republican Citizen. 1796-7.* HU
Virginia Express. 1803-05. AAS, HU
Virginia Herald. 1796-1800,* 1801, 1802,* 1803, 1804-10,* 1811, 1812-13,* 1814, 1815, January 3-March 30, 1816.* AAS, HU, LC, NYPL, NYHS

Leesburg

True American. December 30, 1800. LC
Washingtonian. 1810-11. AAS

Lexington

Rockbridge Repository. 1801, 1803-05. AAS, HU, LC
Virginia Telegraphe. 1803-04, 1806-08. AAS, HU

Lynchburg

Lynchburg and Farmer's Gazette. 1794-5. AAS
Lynchburg Gazette. February 22, 1804. DU
Lynchburg Press. 1809, 1810, 1813, 1815, January 2, 1816. AAS, LC
Lynchburg Star. 1806,* 1807, 1809, 1812. AAS, LC
Lynchburg Weekly Gazette. 1798-1801. AAS, LC, NYHS, NYPL
Lynchburg Weekly Museum. 1797-8. AAS, HU

Martinsburg

Berkeley Intelligencer. 1799, 1800, 1807. BA, LC
Martinsburgh Gazette. December 14, 1810-1812,* 1813. LC
Potowmac Guardian. 1793-8, 1800. AAS, BPL, HU
Republican Atlas. May 6, 1801. LC

Morgantown

Monongalia Gazette. September 8, 1809. AAS

New Market

Virginische Volksberichter. 1807, 1808-June 7, 1809.* DU

Norfolk

American Beacon. 1815-April, 1816. AAS, LC
American Gazette. 1793-5, 1796,* 1797. AAS, HU, LC
Commercial Register. August 16, 1802-January 11, 1803.* Complete file. AAS
Epitome of the Times. 1798-1802. AAS, HU, LC, NYPL
Norfolk Gazette and Publick Ledger. July 17, 1804-March, 1816.* AAS, BA, HU, LC, NYHS, VSL
Norfolk Herald. 1794-5, 1796-1802,* 1803-13, 1814-15,* January 29, 1816. AAS, HU, LC, NYHS, NYPL

Petersburg

Petersburg Daily Courier. 1814. AAS
Petersburg Intelligencer. 1800-04, 1805-07,* 1808-15. AAS, DU, HU, LC, NYHS, NYPL
Republican. 1801-02, 1803,* 1804-10, 1812-13. AAS, HU, LC, NYPL
Virginia Apollo. 1807. AAS
Virginia Gazette and Petersburg Intelligencer. 1793-6, 1797,* 1798-1800. AAS, HU, LC, NYPL, VSL
Virginia Mercury. 1807-08. AAS

Richmond

Daily Compiler. 1813,* 1814-March, 1816. AAS, LC, NYPL, VSL
Enquirer. 1804-March, 1816.* Complete file. AAS, HU, LC, NYHS, NYPL, VSL
Examiner. 1798-1800, 1801-03,* 1804. AAS, HU, LC, NYHS, VSL
Friend of the People. 1800. AAS, LC
Impartial Observer. 1806-07. AAS, HU, VSL
Observatory. 1797-8. AAS, HU, LC
Press. 1800. AAS, LC
Recorder. 1801, 1802-03.* AAS, BA, HU, VSL
Richmond Chronicle. 1795-6. AAS, HU
Richmond and Manchester Advertiser. 1795, 1796.* AAS, HU, LC
Spirit of 'Seventy-Six. September 13-December 30, 1808,* 1809. AAS, HU, LC, NYPL, VSL
Virginia Argus. November 19-December 30, 1796,* 1797-8, 1799-March, 1816.* AAS, DU, HU, LC, NYHS, NYPL, VSL
Virginia Federalist. 1799-1800. AAS, HU, LC
Virginia Gazette and General Advertiser. 1794-5, 1796,* 1797-8, 1799,* 1800-01, 1802-08,* 1809. AAS, BA, HU, LC, NYHS, NYPL, VSL
Virginia Gazette. And Richmond and Manchester Advertiser. 1794-5. AAS
Virginia Gazette and Weekly Advertiser. 1794-5, 1796-April 22, 1797.* AAS, HU
Virginia Patriot. December 26, 1809-February 28, 1816.* AAS, LC, VSL
Virginian. 1808.* AAS, LC, VSL

Shepherdstown

Impartial Observer. 1797. HU

Staunton

Candid Review. 1805, 1807. HU, LC
Observer. 1814. AAS
People's Friend. 1812-13. AAS
Phenix. 1798-9, 1804. AAS, HU
Political Mirror. 1800-01. AAS, LC
Republican Farmer. 1810-11, 1814. AAS, LC
Spirit of the Press. May 18, 1811. AAS
Staunton Eagle. August 14-December 25, 1807,* 1808-10. AAS, BA, HU, LC, NYHS

Staunton Political Censor. 1808-09. AAS
Virginia Gazette. 1796-7. HU, VSL

Winchester

Centinel and Winchester Gazette. 1793-5, 1796,* 1797-8, 1800-01, 1805-11, 1813, 1815. AAS, HU, LC
Democratic Lamp. November 21, 1809. LC
Independent Register. 1804. AAS, HU
Philanthropist. 1806-09. AAS, BA, HU, LC
Republican Constellation. 1813-14. AAS
Winchester Triumph of Liberty. May 13, 1801. LC

2. *Non-Virginia*

Boston

Columbian Centinel. 1800-01,* 1806-07.* NYPL
Independent Chronicle. 1800,* 1806.* NYHS, NYPL

Philadelphia

Gazette of the United States. 1800,* 1801. NYPL

Washington, D. C.

National Intelligencer. March 4, 1801-1815.* LC, NYHS, NYPL

F. PERIODICALS

Lexington

Virginia Religious Magazine. Published Under The Patronage Of The Synod Of Virginia. Vols. II-III, 1806-07. YU

Richmond

National Magazine; Or A Political, Historical, Biographical, And Literary Repository. Vols. I-II, nos. 1-8. Richmond, 1799-1800. AAS, CU, LC, NYHS
Visitor. Vols. I-II, February 11, 1809-August 18, 1810. AAS, LC

Winchester

Monthly Magazine and Literary Journal. Vols. I-II, May, 1812-April, 1813. LC

III. SECONDARY WORKS

A. GEOGRAPHICAL

Paullin, Charles O. Atlas Of The Historical Geography Of The United States. Edited by John K. Wright. 1932. (Publications of the Carnegie Institution of Washington and the American Geographical Society of New York.)
Robinson, Morgan P. Virginia Counties: Those Resulting from Virginia Legislation. Richmond, 1916. (Bulletin of the Virginia State Library, vol. IX, nos. 1-3, January-July, 1816.)

Surface, George T. Studies on the Geography of Virginia. Thesis, University of Pennsylvania, 1907.

B. ECONOMIC AND SOCIAL

Abernethy, Thomas P. "Democracy and the Southern Frontier," *Journal of Southern History*, vol. IV, 1938, pp. 3-13.

——. Three Virginia Frontiers. Louisiana State University Press, 1940.

Ames, Susie M. "A Typical Virginia Business Man Of The Revolutionary Era: Nathaniel Little Savage And His Account Book," *Journal of Economic and Business History*, vol. III, 1930-31, pp. 407-23.

Ballagh, James C., ed. Economic History, 1607-1865. Richmond, 1909. (The South in the Building of the Nation, vol. V.)

Bassett, John S. "The Relation between the Virginia Planter and the London Merchant," *Annual Report Of The American Historical Association For The Year 1901*, vol. I (Washington, 1902), pp. 551-75.

Bezanson, Anne, Gray, R. D., Hussey, M. [Part I:] Wholesale Prices in Philadelphia, 1784-1861. Part II: Series of Relative Monthly Prices. (Pennsylvania University. Wharton School of Finance and Commerce, Industrial Research Department. Research Studies, XXIX-XXX, 1936-7.)

Brooks, Jerome E. Tobacco, Its History Illustrated By The Books, Manuscripts and Engravings In the Library of George Arents, Jr., Together with an introductory essay, A Glossary and Bibliographical Notes. New York, 1937 ff. 4 v.

Bruce, Kathleen. "Virginian Agricultural Decline To 1860: A Fallacy," *Agricultural History*, vol. VI, no. 1, January, 1932, pp. 3-13.

——. Virginia Iron Manufacture In The Slave Era. New York, 1931.

Bruce, Philip A. Economic History of Virginia in the Seventeenth Century... New York, 1907. 2 v.

——. Social Life of Virginia in the Seventeenth Century... Richmond, 1907.

Buron, Edmond. "Notes and Documents. Statistics on Franco-American Trade, 1778-1806," *Journal of Economic and Business History*, vol. IV, November, 1931-August, 1932, pp. 571-80.

Cabell, N. F. (With Notes by E. G. Swem). "Some Fragments of an intended report on the post revolutionary history of agriculture in Virginia," *William and Mary College Quarterly Historical Magazine*, vol. XXVI, no. 3, January, 1918, pp. 145-64.

Carman, Harry J. Social And Economic History Of The United States. Vols. I-II. Boston and New York, 1930, 1934.

Clark, Victor S. History of Manufactures in the United States. New York, 1929. Vols. I, III. (Carnegie Institution of Washington, Publications.)

Cole, Arthur H. Wholesale Commodity Prices In The United States, 1700-1861. Cambridge, 1938.

——. Statistical Supplement. Actual Wholesale Prices of Various Commodities. Cambridge, 1938.

Craven, Avery O. Soil Exhaustion as a factor in the agricultural history of Virginia and Maryland, 1606-1860. Urbana, Ill., 1926.

Galpin, W. Freeman. "The American Grain Trade to the Spanish Peninsula, 1810-1814," *American Historical Review*, vol. XXVIII, October, 1922-July, 1923, pp. 24-44.

——. "The American Grain Trade Under The Embargo of 1808," *Journal of Economic and Business History*, vol. II, 1929-30, pp. 71-100.

——. The Grain Supply Of England During The Napoleonic Period. New York, 1925. (University of Michigan Publications. History And Political Science. Vol. VI.)

——. "The Grain Trade of Alexandria, Virginia, 1801-1815," *North Carolina Historical Review*, vol. IV, October, 1927, pp. 404-27.

——. "Grain Trade of New Orleans, 1804-14," *Mississippi Valley Historical Review*, vol. XIV, March, 1928, pp. 496-507.

Gray, Lewis C. Assisted by Esther K. Thompson. With an introductory note by Henry C. Taylor. History of Agriculture in the Southern United States To 1860. New York, 1941. 2 v.

Hess, Sister Mary A. American Tobacco And Central European Policy: Early Nineteenth Century. Washington, 1948.

Holmes, George K. Tobacco Crop Of The United States, 1612-1911. Washington, 1912. (United States Department of Agriculture. Bureau of Statistics. Circular 33.)

Jacobstein, Meyer. The Tobacco Industry In The United States. New York, 1907.

Johnson, Emory R., Van Metre, T. W., Huebner, G. G., and Hanchett, D. S. History of Domestic and Foreign Commerce of the United States. Washington, 1922. 2 v. in 1. (Publications of the Carnegie Institution of Washington.)

Morton, Louis. Robert Carter of Nomini Hall, A Virginia Tobacco Planter of the Eighteenth Century. Williamsburg, Va., 1941.

Peterson, Arthur G. "The Alexandria Market Prior To The Civil War," *William and Mary College Quarterly Historical Magazine*, 2nd ser., vol. XII, 1932, pp. 104-14.

——. "Commerce of Virginia, 1789-1791," *ib.*, 2nd ser., vol. X, October, 1930, pp. 302-9.

——. "Flour and grist milling in Virginia. A Brief History," *Virginia Magazine Of History And Biography*, vol. XLIII, no. 2, April, 1935, pp. 98-108.

——. Historical Study of Prices Received by Producers of Farm Products in Virginia, 1801-1927. Blacksburg, Va., March, 1929. (Virginia Polytechnic Institute. Virginia Agricultural Experiment Station. Technical Bulletin 37.)

Phillips, Ulrich B. American Negro Slavery. A Survey of the Supply, Employment and Control of Negro Labor as Determined by the Plantation Régime. New York, 1929.

——. " The Economic Cost of Slaveholding in the Cotton Belt," *Political Science Quarterly*, vol. XX, no. 2, June, 1905, pp. 257-75.

——. Life And Labor In The Old South. Boston, 1930.

——. " The Origin And Growth Of The Southern Black Belts," *American Historical Review*, vol. XI, October, 1905-July, 1906, pp. 798-816.

——. Plantation and Frontier, vols. I and II of: A Documentary History Of American Industrial Society, ed. by John R. Commons, U. B. Phillips, *et al.* Cleveland, 1910.

Robert, Joseph C. The Tobacco Kingdom. Plantation, Market, and Factory In Virginia and North Carolina, 1800-1860. Durham, No. Car., 1938.

Smith, W. B. " Wholesale Commodity Prices In The United States, 1795-1824," *Review of Economic Statistics*, vol. IX, 1927, pp. 171-84.

Smith, Walter B. and Arthur H. Cole. Fluctuations in American Business, 1790-1860. Cambridge, 1935.

" The Story of the Development of the Present-Day Varieties of Tobacco," *Yearbook of Agriculture*, 1936, pp. 805-22. (U. S. Department of Agriculture.)

Taylor, George R. "Agrarian Discontent In The Mississippi Valley preceding the War of 1812," *Journal of Political Economy*, vol. XXXIX, February-December, 1931, pp. 471-505.

——. " Prices in the Mississippi Valley Preceding the War of 1812," *Journal of Economic and Business History*, vol. III, 1930-31, pp. 148-63.

——. " Wholesale Commodity Prices At Charleston, South Carolina, 1796-1861," *ibid.*, vol. IV, 1931-2, pp. 848-68 and appendix.

Tyler, Lyon G. "Aristocracy in Massachusetts and Virginia," *William and Mary College Quarterly Historical Magazine*, vol. XXVI, no. 4, April, 1918, pp. 277-81.

——. " Society in East Virginia," *ib.*, vol. XXII, no. 4, April, 1914, pp. 221-8.

U. S. Senate Report, 53 Cong., 2 Sess., vol. IV, no. 259, pt. II. General Statement by articles of Exports, The Growth, Produce, and Manufacture of the United States To Foreign Countries, By Fiscal Years and Decades, From 1789 to 1893, Inclusive. Washington, 1895.

Wertenbaker, Thomas J. Patrician and Plebeian in Virginia or the Origin and Development of the Social Classes of the Old Dominion. Charlottesville, Va., 1910.

——. The Planters of Colonial Virginia. Princeton, 1922.

C. POLITICAL

Beach, Rex. " Spencer Roane and the Richmond Junto," *William and Mary College Quarterly Historical Magazine*, 2nd ser., vol. XXII, no. 1, January, 1942, pp. 1-17.

Beard, Charles A. An Economic Interpretation of the Constitution of the United States. New York, 1929.

——. Economic Origins of Jeffersonian Democracy. New York, 1936.

Chandler, Julian A. C. The History of Suffrage in Virginia. Baltimore, 1901. (Johns Hopkins University Studies In Historical and Political Science. Ninth series, nos. VI-VII.)

——. Representation In Virginia. Baltimore, 1896. (Johns Hopkins University Studies in Historical and Political Science. Fourteenth series, VI-VII.)

Drell, Bernard. "John Taylor of Caroline and the Preservation of an old social order," *Virginia Magazine Of History And Biography*, vol. XLVI, no. 4, October, 1938, pp. 285-98.

Ferguson, Isabel. "County Court In Virginia, 1700-1830," *North Carolina Historical Review*, vol. VIII, no. 1, January, 1931, pp. 14-40.

Harrell, Isaac S. "Some Neglected Phases Of The Revolution In Virginia," *William and Mary College Quarterly Historical Magazine*, 2nd ser., vol. V, no. 2, April, 1925, pp. 159-70.

——. Loyalism In Virginia. Chapters in the Economic History of the Revolution. Durham, 1926.

Honeywell, Roy J. "President Jefferson and his Successor," *American Historical Review*, vol. XLVI, no. 1, October, 1940, pp. 64-75.

Prufer, Julius F. "The Franchise In Virginia From Jefferson Through The Convention Of 1829," *William and Mary College Quarterly Historical Magazine*, 2nd ser., vol. VII, no. 4, October, 1927, pp. 255-70; vol. VIII, no. 1, January, 1928, pp. 17-32.

D. CULTURAL

Becker, Carl. "What Is Still Living in the Political Philosophy of Thomas Jefferson," *American Historical Review*, vol. XLVIII, no. 4, July, 1943, pp. 691-706.

Curti, Merle. The Growth Of American Thought. 2nd ed. New York, 1943.

Dorfman, Joseph. "The Economic Philosophy Of Thomas Jefferson," *Political Science Quarterly*, vol. LV, March, 1940, pp. 98-121.

Hofstadter, Richard. "Parrington And The Jeffersonian Tradition," *Journal of the History of Ideas*, vol. II, no. 4, October, 1941, pp. 391-400.

Hubbell, Jay B. "William Wirt and the Familiar Essay in Virginia," *William and Mary College Quarterly Historical Magazine*, ser. 2, vol. XXIII, no. 2, April, 1943, pp. 136-52.

Jenkins, William S. Pro-Slavery Thought In The Old South. Chapel Hill, No. Car., 1935.

Koch, Adrienne. The Philosophy Of Thomas Jefferson. New York, 1943.

Lee, James M. History of American Journalism. New ed., revised. Boston and New York, 1923.

McMurtrie, Douglas C. The Beginnings of Printing in Virginia. Lexington, Va., 1935.

——. The Beginnings of Printing in West Virginia... Charleston, W. Va., 1935.

——. A History Of Printing In The United States. The Story of the Introduction of the press and of its history and influence during the pioneer period in each state of the union. Vol. II, Middle & South Atlantic States. New York, 1936.

Martin, Benjamin E. "Transition Period Of The American Press. Leading Editors Early In This Century," *Magazine Of American History*, vol. XVII, no. 4, April, 1887, pp. 273-94.

Mott, Frank L. A History Of American Magazines, vol. I, 1741-1850. New York and London, 1930.

——. American Journalism, A History Of Newspapers In The United States Through 250 Years, 1690 to 1940. New York, 1941.

Painter, F. V. N. Poets Of Virginia. Richmond, 1907.

Parrington, Vernon L. Main Currents in American Thought, An Interpretation Of American Literature From The Beginnings To 1920. Vols. I, II. New York, 1927.

Trent, William P. English Culture in Virginia. A Study Of The Gilmer Letters And An Account Of The English Professors Obtained By Jefferson For The University Of Virginia. Baltimore, 1889. (Johns Hopkins University Studies in Historical and Political Science. Herbert B. Adams, ed. Seventh Series, nos. V-VI.)

E. BIOGRAPHICAL

Adair, Douglass. "The New Jefferson," *William and Mary Quarterly*, 3rd ser., vol. III, no. 1, January, 1946, pp. 123-33.

Ambler, Charles H. Thomas Ritchie, A Study in Virginia Politics. Richmond, 1913.

Anderson, Dice R. William Branch Giles: A Study in the Politics of Virginia and the Nation from 1790 to 1830. Menasha, Wisconsin, 1914.

Beveridge, Albert J. The Life Of John Marshall. Boston, 1916-9. 4 v.

Biographical Directory Of The American Congress, 1774-1927... United States Printing Office, 1928. (Sixty-Ninth Congress, Second Session, House Document No. 783.)

Boyd, Thomas. Light-horse Harry Lee. New York, 1931.

Brant, Irving. James Madison, Father of the Constitution, 1783-1800. New York, 1950.

Bruce, William C. John Randolph of Roanoke, 1773-1833, A Biography Based Largely On New Material. New York, 1922. 2 v.

Chinard, Gilbert. Thomas Jefferson, The Apostle Of Americanism. 2nd ed., revised. Boston, 1943.

Conway, Moncure D. Omitted Chapters Of History Disclosed In The Life And Papers Of Edmund Randolph. 2nd ed. New York, 1889.

Dictionary of American Biography. Under the Auspices of the American Council of Learned Societies. Edited by Allen Johnson and Dumas Malone. New York, 1928-37. 20 v. and an index.

Dodd, William E. "John Taylor, of Caroline, Prophet of Secession," *John P. Branch Historical Papers of Randolph-Macon College*, vol. II, nos. 3-4, Richmond, 1908, pp. 214-52.

Encyclopedia of Virginia Biography. Lyon G. Tyler, ed. Vol. II. New York, 1915.

Garland, Hugh A. The Life Of John Randolph Of Roanoke. 2 v. in 1. 11th ed. New York, 1857.

Henry, William Wirt. Patrick Henry, Life, Correspondence and Speeches. Vols. II-III. New York, 1891.

Hilldrup, Robert L. The Life and Times of Edmund Pendleton. Chapel Hill, No. Car., 1939.

Hunt, Gaillard. The Life of James Madison. New York, 1902.

Kennedy, John. Memoirs Of The Life Of William Wirt, Attorney General Of The United States. Philadelphia, 1849. 2 v.

Long, W. S. "James Barbour," *John P. Branch Historical Papers of Randolph-Macon College,* vol. IV, no. 2, June, 1914, pp. 34-64.

Malone, Dumas. Jefferson And His Time. Vol. I: Jefferson the Virginian. Boston, 1948.

Mayo, Bernard. Henry Clay, Spokesman Of The New West. Cambridge, 1937.

Morgan, George. The Life Of James Monroe. Boston, 1921.

Pickering, Octavius and Upham, Charles W. The Life of Timothy Pickering. Vols. III-IV. Boston, 1873.

Powell, Robert C. A Biographical Sketch Of Col. Leven Powell, Including His Correspondence During The Revolutionary War. Alexandria, Va., 1877.

Quincy, Edmund. Life Of Josiah Quincy Of Massachusetts. Boston, 1867.

Randall, Henry S. The Life Of Thomas Jefferson. New York, 1858. 3 v.

Ryland, Elizabeth H. *Résumé* of the Henry Banks Papers in the Virginia Historical Society. (Typescript; in my possession.)

Simms, Henry H. Life Of John Taylor, The Story of a Brilliant Leader in the Early Virginia State Rights School. Richmond, 1932.

Smith, Harry K. "Daniel Sheffey," *John P. Branch Historical Papers of Randolph-Macon College,* vol. IV, no. 4, June, 1916, pp. 364-71.

Wyatt IV, Edward A. John Daly Burk, Patriot-Playwright-Historian. Charlottesville, Va., 1936. (Southern Sketches, no. 7, 1st series.)

F. INTERNATIONAL

Bemis, Samuel F. A Diplomatic History Of The United States. Revised ed. New York, 1942.

Benns, F. Lee. The American Struggle For The British West-India Carrying Trade, 1815-1830. n.p. (Indiana University Studies. Vol. X, Study no. 56, March, 1923.)

Broadley, A. M. Napoleon In Caricature, 1795-1821. With an introductory essay on pictorial satire as a factor in Napoleonic History by J. Holland Rose. London, 1911. 2 v.

Darling, Arthur B. Our Rising Empire, 1763-1803. New Haven, 1940.

Faÿ, Bernard. The Revolutionary Spirit In France And America, A Study of moral and intellectual relations between France and the United States at the end of the eighteenth century. Trans. by Ramon Guthrie. New York, 1927.

Giddens, Paul H. "Contemporary American Opinion of Napoleon," *Journal of American History*, vol. XXVI, 1932, pp. 189-204.

Goodman, Warren H. "The Origins of the War of 1812: A Survey of Changing Interpretations," *Mississippi Valley Historical Review*, vol. XXVIII, no. 2, September, 1941, pp. 171-86.

Hartfield, Clara V. Contemporary American Opinion Of Napoleon I. Unpublished dissertation, Johns Hopkins University, 1925.

Hazen, Charles D. Contemporary American Opinion of the French Revolution. Baltimore, 1897. (Johns Hopkins University Studies in History and Political Science. Herbert B. Adams, ed. Extra vol. XVI.)

Heckscher, Eli F. The Continental System, An Economic Interpretation. Edited by Harold Westergaard. Oxford, 1922. (Publications of the Carnegie Endowment for International Peace. Division of Economics and History.)

Hunt, Gaillard. "Joseph Gales on the War Manifesto of 1812," *American Historical Review*, vol. XIII, no. 2, January, 1908, pp. 303-10.

Jones, Howard M. America And French Culture, 1750-1848. Chapel Hill, 1927.

Jones, Howard M. and Aaron, Daniel. "Notes on the Napoleonic Legend in America," *Franco-American Review*, vol. II, 1937-8, pp. 10-26.

Lyon, E. Wilson. "The Directory and the United States," *American Historical Review*, vol. XLIII, no. 3, April, 1938, pp. 514-32.

——. "The Franco-American Convention of 1800," *Journal of Modern History*, vol. XII, no. 3, September, 1940, pp. 305-33.

——. Louisiana in French Diplomacy, 1759-1804. Norman, Okla., 1934.

Maccunn, F. J. The Contemporary English View Of Napoleon. London, 1914.

Melvin, Frank E. Napoleon's Navigation System, A Study of trade control during the Continental Blockade. New York, 1919.

Ogg, Frederic A. "Jay's Treaty and the slavery interests of the United States," *Annual Report of the American Historical Association for the Year 1901*, vol. I, pp. 273-98.

Pelzer, Louis. "Economic Factors in the Acquisition of Louisiana," *Proceedings of the Mississippi Valley Historical Association for the Year 1912-1913*, vol. VI, pp. 109-28.

Philips, Edith. Louis Hue Girardin and Nicholas Gouin Dufief And Their Relations With Thomas Jefferson. An Unknown Episode Of The French Emigration In America. Baltimore, 1926. (Johns Hopkins Studies In Romance Literatures And Languages. Extra vol. no. III.)

Pratt, Julius W. Expansionists Of 1812. New York, 1925.

Savelle, Max. "The Appearance of an American Attitude toward External Affairs, 1750-1775," *American Historical Review*, vol. LII, no. 4, July, 1947, pp. 655-66.

Shulim, Joseph I. "Henry Banks: A Contemporary Napoleonic Apologist in the Old Dominion," *Virginia Magazine Of History And Biography*, vol. LVIII, no. 3, July, 1950, pp. 335-45.

——. "Napoleon I As The Jewish Messiah: Some Contemporary Conceptions In Virginia," *Jewish Social Studies*, vol. VII, no. 3, July, 1945, pp. 275-80.

Whitaker, Arthur P. The Mississippi Question, 1795-1803, A Study in Trade, Politics, and Diplomacy. New York, 1934.

Wiltse, Charles M. "The Authorship of the War Report of 1812," *American Historical Review*, vol. XLIX, no. 2, January, 1944, pp. 253-9.

G. GENERAL AND MISCELLANEOUS

1. *National*

Abernethy, Thomas P. Western Lands and the American Revolution. New York, 1937.

Adams, Henry. History Of The United States Of America During The Administration Of Thomas Jefferson. New York, 1930. Books I-IV.

——. History Of The United States Of America During The Administration Of James Madison. New York, 1930. Books V-IX.

Channing, Edward. A History Of The United States. Vols. III-V, New York, 1935-8.

——. The Jeffersonian System, 1801-11. New York and London, 1906. (The American Nation, A History, edited by A. B. Hart, vol. XII.)

Krout, John A. and Fox, Dixon R. The Completion Of Independence, 1790-1830. New York, 1944. (A History Of American Life, vol. V.)

Link, Eugene P. Democratic-Republican Societies, 1790-1800. New York, 1942.

McMaster, John B. A History Of The People Of The United States, From the Revolution to the Civil War, vols. II-IV. New York, 1885-95.

2. *State*

Ambler, Charles H. A History Of West Virginia. New York, 1933.

——. Sectionalism in Virginia from 1776 to 1861. Chicago, 1910.

Burton, H. W. The History Of Norfolk, Virginia. Norfolk, 1877.

Caton, James R. Legislative Chronicles of the City of Alexandria. Alexandria, Va., 1933.

Craven, Avery, ed. Essays In Honor of William E. Dodd By His Former Students At The University of Chicago. Chicago, 1935.

Evans, Willis F. History of Berkeley County, West Virginia. n. p., 1928.

Hart, Freeman H. The Valley of Virginia In The American Revolution, 1763-1789. Chapel Hill, No. Car., 1942.

History Of Virginia. Vol. I, Colonial Period, 1607-1763, by Philip A. Bruce. Vol. II, The Federal Period, 1763-1861, by Lyon G. Tyler. New York, 1924.

Lewis, Virgil A. First Biennial Report of the Department of Archives and History of the State of West Virginia. Charleston, 1906.

——. Second Biennial Report of the Department of Archives and History of the State of West Virginia. Charleston, 1908.

Meade, Bishop William. Old Churches, Ministers, And Families Of Virginia. Philadelphia, 1900. 2 v.

Mordecai, Samuel. Virginia, Especially Richmond, In By-Gone Days; With A Glance At The Present: Being Reminiscences And Last Words Of An Old Citizen. 2nd ed., with many corrections and additions. Richmond, 1860.

Wertenbaker, Thomas J. Norfolk, Historic Southern Port. Durham, No. Car., 1931.

Wingfield, Marshall. A History Of Caroline County, Virginia. Richmond, 1924.

H. PERIODICALS

The Lower Norfolk County Virginia Antiquary. Baltimore, 1897-1906. 5 v.

Tyler's Quarterly Historical and Genealogical Magazine. 1920 to date.

The Virginia Historical Register and Literary Advertiser. Edited by William Maxwell. Vols. I-III, V. Richmond, 1848-50, 1852.

The Virginia Magazine Of History And Biography. Published quarterly by the Virginia Historical Society. Richmond, 1894 to date.

William and Mary College Quarterly Historical Papers, vols. I-II. Then: William and Mary College Quarterly Historical Magazine. Beginning in 1944: The William and Mary Quarterly. Williamsburg, Va., 1892 to date.

PERIODICALS

INDEX